MW00442083
LOVE FOR HORSES
SEX
MUD
VIOLENCE
AIRBRUSH
LOG
NUTS
OH SWEET NUTS
'BOOTS'

WHAT THE HELL ARE YOU DOING ?

WHAT THE HELL ARE YOU DOING?

THE ESSENTIAL DAVID SHRIGLEY

CANONGATE

EDINBURGH - LONDON - NEW YORK - MELBOURNE

PUBLISHED BY CANONGATE BOOKS IN 2010

2

FIRST PUBLISHED IN GREAT BRITAIN IN 2010
BY CANONGATE BOOKS LTD.
14 HIGH STREET, EDINBURGH EH1 1TE

WWW.MEETATTHEGATE.COM

BRITISH LIBRARY CATALOGUING-IN-PUBLICATION DATA
A CATALOGUE RECORD FOR THIS BOOK IS
AVAILABLE ON REQUEST FROM THE
BRITISH LIBRARY

ISBN 978 1 84767 859 1

PRINTED AND BOUND BY ROBOTS

Introduction by Will Self

I am a regular if not exactly enthusiastic patron of my local bookshop. I try to buy at least some books there, because I cling to the belief that it's important to maintain those businesses that put a human face on the exchange of money for goods and services. If we bought everything on the internet, our eyes and mouths and nostrils would probably begin to film over with a tegument – initially tissue-thin and capable of being removed each morning, it would gradually thicken and harden until we were imprisoned in our own tiny minds.

Anyway, over the years I've not exactly grown friendly with the staff of the bookshop, but we do tolerate one another. They know I'm a writer – obviously – and they do me the kindness of displaying signed copies of my books in their window. On a couple of occasions I've even given readings at the shop. What I'm trying to say here is that, basically, this is a functioning relationship, albeit one of a circumscribed kind: I write books; they sell books; I buy books from them (although not my own, because I know what's in those ones already).

Then, I don't know, perhaps a year or two ago, one of the men who works in the bookshop told me he had written a book, and asked me if I would take a look at it. This happens to me quite a lot – some people are looking for advice or concrete assistance to get their work published, others simply require a generalised affirmation. None of them, I suspect, is looking for genuine and heartfelt criticism such as: Your book is dreadful, you are wholly without talent; please, never try to do this again – although I'm glad you showed me this, for, having established just how vile it is, I have been able to burn it and so prevent it from falling into the hands of someone less worldly-wise and more vulnerable than I am, someone who might be so depressed by your execrable efforts that they self-harmed or committed suicide.

I was a bit put out by the way the parameters of my relationship with the people who work in the bookshop were being altered, but despite knowing full well that I'd probably be unable to respond to the material with any great honesty, I still found myself unable to refuse. As it transpired, the book turned out to be pretty good. It consisted of a series of drawings executed in a style that was at once childlike and sinisterly knowing, and the drawings were accompanied by texts of different lengths – some little more than captions, others taking up the whole page – that also disturbingly married the infantile to the cynical. Overall, the impression the book left me with was of a small and dirty window being opened on to an alien world of compelling familiarity – not a bad effect, I'm sure you'll agree, for an artist-cum-writer to have achieved.

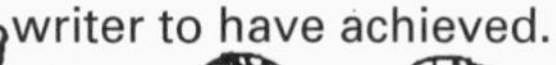

A few days later I went back to the bookshop and returned the book to its creator. I like your work, I told him, then said the nice things about it that I've written here. But, I continued, I also have a problem with it. Oh, said the bookshop man, really? Yes, I said. I don't exactly know how to put this, but has anyone who's seen your work ever pointed out to you that it bears a strong resemblance to the work of someone else? Do you mean David Shrigley? said the man. Yes, I replied, that is exactly who I mean. Well, said the bookshop man, a little abashed but putting a brave face on things, I know my work is very like David Shrigley's, but, you see, it is my work, work I've been doing for years now, since long before I was ever aware of David Shrigley's work. I accept that, I said – although at the time of speaking I did, in fact, retain ignoble reservations. But what I'm trying to tell you is that I think you'll find it hard to get your work published given its strong similarity to the work of David Shrigley, who is quite well established. And that is where we left it.

As I said, while I was speaking to the bookshop man I had ignoble reservations. It wasn't that I imagined he had plagiarised the work of David Shrigley – the notion was too bizarre. It was rather that I suspected he might have seen some of Shrigley's work, been sort of inadvertently influenced by it and then – quite legitimately – forgotten that he'd ever seen it at all.

However, as I walked away from the bookshop my ignoble reservations dispersed, hanging for a while like a smirch of lorry exhaust against the dull shop fronts of the suburban high street and then disappearing entirely. No, I thought, it's true: this man has been doing these Shrigleyesque drawings and writings for years now, and he is doomed to utter obscurity whereas David Shrigley probably lives high on the hog, sipping Kir Royale cocktails from the bra cups of deeply aroused and admiring Hollywood stars. Yes, this man, and, who knows (because the world is a desperately big place), perhaps thousands of other men and women, will labour away at their shriggles, yet be unable to gain any purchase on the public realm, a realm bestridden by Shrigley himself. For is it not the case that no summit meeting or international conference is considered viable without him in attendance, usually giving the plenary address? These poor folk, I thought, will be restless and dissatisfied with their lives, while from moment to moment Shrigley knows a deep and abiding spiritual joy.

Still, I comforted myself, as I strolled beneath the railway bridge and noted how the pigeons had defied the measures taken against them by shitting liberally on the serried palisades of nylon spikes, might this business with Shrigley and the myriad Shrigley-a-likes be simply another instance of a phenomenon we see all about us in nature? The multitudinous elvers are spawned, but only a few make it to the Sargasso; the legions of sperm are ejaculated, yet it may be that not one manages to fertilise the egg. Untold billions of stars are hurled out into the infinity of space, but on only one of these will the Shrigley evolve.

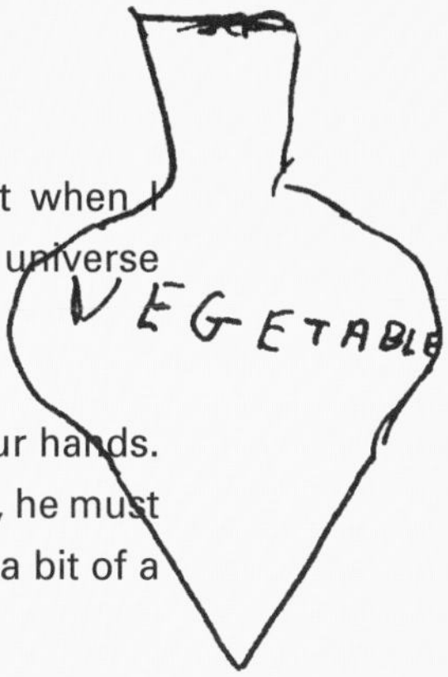

These rarefied speculations sustained me so long as I was walking, but when I reached home I slumped, dejected. How could anyone be sanguine about a universe the ordering principle of which appeared to be such useless profligacy?

I thought of all this as I took up the proofs of the book you now hold in your hands. Was I simply confirming Shrigley's unique fitness to be Shrigley – for surely, he must be that by virtue of his survival alone? Or did I simply want to give myself a bit of a laugh?

A pattern of wonky hexagons, a blot, a scribble – all inky black: 'Unfinished plan for a new and better society', the legend read. Then it struck me: the man in the bookshop's work may have borne a strong resemblance to Shrigley's, but it just wasn't the actualité. There were none of these luridly dull photographs with scrawled-upon signs in the foregrounds, which undermine the basis of not just any society, but precisely this one. Shrigley's photographic works suggest the refined eye of someone sent back from the future beyond the looming apocalypse, charged with assembling images that, while ostensibly of the mundane, nonetheless explain how it came to pass that humanity destroyed itself.

Humans. Humans entire or pared down to heads, or heads equipped with legs: uglified anime you hope won't move. In Shrigley's drawings – and Shrigley's alone – the human body is undifferentiated, as imagined by a child, with sausage limbs and a hammy torso . . . and yet . . . and yet, it is also as acutely visceral as a freshly killed cadaver plastinated by Gunther von Hagens. No wonder the animals depicted in Shrigley's work – and there are a lot of them – have such troubled expressions and pithy thoughts: crouched in their garish colour fields they retain their integrity, while compelled to witness the bewildering juxtapositions of hubris and false humility evinced by the twiggy men and women.

Only Shrigley's world is so furtively inhabited; hesitantly, his vision emerges from behind a palisade of penstrokes, advances on tiptoe towards whimsy, then beats it insensible with a lump of wood. Because they're angry in Shrigley world, angry at the enjambment that splits dimensions across lines of wonky text. And they're unstable in Shrigley-world, their feigned maturity constantly being undermined by the artist's compulsion to show duff workings. It's also quite terrifyingly archaic, this realm the artist has created – an archaism that reveals itself through demons and bogey beasts, and the efforts of the stick-figure shamans to magic remote effects using a bricolage of pen strokes and blots.

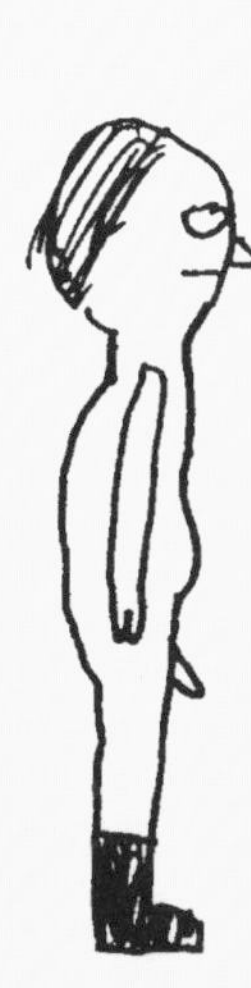

Like other graphic artists who create enclosed worlds of morphs – Dr Seuss, Edwards Gorey and Lear – there is nothing in Shrigley's disconcerting pictorial space which doesn't belong; however, I think he may well be unique in the fine balance he creates

between image and caption. At his best, John Glashan got close to what Shrigley achieves, but he never had quite the same range and fluency: on the kink of his line Shrigley can shift effortlessly from pathos to paranoia.

And his work is funny – very funny; his timing is devastatingly effective while being curiously non-Euclidean (the punch line is located in a separate dimension to the set-up, never alongside). Only Shrigley can pull off such rapid-fire combinations: if the profound fist don't get you, the prosaic one will; only Shrigley can produce effective social commentary using doodles of men down holes: 'It's great down here. I'm really enjoying myself', 'Yes. It's great to be away from our wives'.

We could get more elevated . . . let's. Like others of his contemporaries – Simon Patterson's *The Great Bear* comes to mind – Shrigley is preoccupied by the uncertainty implied in the act of mapping, rather than its technical ability to reduce the large-scale to the intelligible. Shrigley's maps and plans reveal an endemic predisposition on our part to mislabelling: we do not know the names of our own parts, let alone the parts of anything else. Worse still, even the words we use for the legends of these maps and plans are misspelled and misunderstood; they too, if looked at closely enough, are exposed as not denotative but diagrammatic – they are themselves wonky little word maps with their own misspelled legends. Thus, Shrigley takes the picture theory of meaning espoused by Wittgenstein's *Tractatus Logico-Philosophicus*, balls it up and chucks it in the general direction of the bin.

For Shrigley, consciousness can never be explained; it is always deranged, and the things that people do – especially the making of artworks – are monstrous in their complaisant acceptance of this derangement. To quibble over whether Shrigley is a 'fine artist' or a cartoonist is just that: quibbling. He is, perhaps, neither – rather he is the maker of meta-textual chapbooks that simultaneously drag us back to a pre-literate past and flog us forward towards an unutterable future. You can call this art if you like – but don't expect me to like you.

In conclusion, then, there are many, many Shrigleys out there – some of them are mutants, others are not wholly viable, still more may be necessary in their own strange way – but it remains the case that there is only one essential Shrigley. Here it is.

Will Self

THERE IS A LAND NOT FAR AWAY FROM HERE WHERE RABBITS LIVE IN HARMONY WITH ALL OTHER CREATURES
THAT'S A COMPLETE LOAD OF SHIT AND YOU KNOW IT

EXPLOSION
INSIDE YOUR
HEAD MAKES
ALMOST
NO SOUND

LOST

GREY + WHITE
PIDGEON WITH
BLACK BITS.
NORMAL SIZE.
A BIT MANGY
-LOOKING.
DOES NOT HAVE
A NAME.
CALL 257 1964

BUDDHA IS CARRIED OFF BY ANTS

BUDDHA IS RETURNED BY ANTS

CRAP
IT'S BRILLIANT

ARTISTS TALK ABOUT THEIR WORK

I DON'T ACTUALLY DO THE PAINTINGS MYSELF, I GET A BUNCH OF HANDICAPPED KIDS TO DO THEM FOR ME....

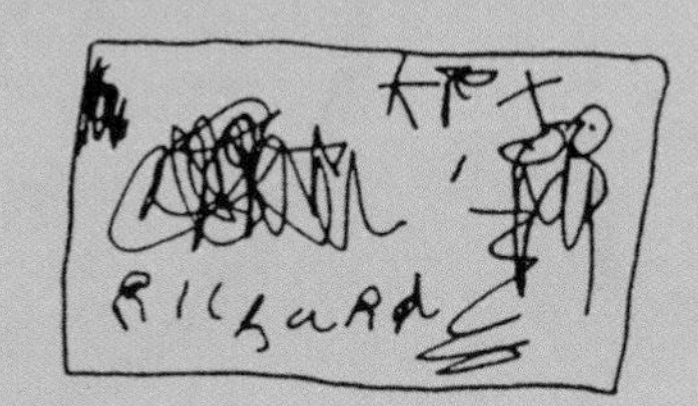

I USE A LOT OF FOUND MATERIALS IN MY WORK. MY LATEST PIECE IS FIFTY IDENTICAL PAIRS OF CHILDRENS SHOES WHICH I FOUND IN A CHARITY SHOP THEY'RE BRILLIANT AND THEY ONLY COST £30.

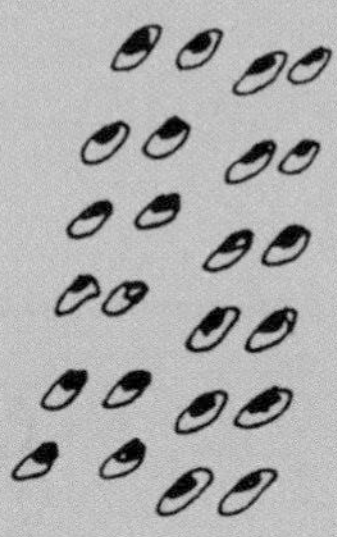

I WENT AROUND TOWN AND ASKED DOSSERS IF I COULD BUY THEIR UNDERPANTS FROM THEM. I GOT SIX PAIRS FOR £5 EACH AND USED THEM FOR MY SHOW IN FRANCE.

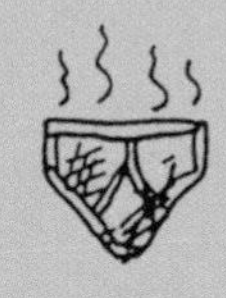

I GO AROUND BARS AT THE WEEKENDS AND DELIBERATELY GET INTO FIGHTS AND GET MY HEAD KICKED IN WHILE A FRIEND OF MINE VIDEOS IT.

THIS
IS ME

THIS IS
ALSO ME

I'M
DEAD

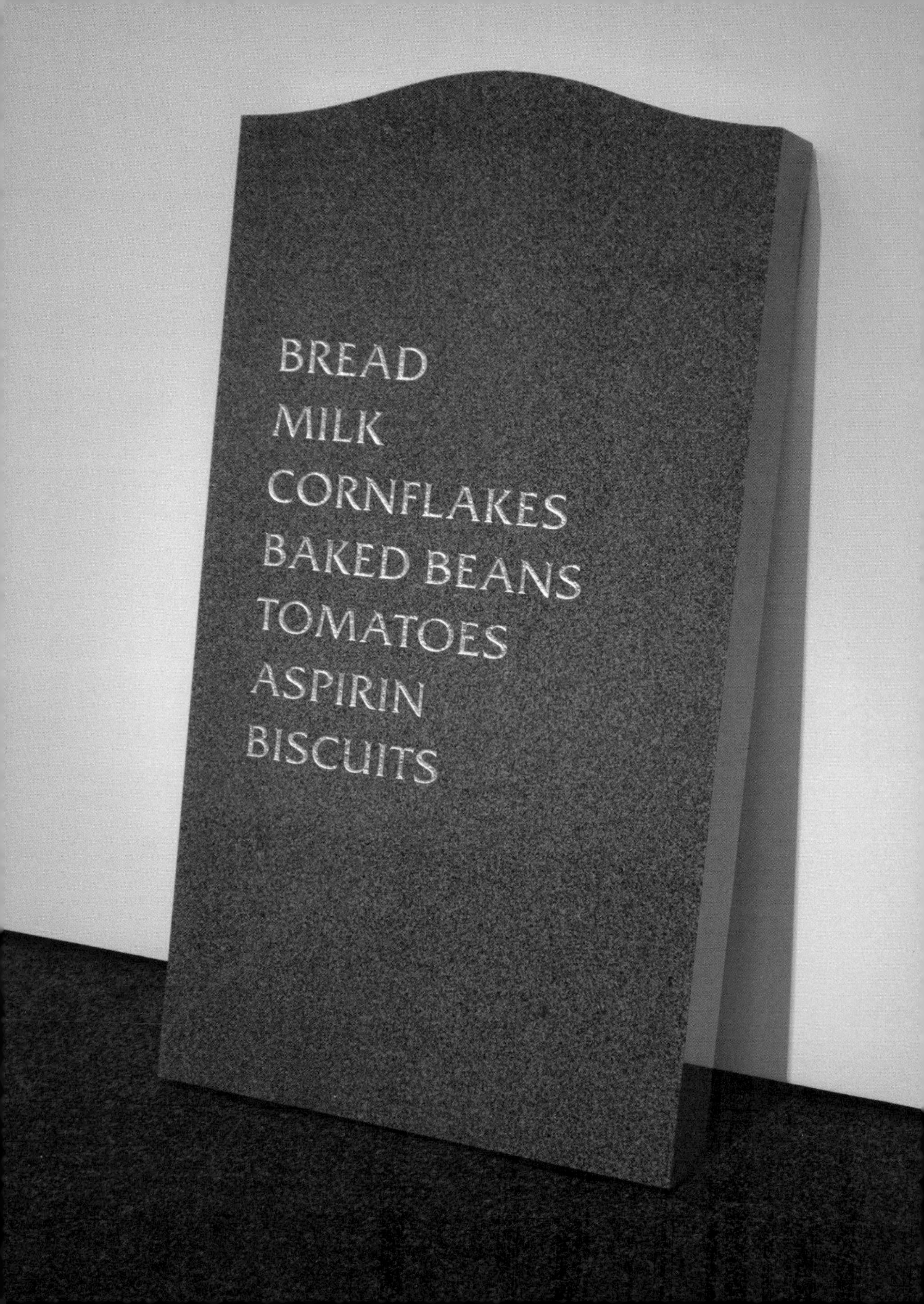

BREAD
MILK
CORNFLAKES
BAKED BEANS
TOMATOES
ASPIRIN
BISCUITS

IT IS ONLY YOUR SMILING FACE THAT KEEPS ME FROM GOING MAD

THIS IS TO TELL YOU ABOUT THE BARN DANCE

IT IS ON SUNDAY AT 8 PM
IN THE BARN

I WILL PLAY

THE OTHER PATIENTS WILL DANCE

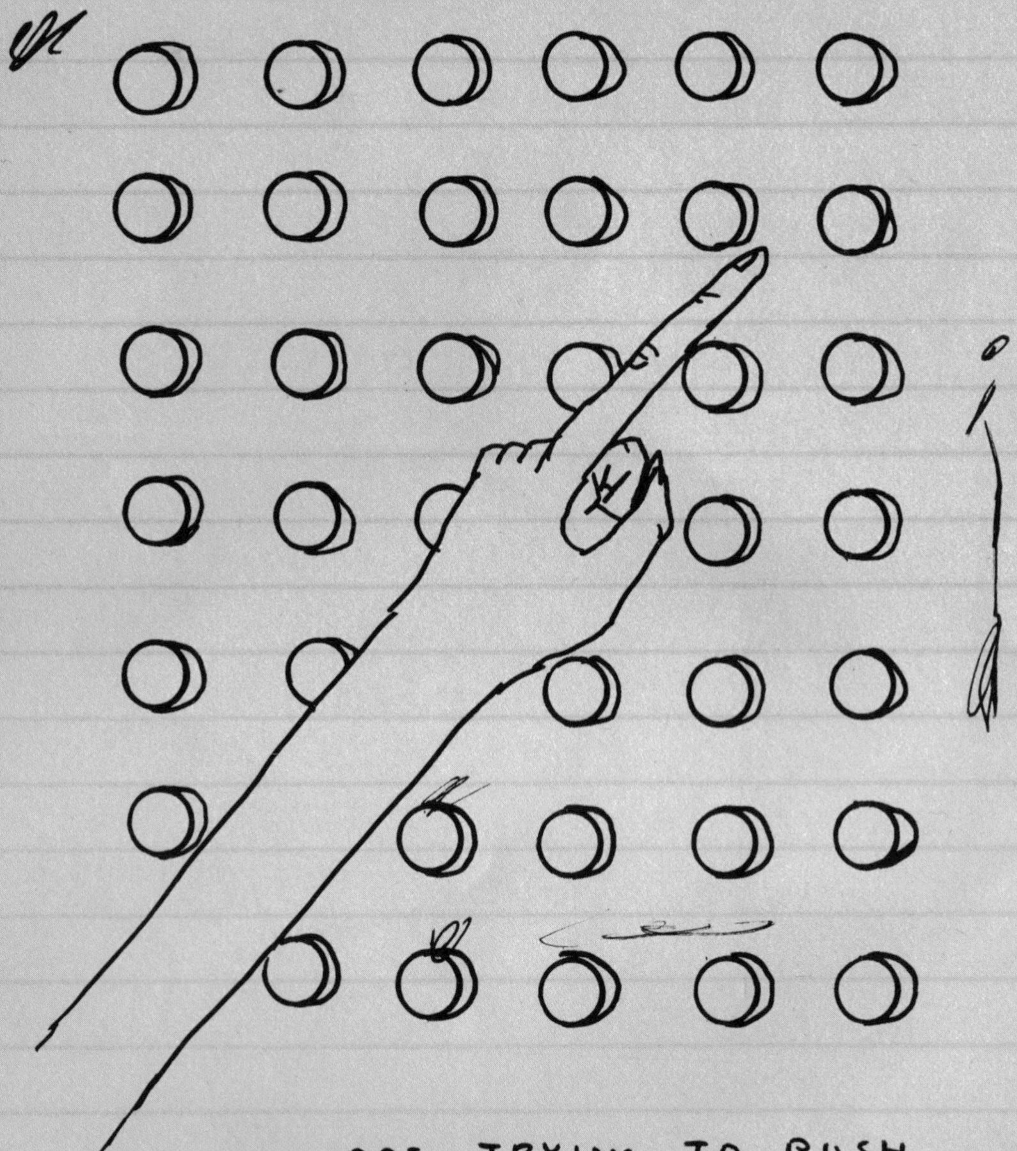

YOU ARE TRYING TO PUSH
THE RIGHT BUTTONS
BUT WHICH ARE THE RIGHT BUTTONS?
IT'S IMPOSSIBLE TO TELL. ISN'T IT?

I FEEL REALLY BAD ABOUT THIS
DON'T WORRY IT'S FINE

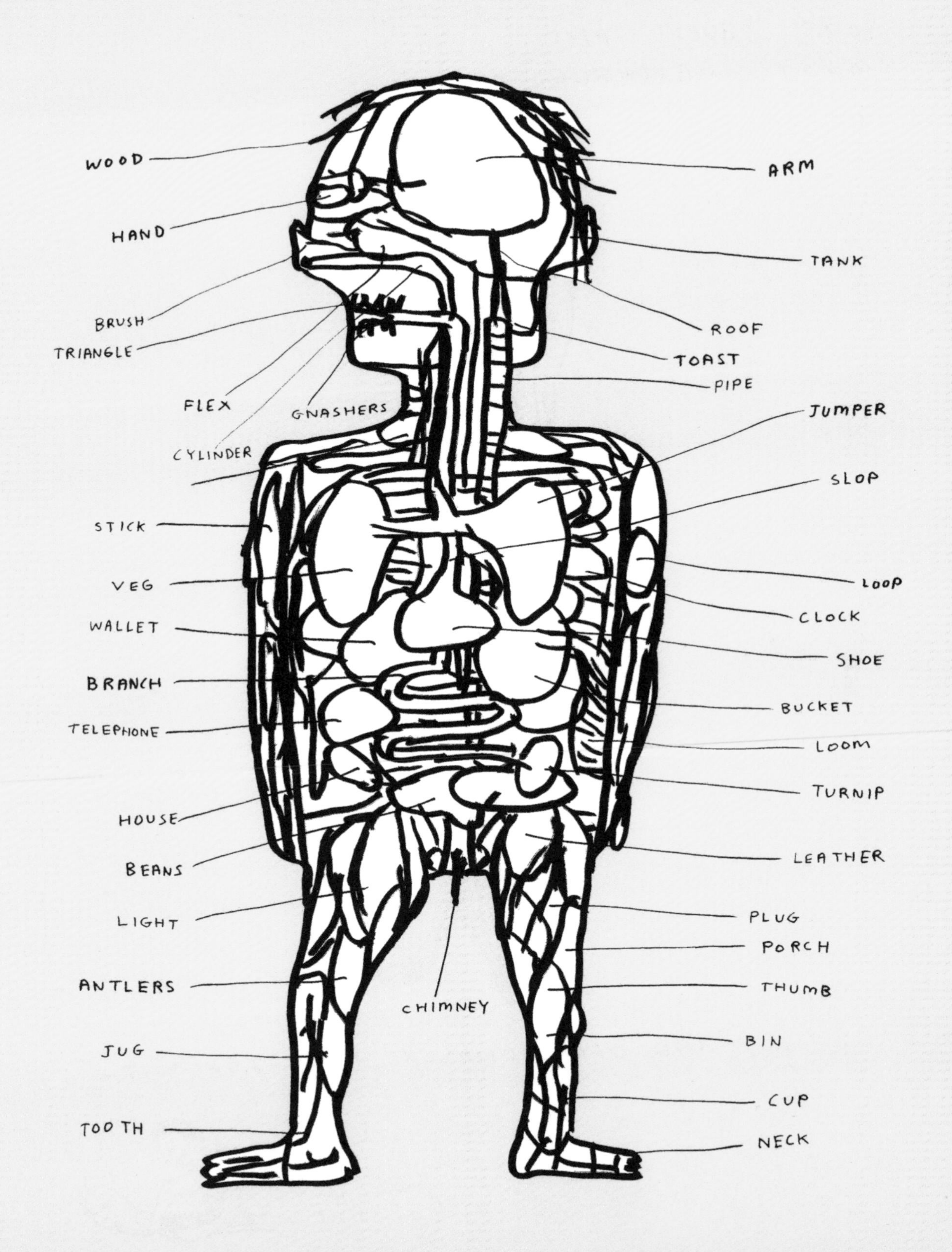
WOOD
ARM
HAND
TANK
BRUSH
ROOF
TRIANGLE
TOAST
PIPE
FLEX
GNASHERS
JUMPER
CYLINDER
SLOP
STICK
LOOP
VEG
CLOCK
WALLET
SHOE
BRANCH
BUCKET
TELEPHONE
LOOM
TURNIP
HOUSE
LEATHER
BEANS
PLUG
LIGHT
PORCH
ANTLERS
THUMB
CHIMNEY
JUG
BIN
CUP
TOOTH
NECK

YOUR TRUEST AND
MOST FAITHFUL FRIEND

WHOM YOU LOVE

AND OCCASIONALLY HAVE SEX WITH

WE THOUGHT WE WOULD WIN EASILY
WE HAD SUCH A HUGE ADVATAGE

BUT IN THE END WE HAD TO SETTLE FOR A DRAW
IT WAS TERRIBLY FRUSTRATING

- RETURN MY CHILD TO ME!
- I AM NOT INCLINED TO RETURN YOUR CHILD
- WHY NOT?
- BECAUSE I THINK I WILL BE A BETTER PARENT THAN YOU

GOD
IS
IDLE

RIVER
FOR
SALE

THY WELLINGTONS
YONDER

MY WELLINGTONS HERE

EXHIBITION OF SPIDERS

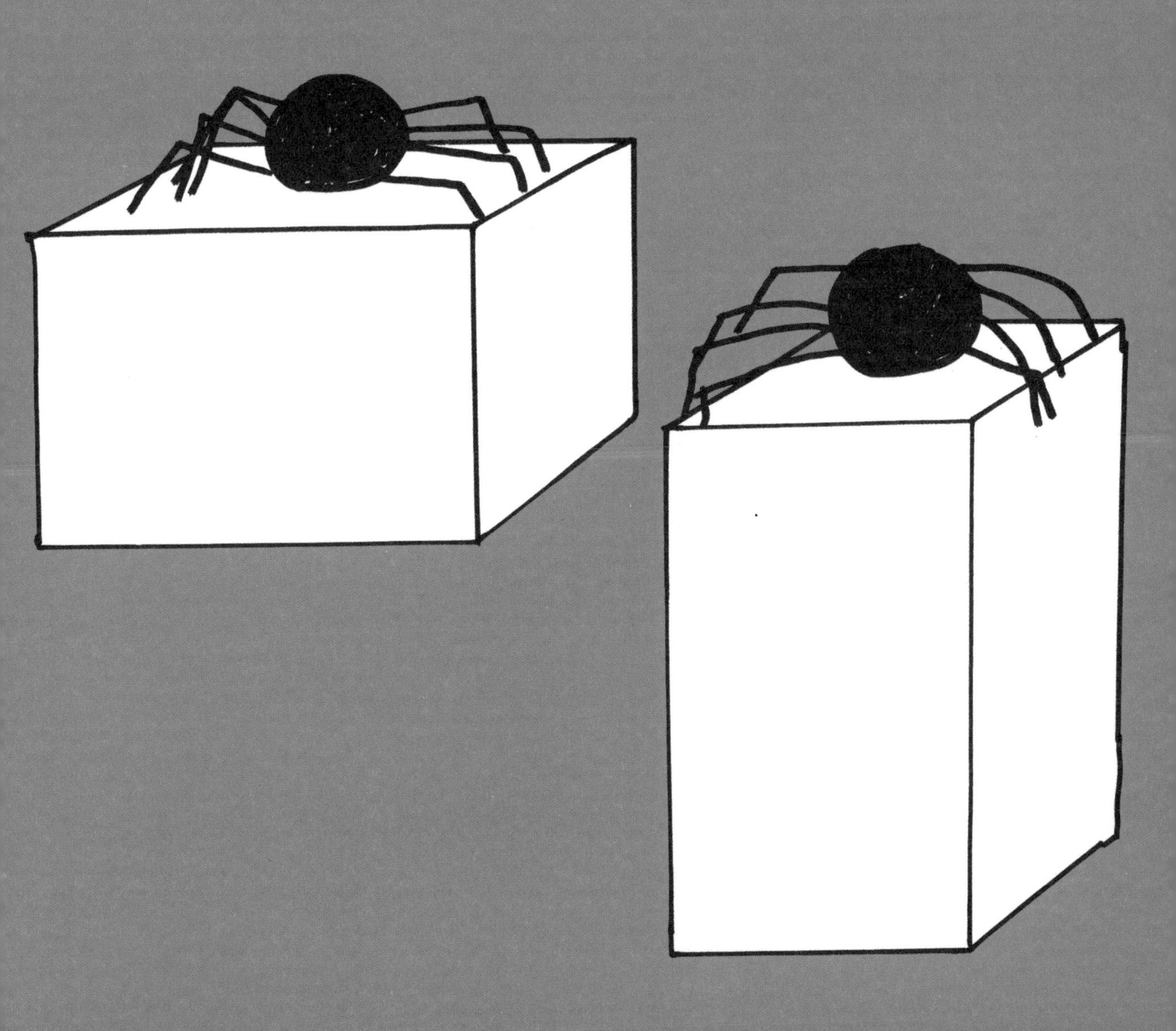

SIX CANS OF COLA

I DRANK SIX CANS OF COLA
ONE AFTER THE OTHER
AND NOW I FEEL FUCKING GREAT

CUP OF TEA FOR SALE

£100 (OR NEAR OFFER)

GOOD CONDITION. MILK, 2 SUGARS

A FREAK

(AERIAL VIEW)

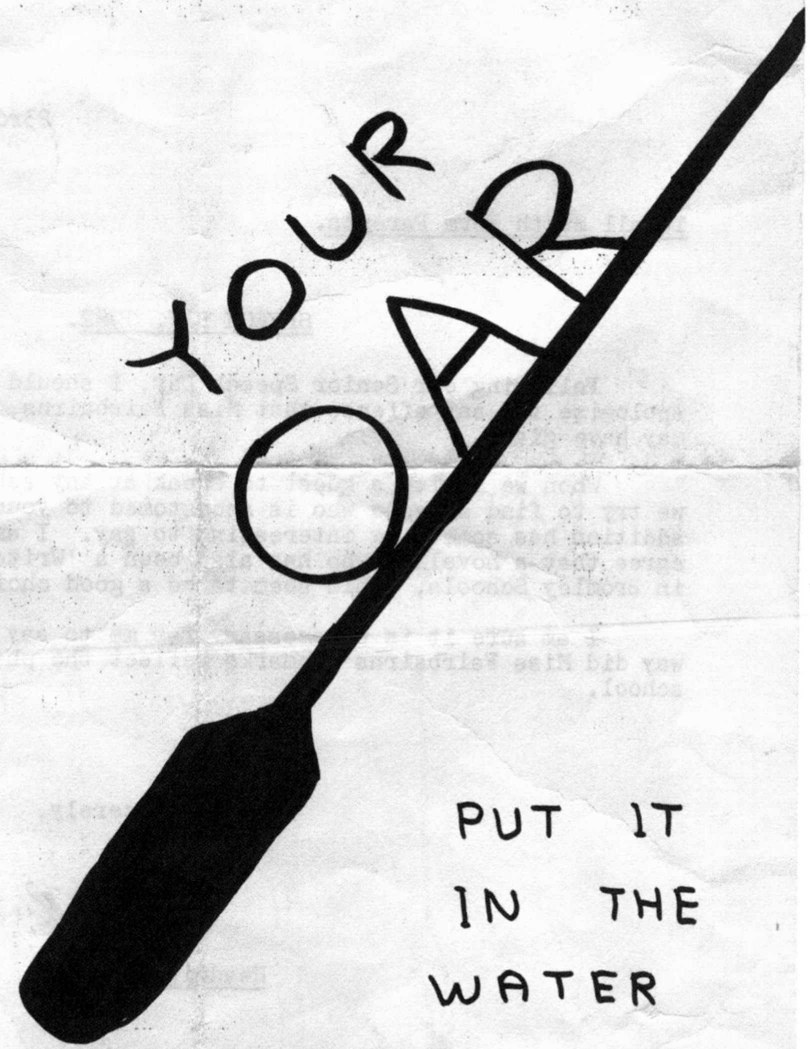

YOUR OAR

PUT IT
IN THE
WATER

OR LOSE IT FOREVER!

ARE YOU AN OLDER VERSION OF ME? SENT BACK IN TIME PERHAPS? TO GIVE ME A MESSAGE?
FUCK OFF

HAIR

DEAR MOTHER,
I DO NOT LIKE
BALLET SCHOOL. THEY
TEACH US TO PRANCE
AROUND LIKE MONKEYS

IT'S A BALL OF WOOL FOR THE FISH TO PLAY WITH

GO DOWN THE HOLE

STAY DOWN THE HOLE

NOT TO BE
RUNG AGAIN
UNTIL JESUS
RETURNS

APPLAUSE
AT FIRST I LOVED THE APPLAUSE.
IT WAS THE MOTIVATION FOR MY PERFORMANCE,
BUT THEN I STARTED TO GROW TIRED OF IT

WHAT IS MY PURPOSE ?

YOUR PURPOSE IS TO LISTEN

BIRD ON A WIRE GETTING ELECTROCUTED

PREVIOUSLY IN THE BIRDS LIFE:

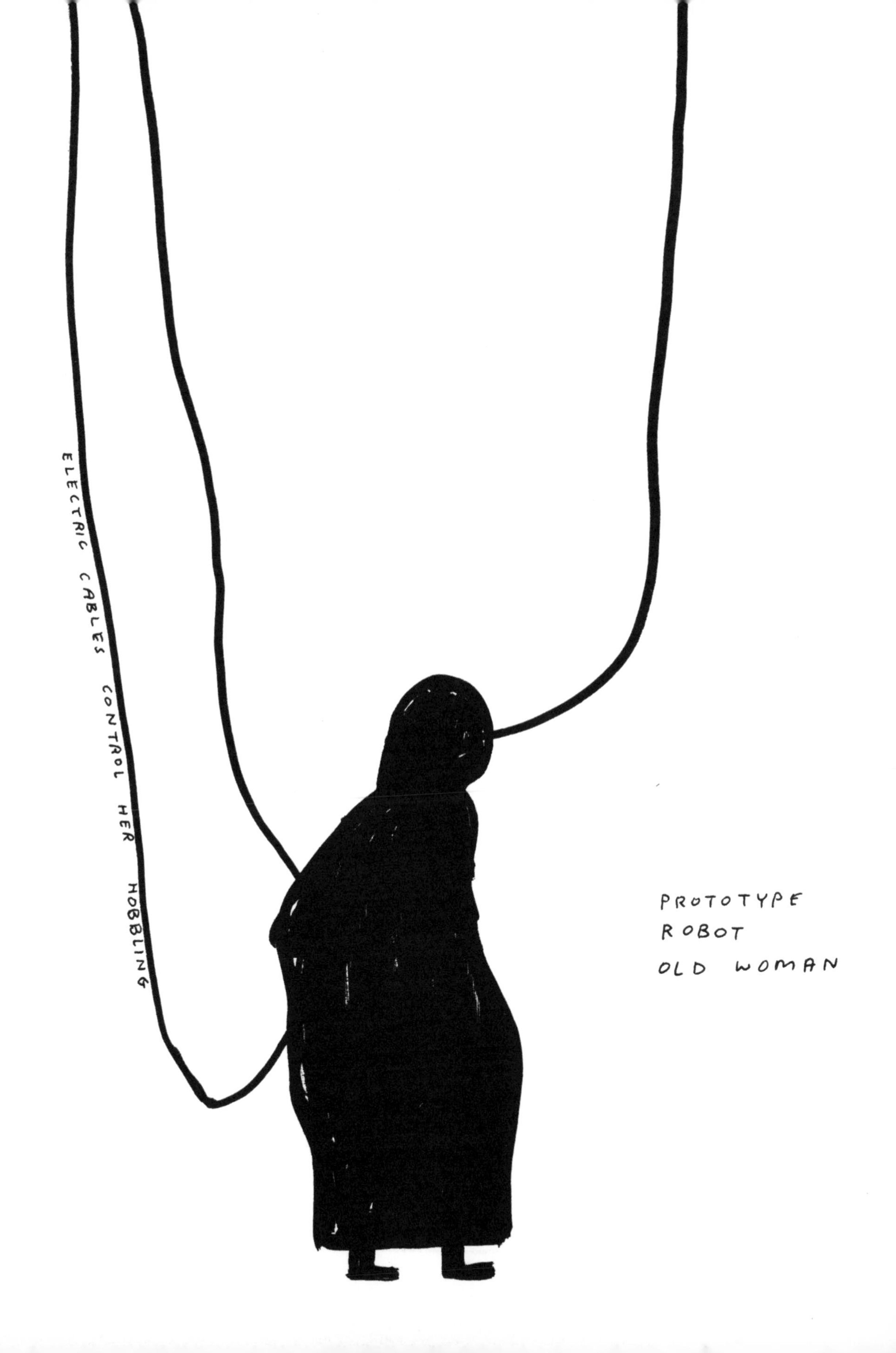
ELECTRIC CABLES CONTROL HER HOBBLING
PROTOTYPE
ROBOT
OLD WOMAN

COME BACK!

1+2=3
TRY
TO BE
HAPPY

DING
DONG

BRAINY BIRD BECOMES A NAZI

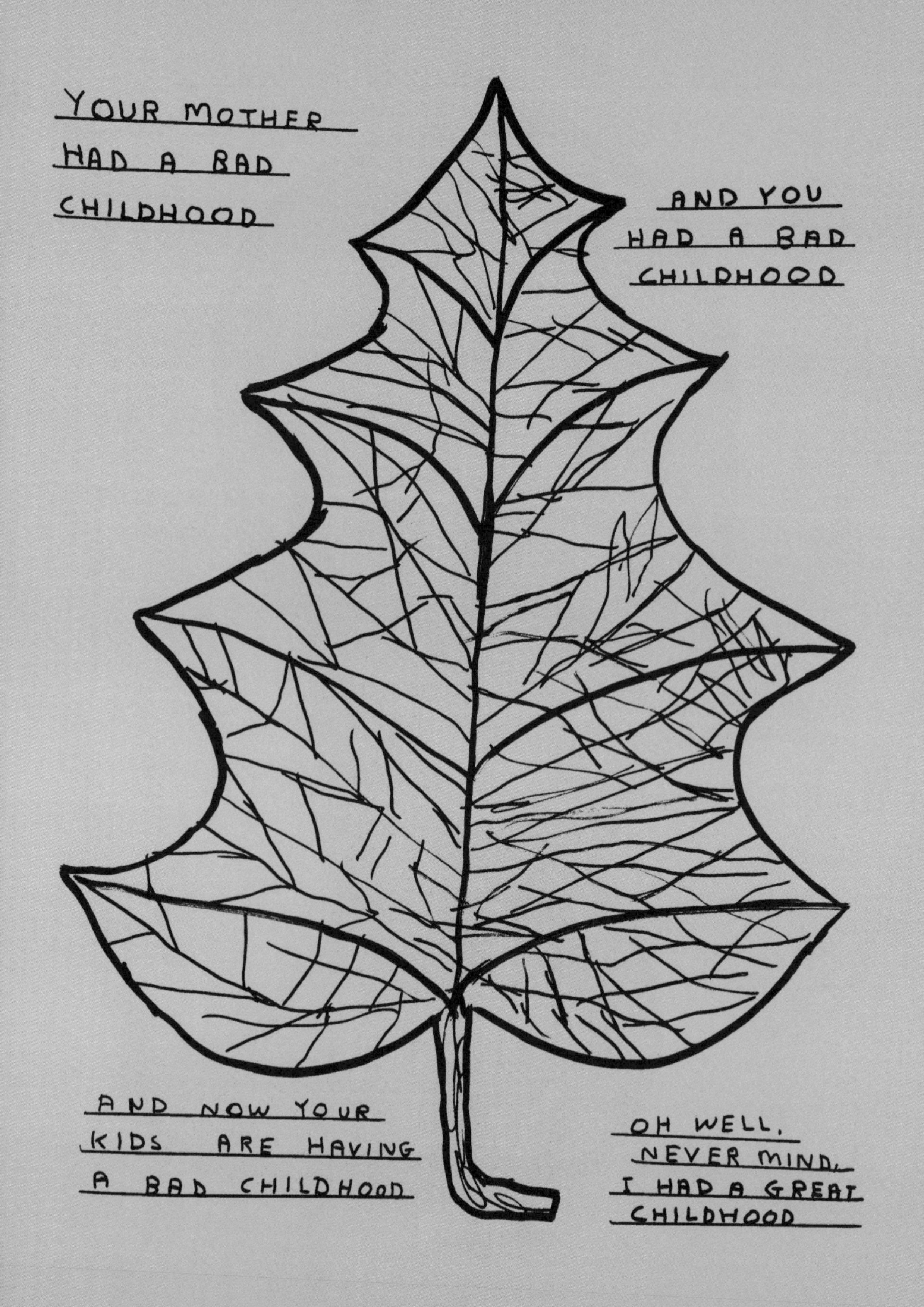
YOUR MOTHER
HAD A BAD
CHILDHOOD
AND YOU
HAD A BAD
CHILDHOOD
AND NOW YOUR
KIDS ARE HAVING
A BAD CHILDHOOD
OH WELL,
NEVER MIND,
I HAD A GREAT
CHILDHOOD

WHAT DOES THE FUTURE HOLD?

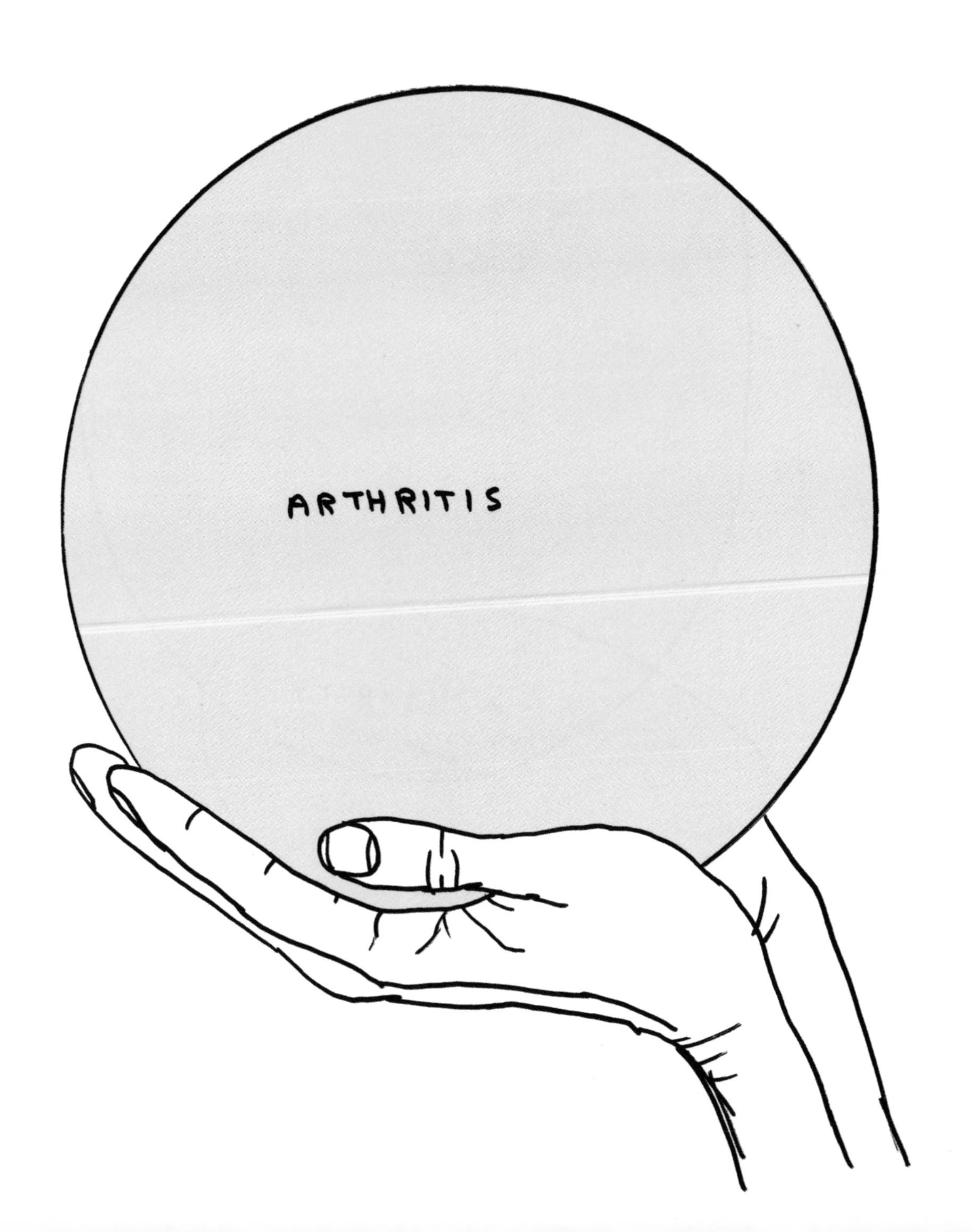

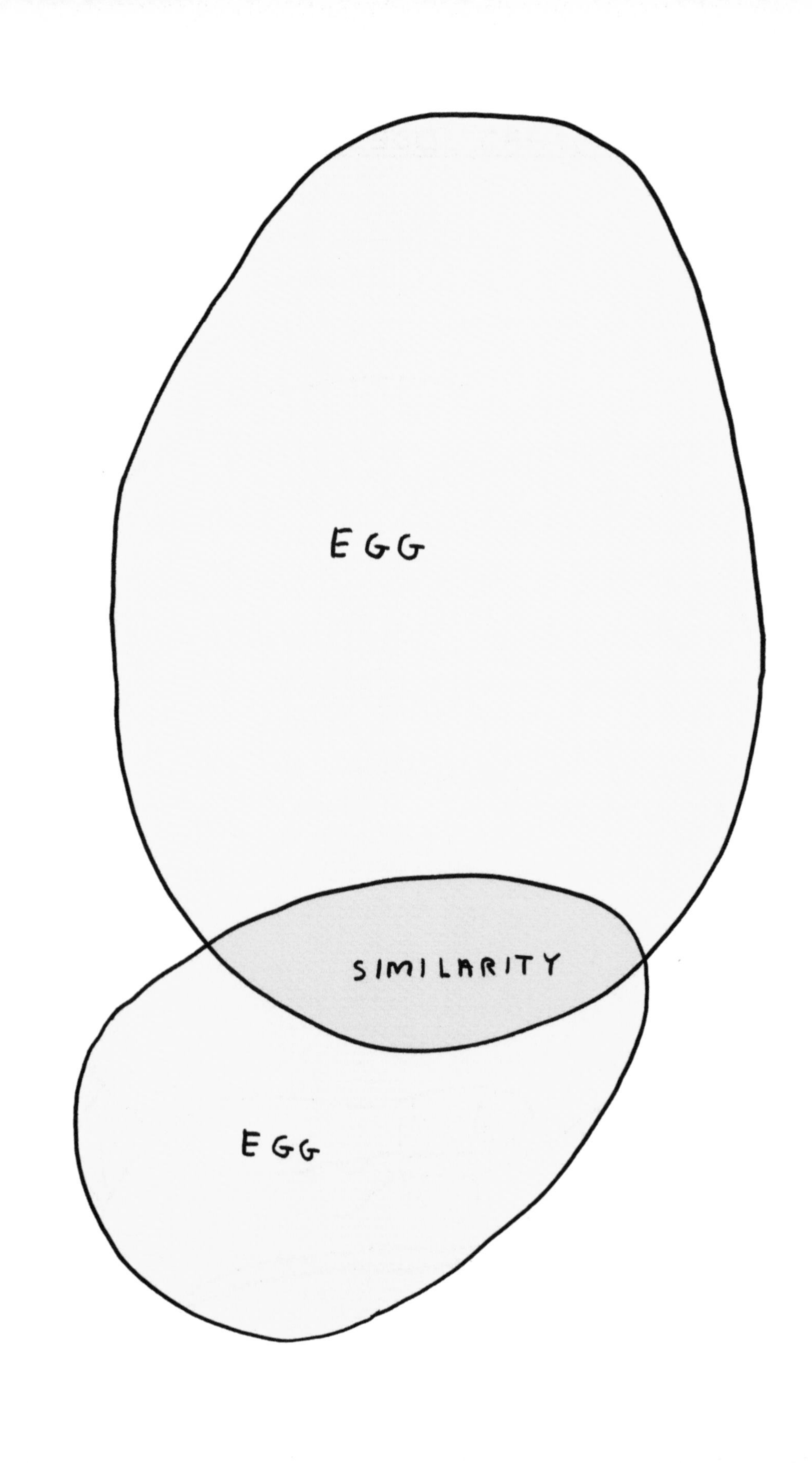
EGG
SIMILARITY
EGG

MEN DOWN A HOLE

IT'S GREAT DOWN HERE. I'M REALLY ENJOYING MYSELF

YES. IT'S GREAT TO BE AWAY FROM OUR WIVES

THE RING
I FOUND THE RING IN THE BUSHES.
I WAS VERY HAPPY TO FIND IT.
I SAW ITS JEWEL GLINTING,
THAT IS HOW I FOUND IT.
IT WAS BEING WORN AT THE
TIME BY A SKELETON.

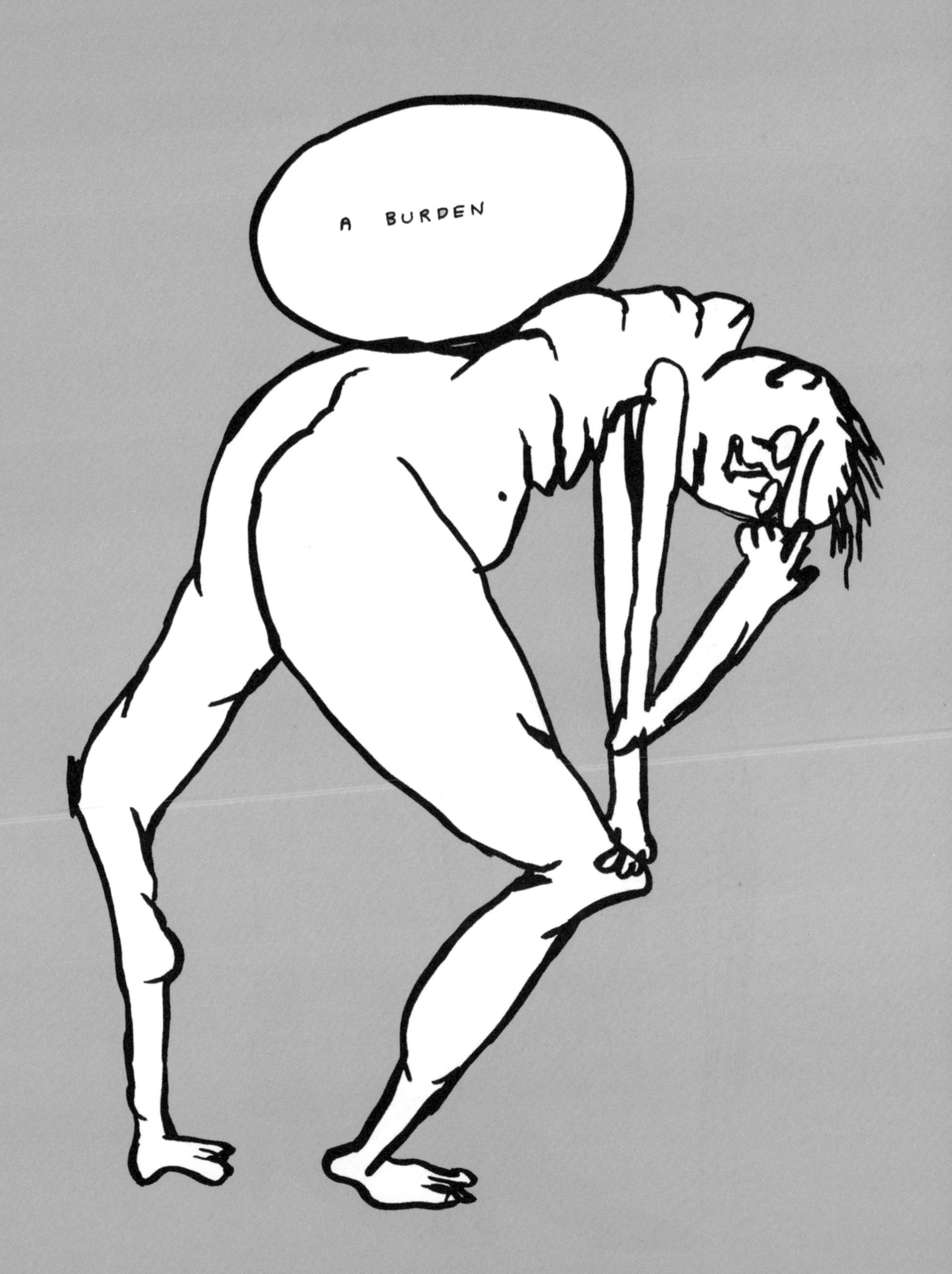
A BURDEN

I WAS ATTRACTED
BY THE LUSTRE
OF MY OWN
BOOTS

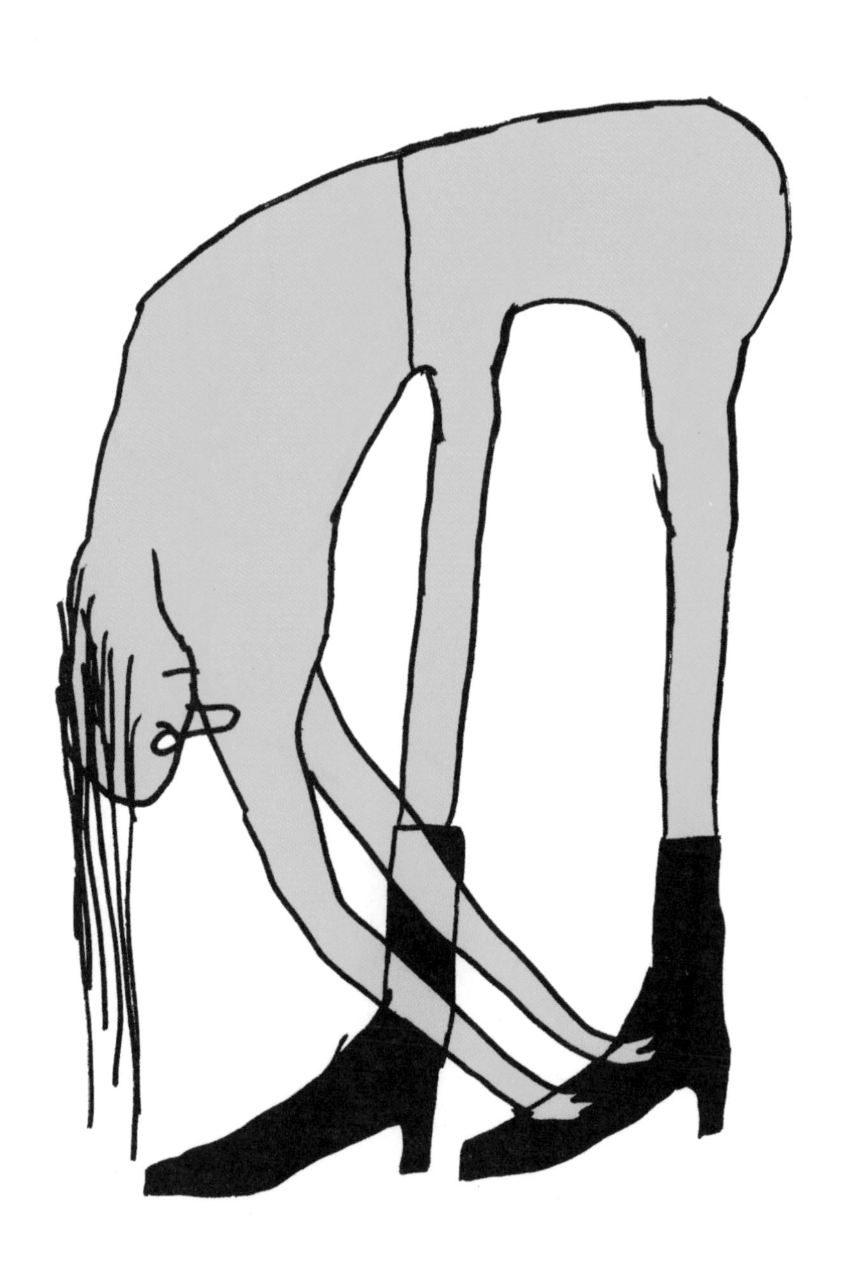

PILE OF SHIT

MR. TURNIP

ON ONE HAND
HE IS ENTERTAINING
AND GOOD HUMOURED

ON THE OTHER
HAND HE IS
NOT ENTERTAINING
OR GOOD
HUMOURED
IN FACT HE
IS A
BASTARD

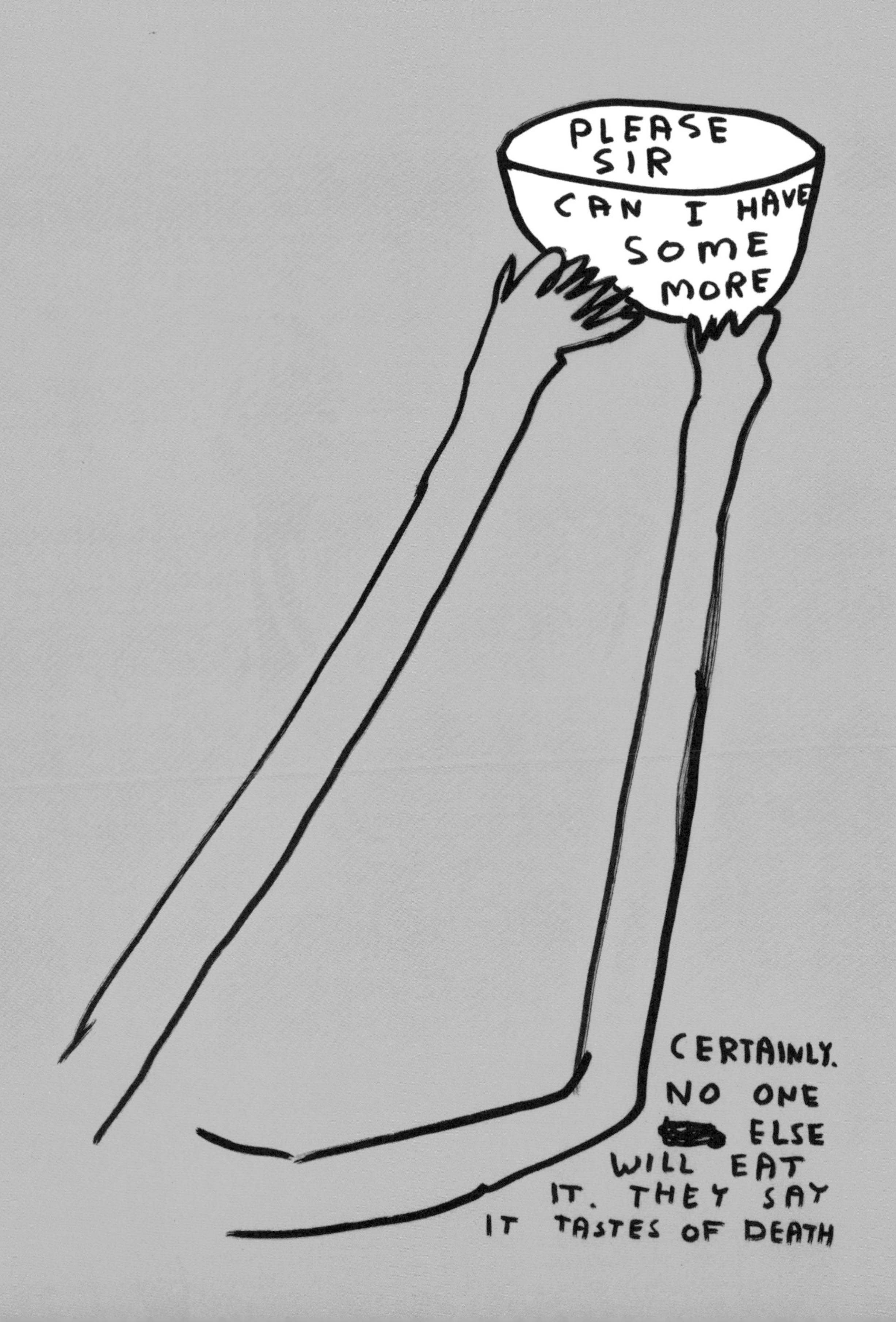
PLEASE SIR
CAN I HAVE
SOME
MORE
CERTAINLY.
NO ONE
ELSE
WILL EAT
IT. THEY SAY
IT TASTES OF DEATH

YOU ARE ABOUT TO MEET YOURSELF

ROLL OUT THE BARREL
WE'LL HAVE A BARREL OF FUN
THE BARREL CONTAINS MIDGETS
WHO WILL DANCE

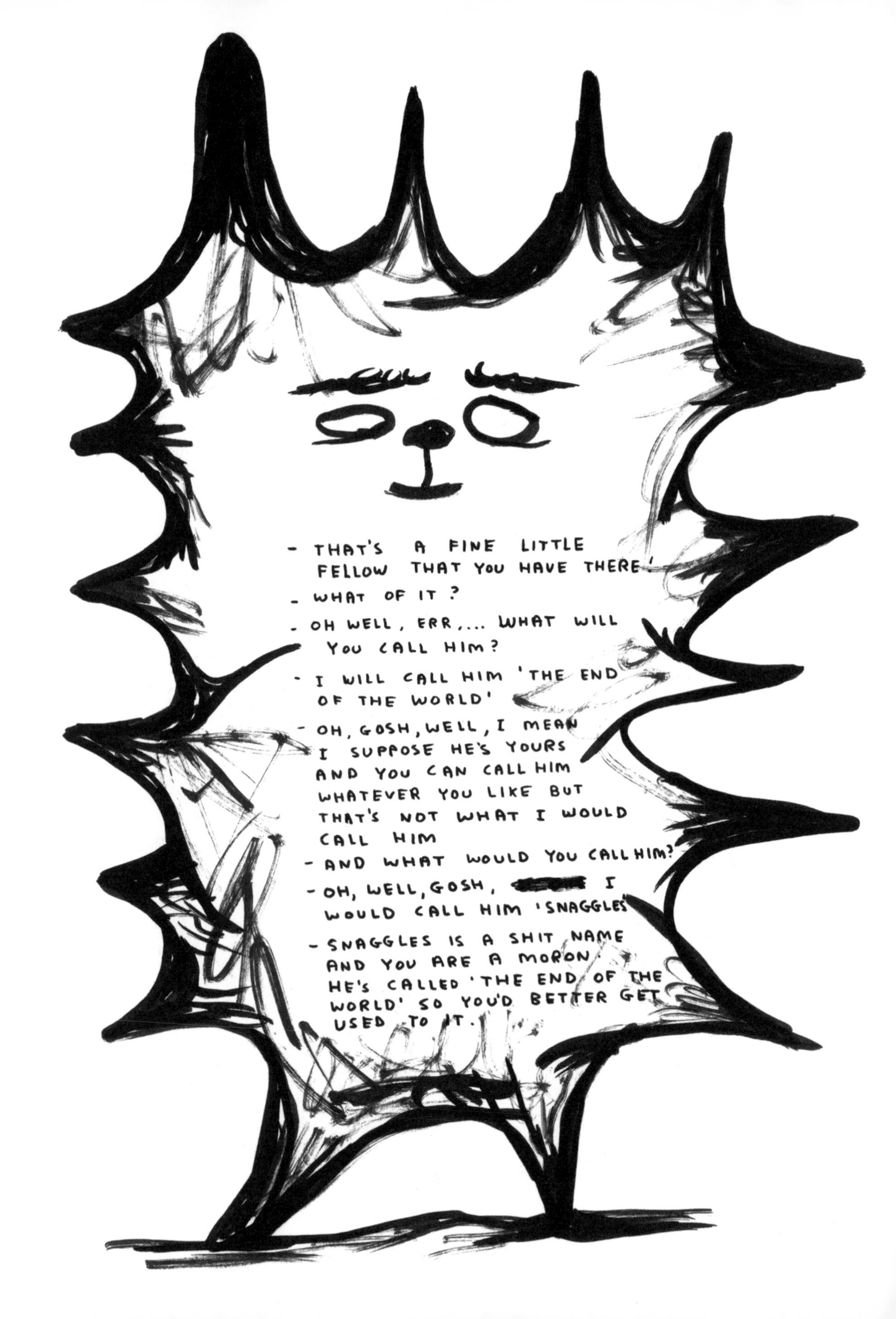
- THAT'S A FINE LITTLE FELLOW THAT YOU HAVE THERE!
- WHAT OF IT ?
- OH WELL, ERR,... WHAT WILL YOU CALL HIM?
- I WILL CALL HIM 'THE END OF THE WORLD'
- OH, GOSH, WELL, I MEAN I SUPPOSE HE'S YOURS AND YOU CAN CALL HIM WHATEVER YOU LIKE BUT THAT'S NOT WHAT I WOULD CALL HIM
- AND WHAT WOULD YOU CALL HIM?
- OH, WELL, GOSH, I WOULD CALL HIM 'SNAGGLES'
- SNAGGLES IS A SHIT NAME AND YOU ARE A MORON. HE'S CALLED 'THE END OF THE WORLD' SO YOU'D BETTER GET USED TO IT.

UNFINISHED DRAWING OF CAMPSITE

HOMEMADE BAT
I HAVE WON MANY
CONTESTS
USING THE HOMEMADE
BAT. MY OPPONENTS
ARE OFTEN FORCED
TO RETIRE THROUGH
INJURY
MADE OF
METAL
TWINE AROUND
THE HANDLE

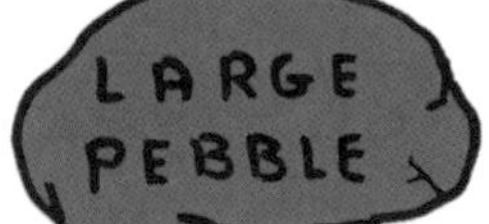
LARGE
PEBBLE

HOMOSEXUAL

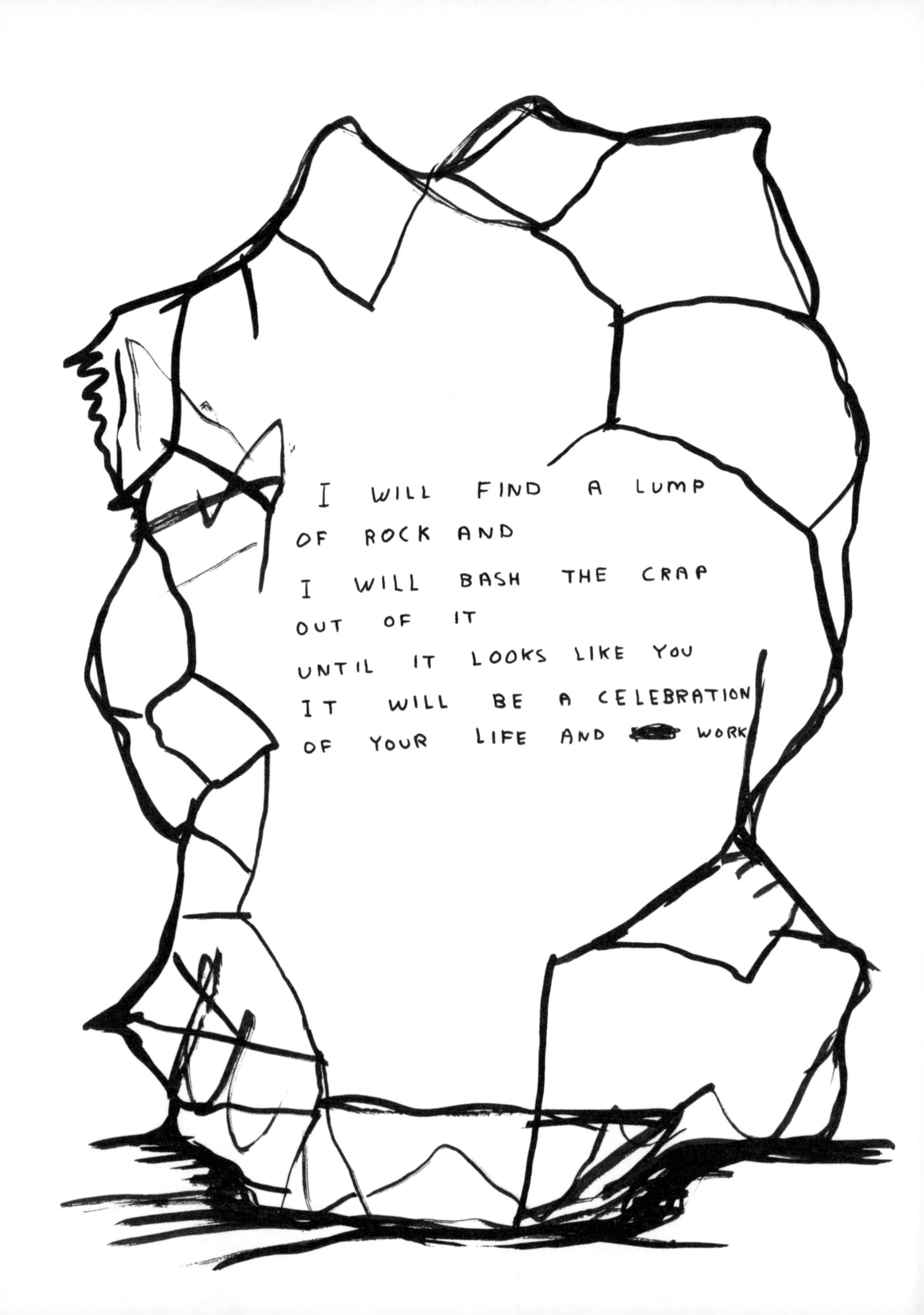
I WILL FIND A LUMP
OF ROCK AND
I WILL BASH THE CRAP
OUT OF IT
UNTIL IT LOOKS LIKE YOU
IT WILL BE A CELEBRATION
OF YOUR LIFE AND WORK

SEE ALL THIS AND MORE

HAPPY BIRTHDAY

FUCK OFF YOU FUCKING UGLY RETARD
GO ON FUCK OFF YOU RETARD
YOU RETARDED FUCKER GET THE FUCK OFF WITH THEE
THAT'S RIGHT FUCK OFF YOU RETARD SHIT AND STOP CRYING
KEEP GOING YOU UGLY RETARD FUCKER
I THOUGHT I TOLD YOU TO FUCK OFF
I FORGOT TO WISH YOU A HAPPY BIRTHDAY

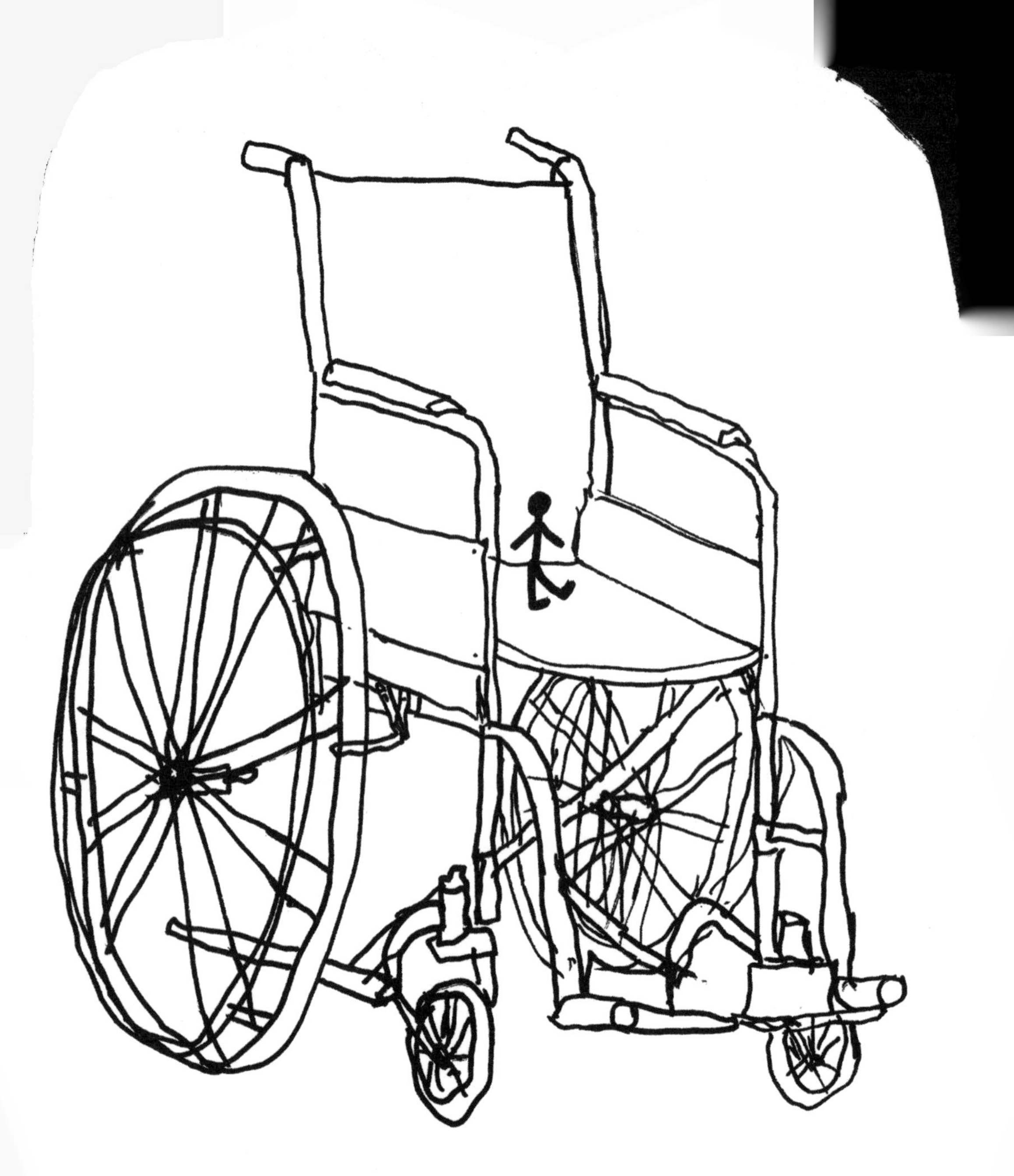

THE INCREDIBLE SHRINKING DISABLED MAN

WANTED

DEAD OR ALIVE

REWARD £5

HE STOLE MY PENCIL

THE TIME COMETH

ONE DAY
A BIG WIND
WILL COME
AND

YOU MUST TRAVEL THROUGH THE WILDERNESS

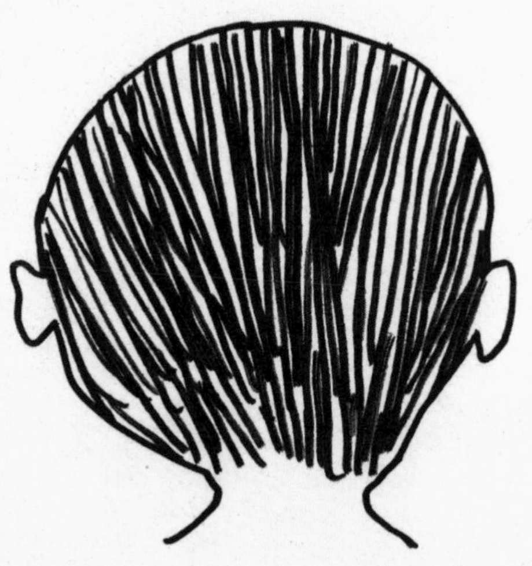

YOU BUILD BRIDGES, I BUILD WALLS

YOU

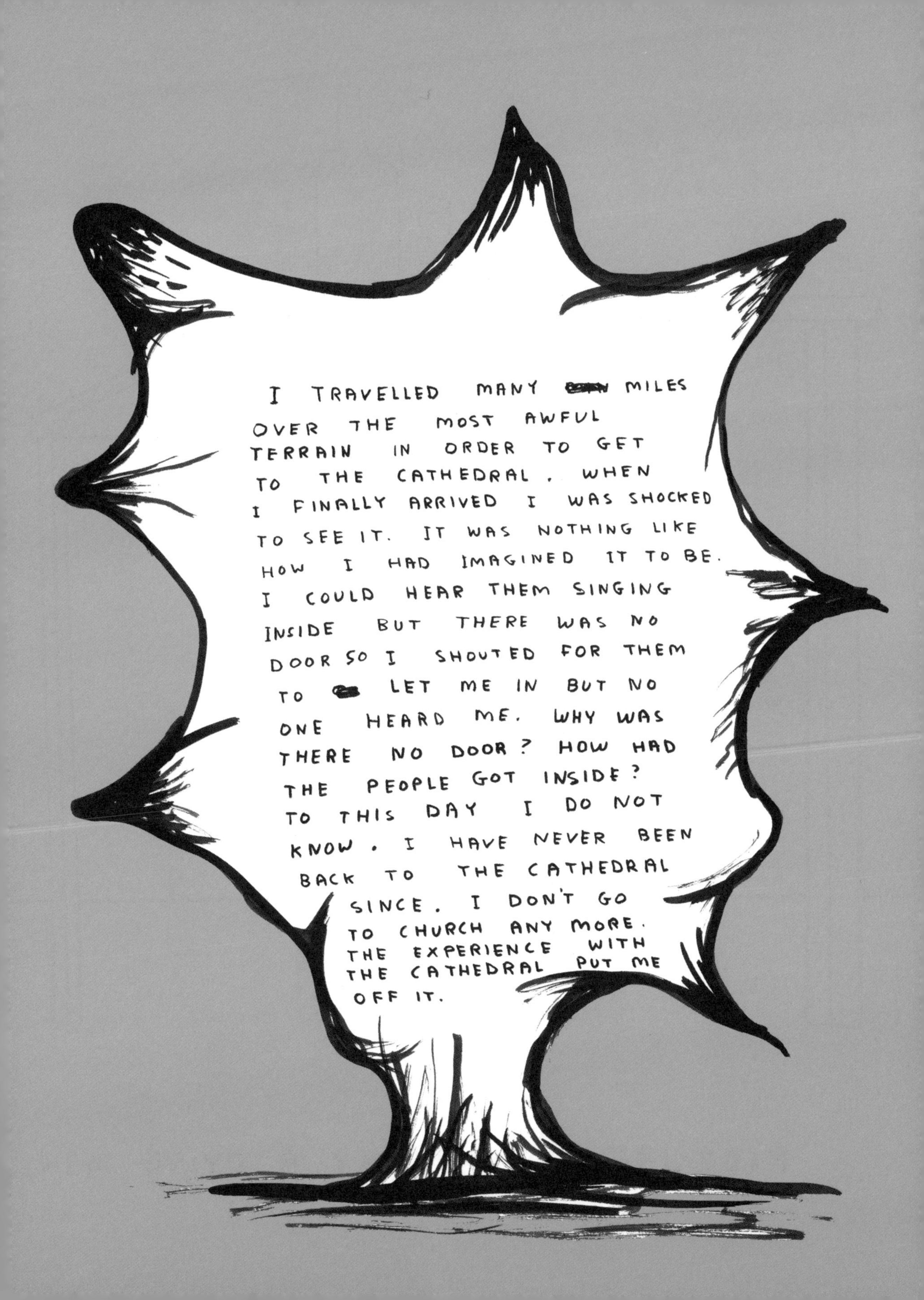
I TRAVELLED MANY MILES
OVER THE MOST AWFUL
TERRAIN IN ORDER TO GET
TO THE CATHEDRAL. WHEN
I FINALLY ARRIVED I WAS SHOCKED
TO SEE IT. IT WAS NOTHING LIKE
HOW I HAD IMAGINED IT TO BE.
I COULD HEAR THEM SINGING
INSIDE BUT THERE WAS NO
DOOR SO I SHOUTED FOR THEM
TO LET ME IN BUT NO
ONE HEARD ME. WHY WAS
THERE NO DOOR? HOW HAD
THE PEOPLE GOT INSIDE?
TO THIS DAY I DO NOT
KNOW. I HAVE NEVER BEEN
BACK TO THE CATHEDRAL
SINCE. I DON'T GO
TO CHURCH ANY MORE.
THE EXPERIENCE WITH
THE CATHEDRAL PUT ME
OFF IT.

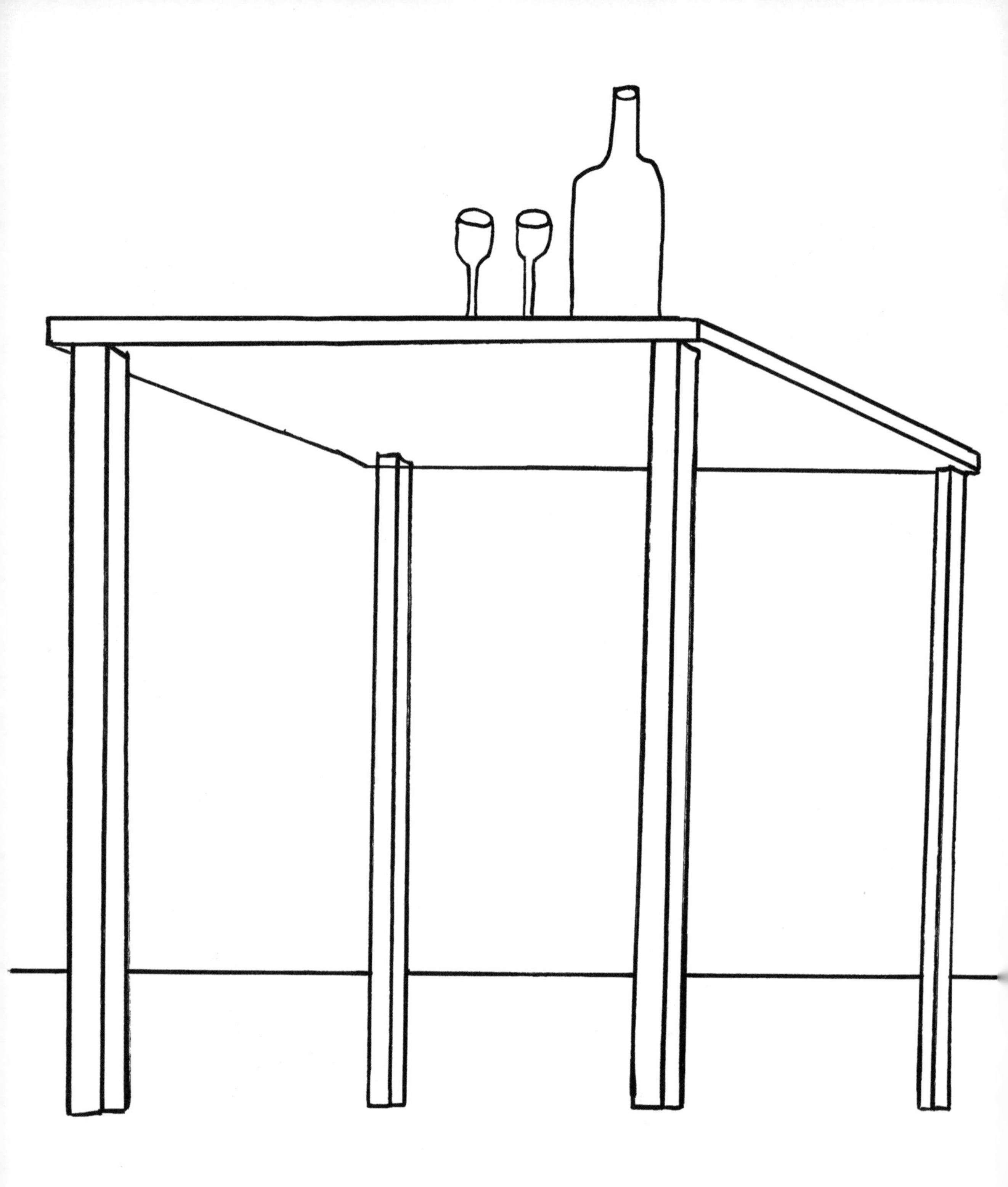

PICTURE DRAWN BY A DYING MAN

WHERE ARE OUR TEETH?

DRUNK AGAIN
I'M NOT DRUNK - I HAVE BEEN HARPOONED

IS HE READY TO BE SLAUGHTERED?

- YES HE IS READY

DO YOU THINK HE KNOWS HE IS ABOUT TO DIE?

- NO HE DOES NOT KNOW. HE IS STUPID.

T R U S T
T R U S T
T R U S T
T R U S T
T R U S T
T R U S T
T R U S T
T R U S T
T R U S T
T R U S T
TRUST
TRUST
TRUST
TRUST
TRUST
TRUST
TRUST
TRUST
TRUST
TRUST
TRUST
TRUST
TRUST
TRUST YOURSELF

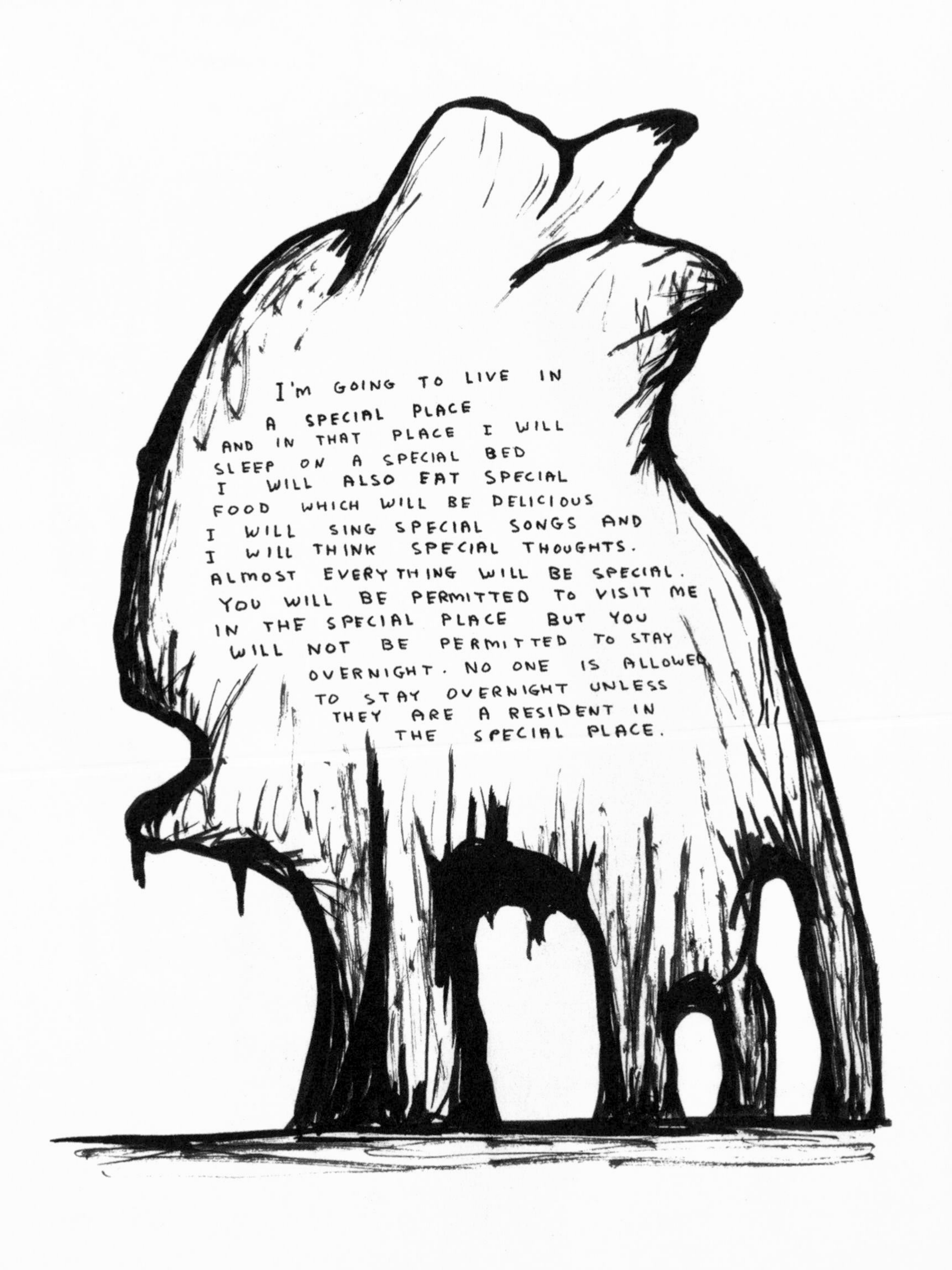
I'M GOING TO LIVE IN
A SPECIAL PLACE
AND IN THAT PLACE I WILL
SLEEP ON A SPECIAL BED
I WILL ALSO EAT SPECIAL
FOOD WHICH WILL BE DELICIOUS
I WILL SING SPECIAL SONGS AND
I WILL THINK SPECIAL THOUGHTS.
ALMOST EVERYTHING WILL BE SPECIAL.
YOU WILL BE PERMITTED TO VISIT ME
IN THE SPECIAL PLACE BUT YOU
WILL NOT BE PERMITTED TO STAY
OVERNIGHT. NO ONE IS ALLOWED
TO STAY OVERNIGHT UNLESS
THEY ARE A RESIDENT IN
THE SPECIAL PLACE.

SPIRITS
~~FEELINGS~~
NICEST OF ALL ~~CREATURES~~
YOU ARE WELCOME
THIS DAY IN MY
HOUSE
YOU GIVE ME
GUIDANCE AND
KEEP ME IN
A REASONABLE
ORBIT
I HAVE
~~BEEN~~ FELT
LOST BUT
NOW FEEL
MUCH
BETTER

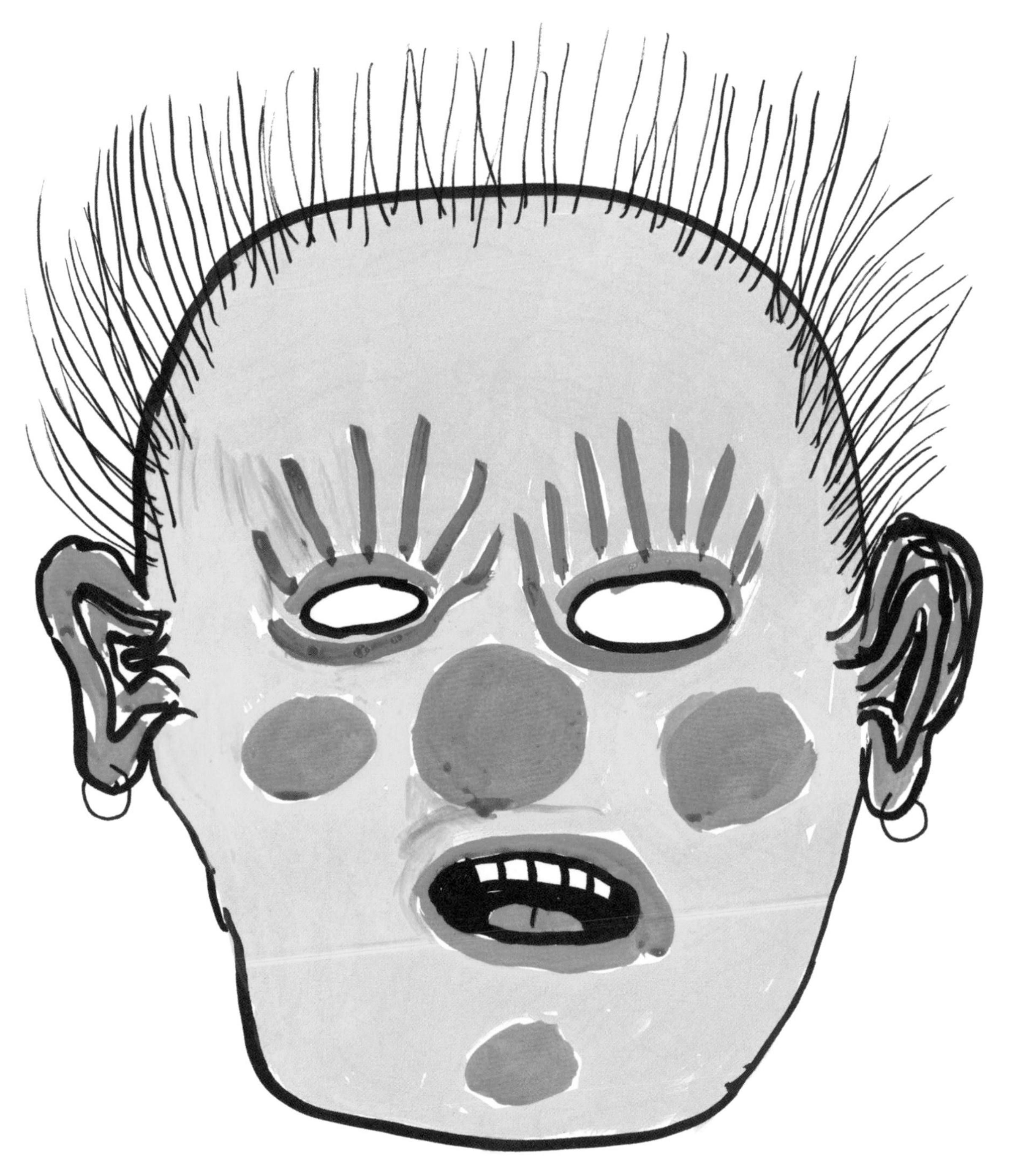

HA HA HA HA HA HA HA HA HA HA
HA HA HA HA HA HA HA HA HA HA
HA HA HA HA HA HA HA HA HA HA
HA HA HA HA HA HA HA HA HA HA
HA HA HA HA HA HA HA HA HA HA
HA HA HA HA

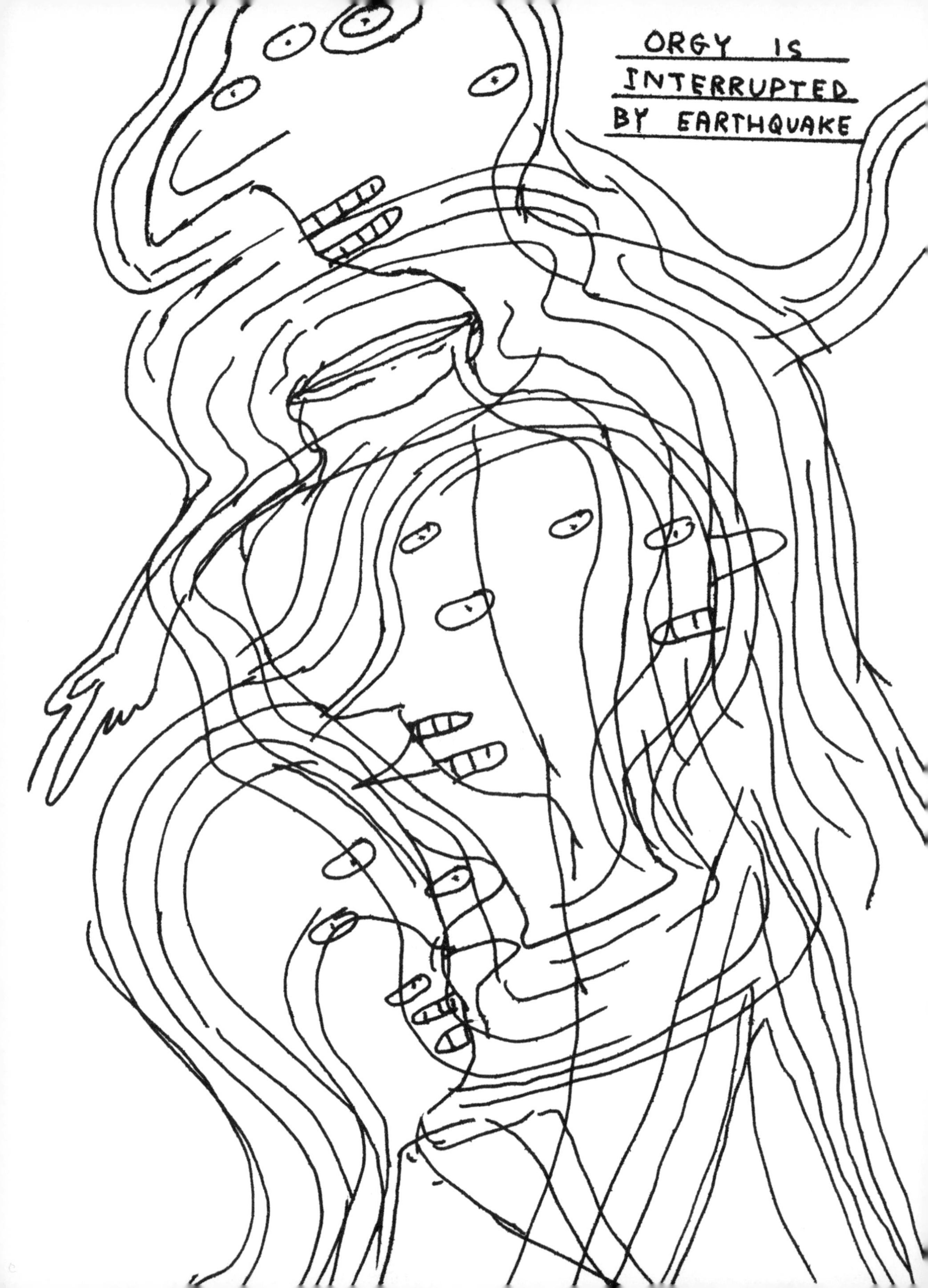
ORGY IS
INTERRUPTED
BY EARTHQUAKE

MY HOUSE

WAS SET

ON FIRE BY

HOOLIGANS

SHE SAID

THE LECTURE YOU GAVE WAS NOT WELL RECEIVED

THE NORTH WIND
DOTH BLOW

THINKING

NOT THINKING

THINKING

NOT THINKING

THINKING

NOT THINKING

THINKING

NOT THINKING

THINKING

NOT THINKING

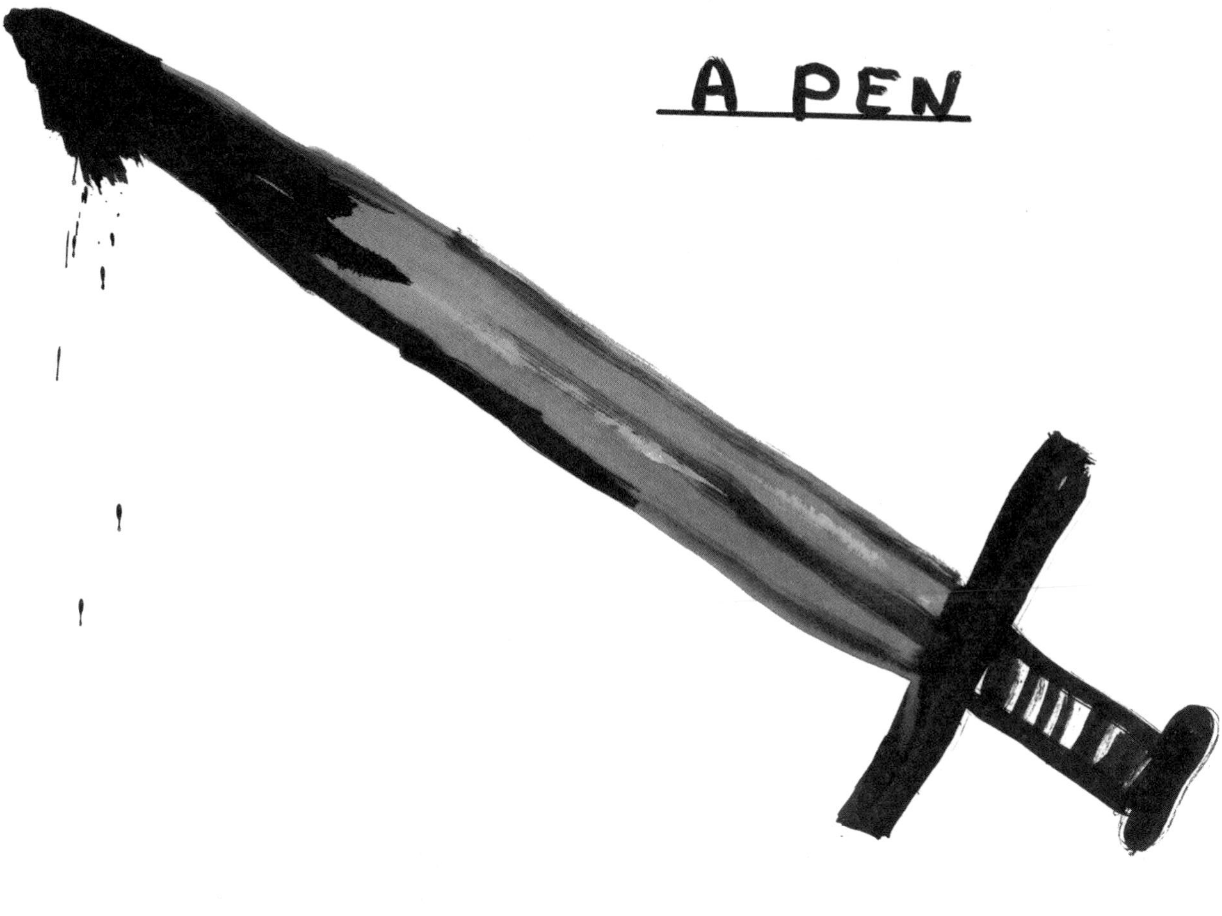

A PEN

ARTIST
EATEN BY
A WOLF

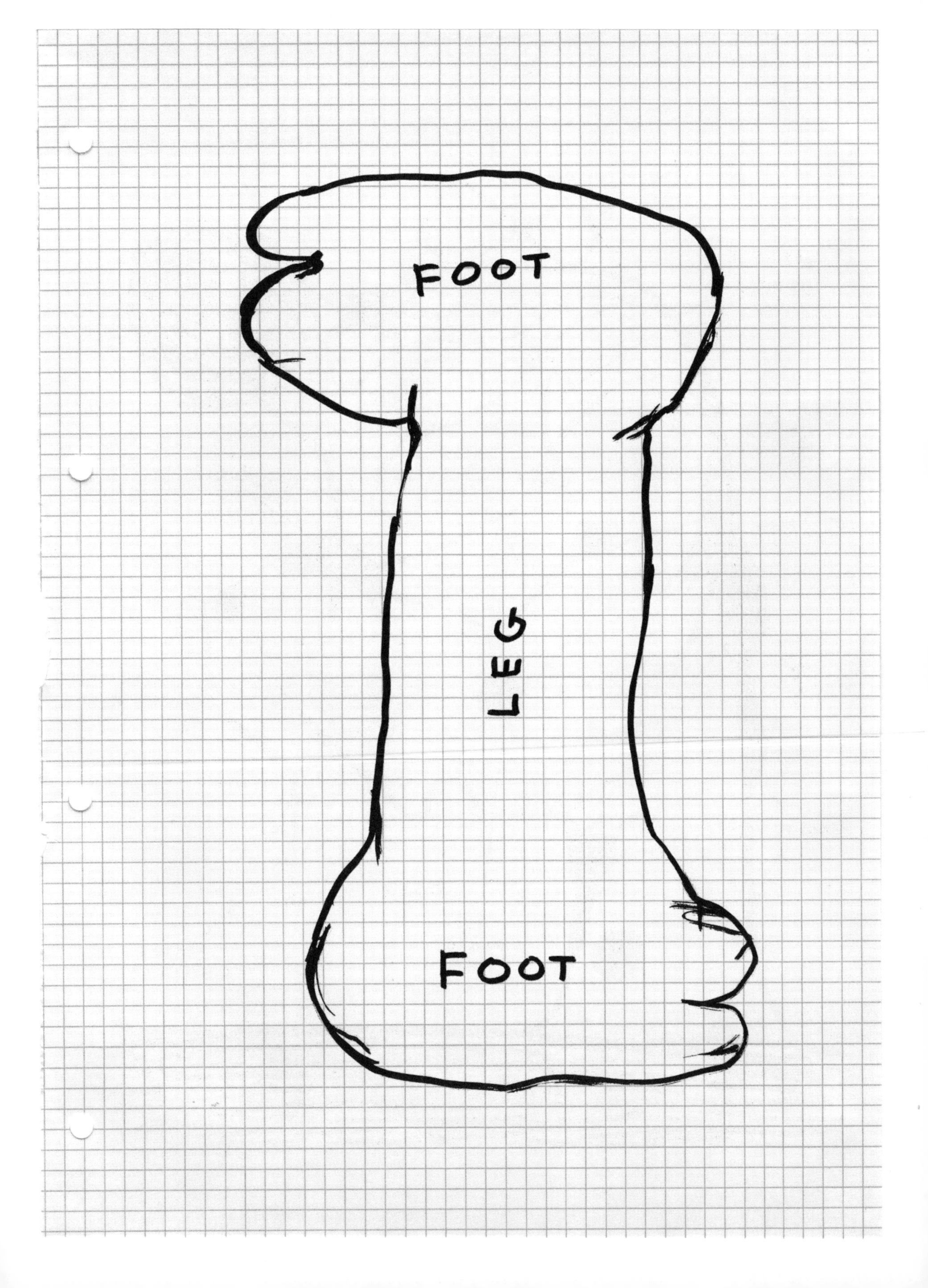
FOOT
LEG
FOOT

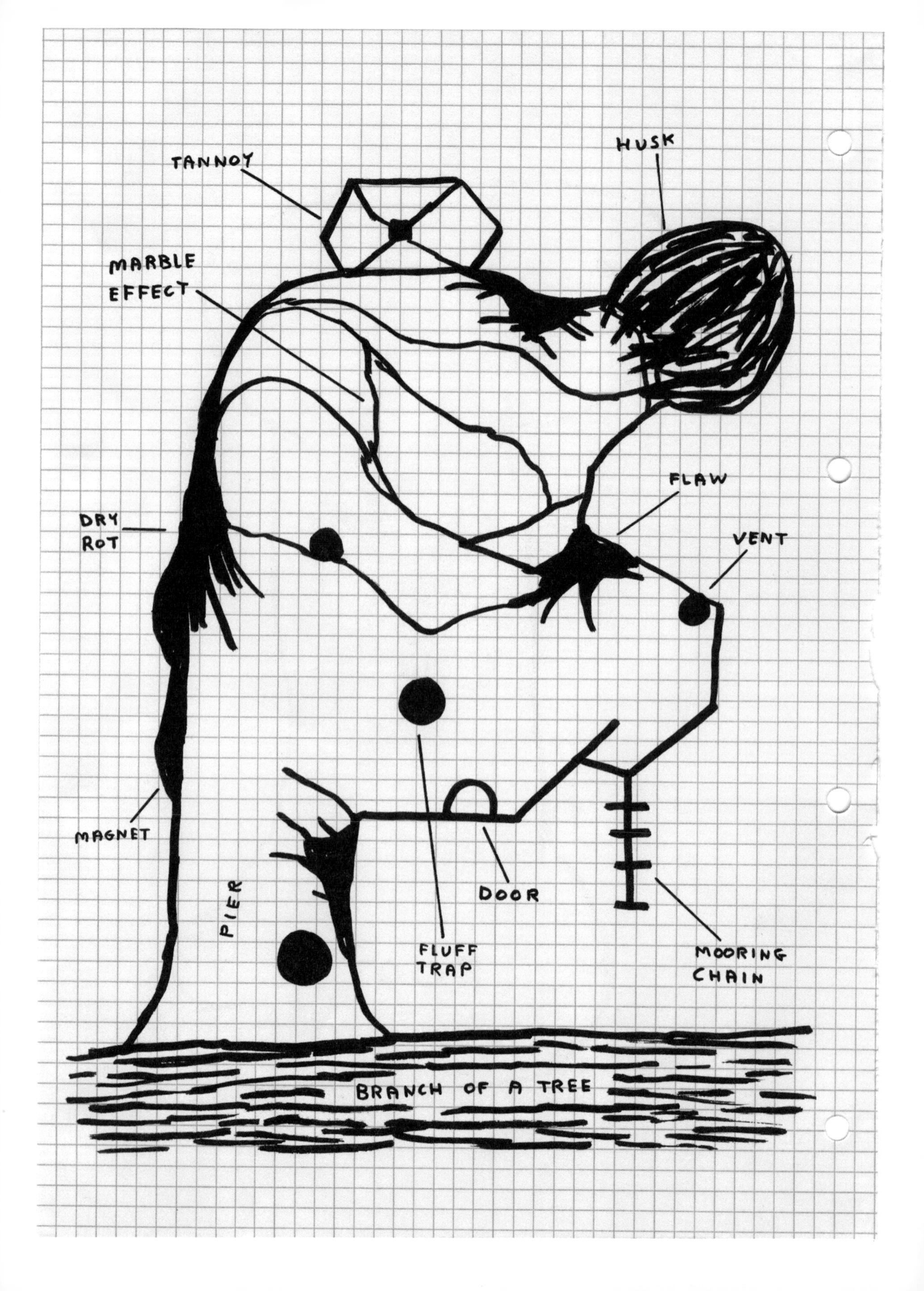
TANNOY
HUSK
MARBLE
EFFECT
FLAW
VENT
DRY
ROT
MAGNET
PIER
DOOR
FLUFF
TRAP
MOORING
CHAIN
BRANCH OF A TREE

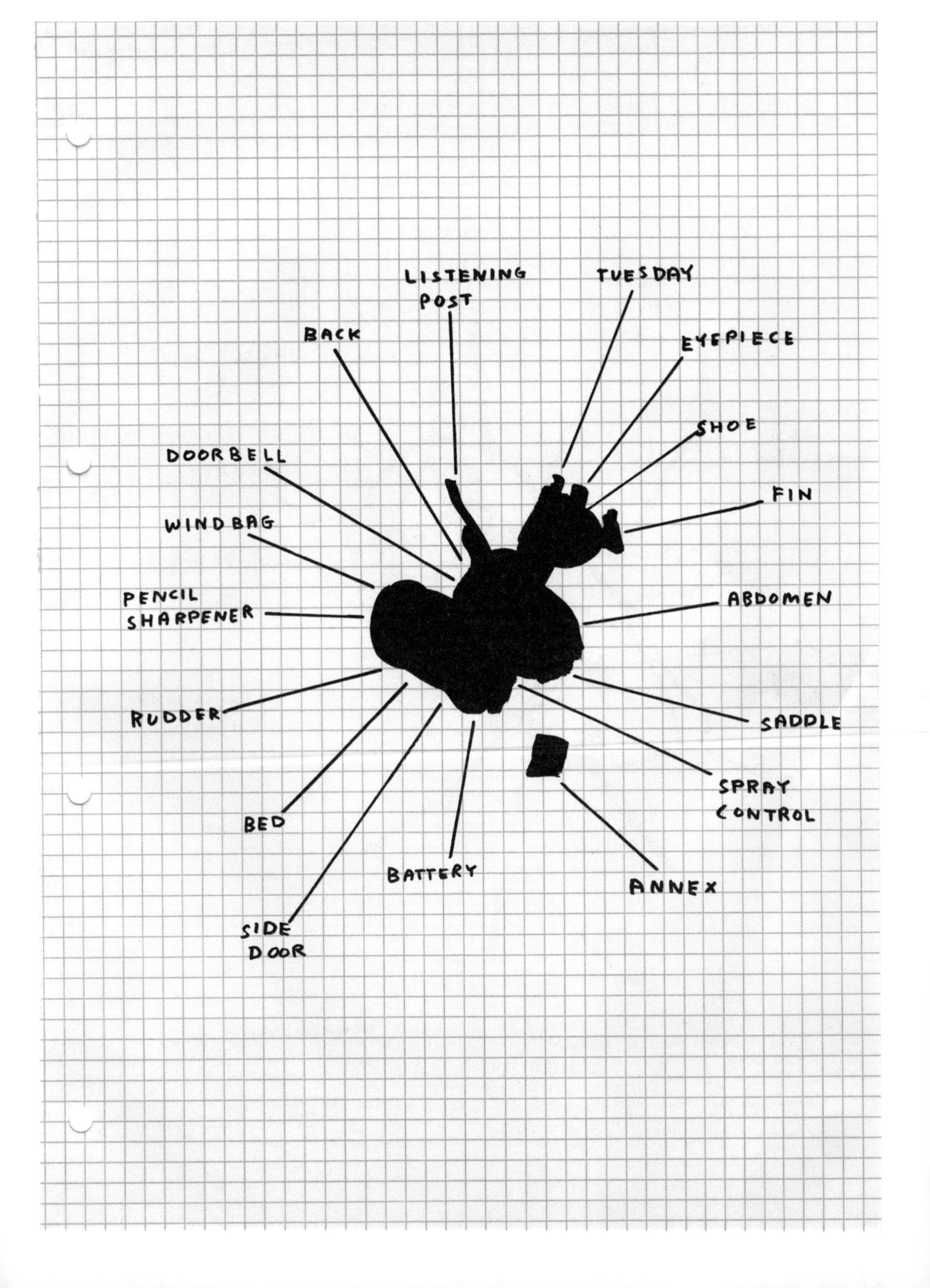
LISTENING POST
TUESDAY
BACK
EYEPIECE
SHOE
DOORBELL
FIN
WINDBAG
PENCIL SHARPENER
ABDOMEN
RUDDER
SADDLE
SPRAY CONTROL
BED
BATTERY
ANNEX
SIDE DOOR

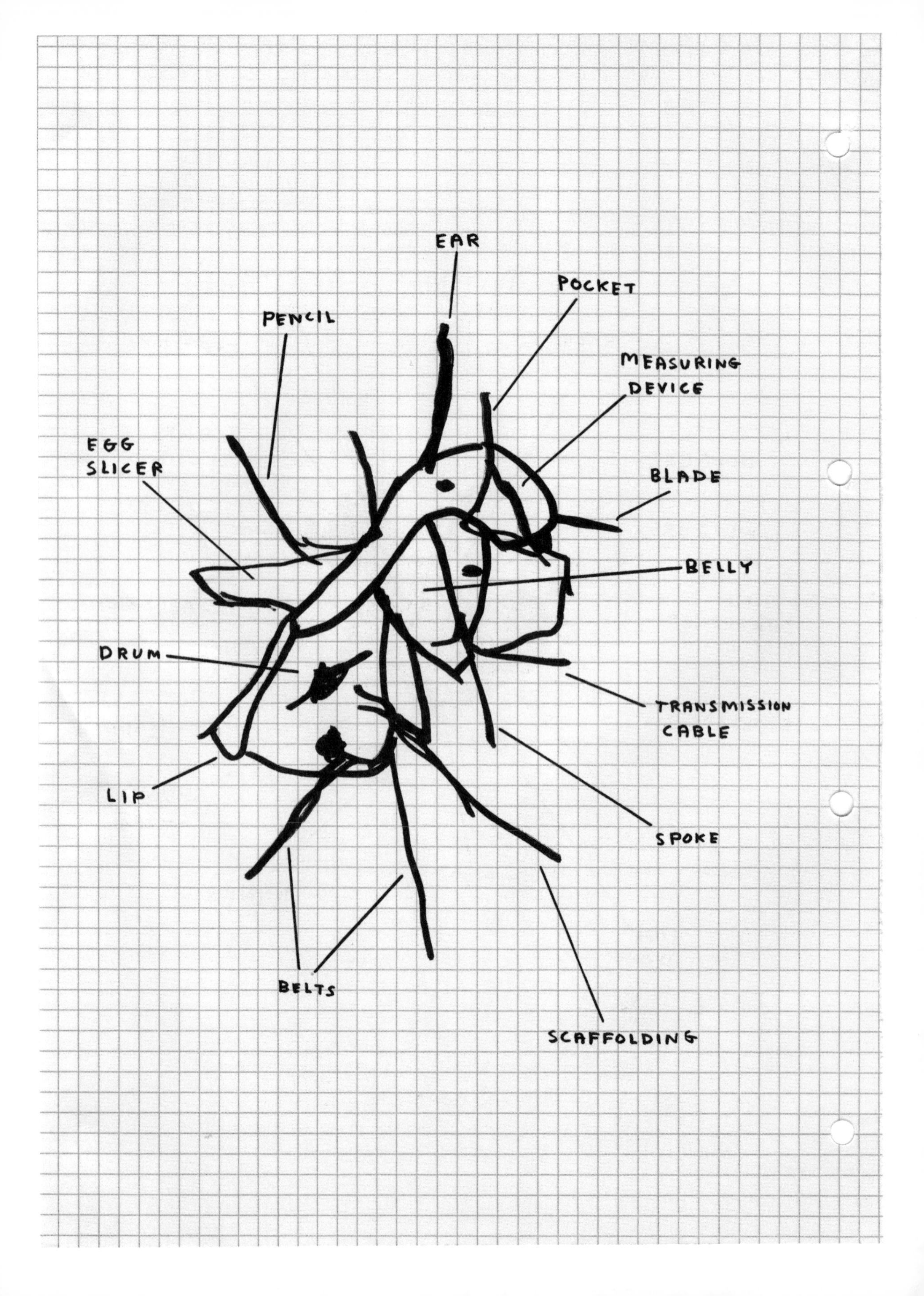
EAR
POCKET
PENCIL
MEASURING DEVICE
EGG SLICER
BLADE
BELLY
DRUM
TRANSMISSION CABLE
LIP
SPOKE
BELTS
SCAFFOLDING

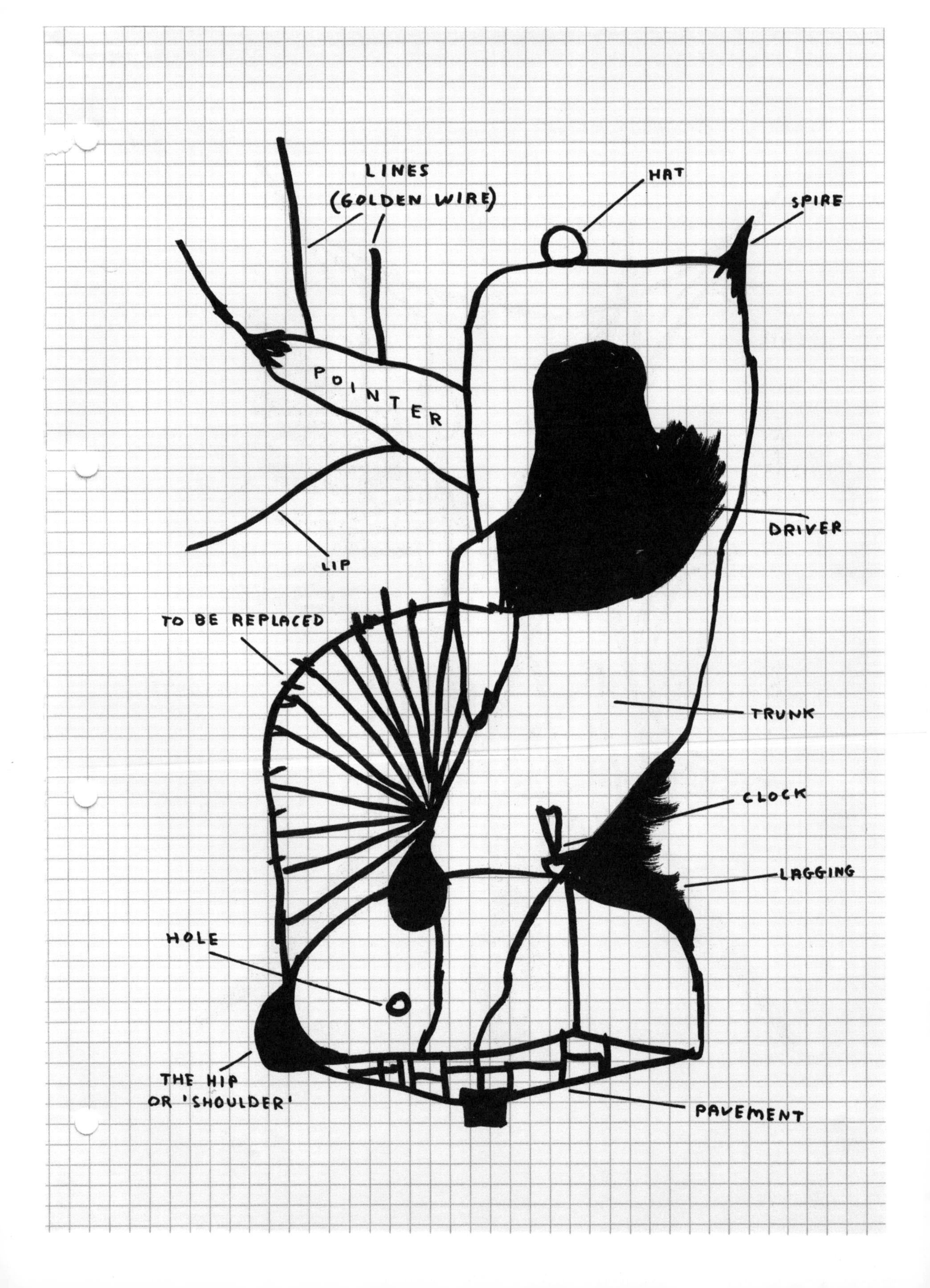

LINES
(GOLDEN WIRE)
HAT
SPIRE
POINTER
DRIVER
LIP
TO BE REPLACED
TRUNK
CLOCK
LAGGING
HOLE
THE HIP
OR 'SHOULDER'
PAVEMENT

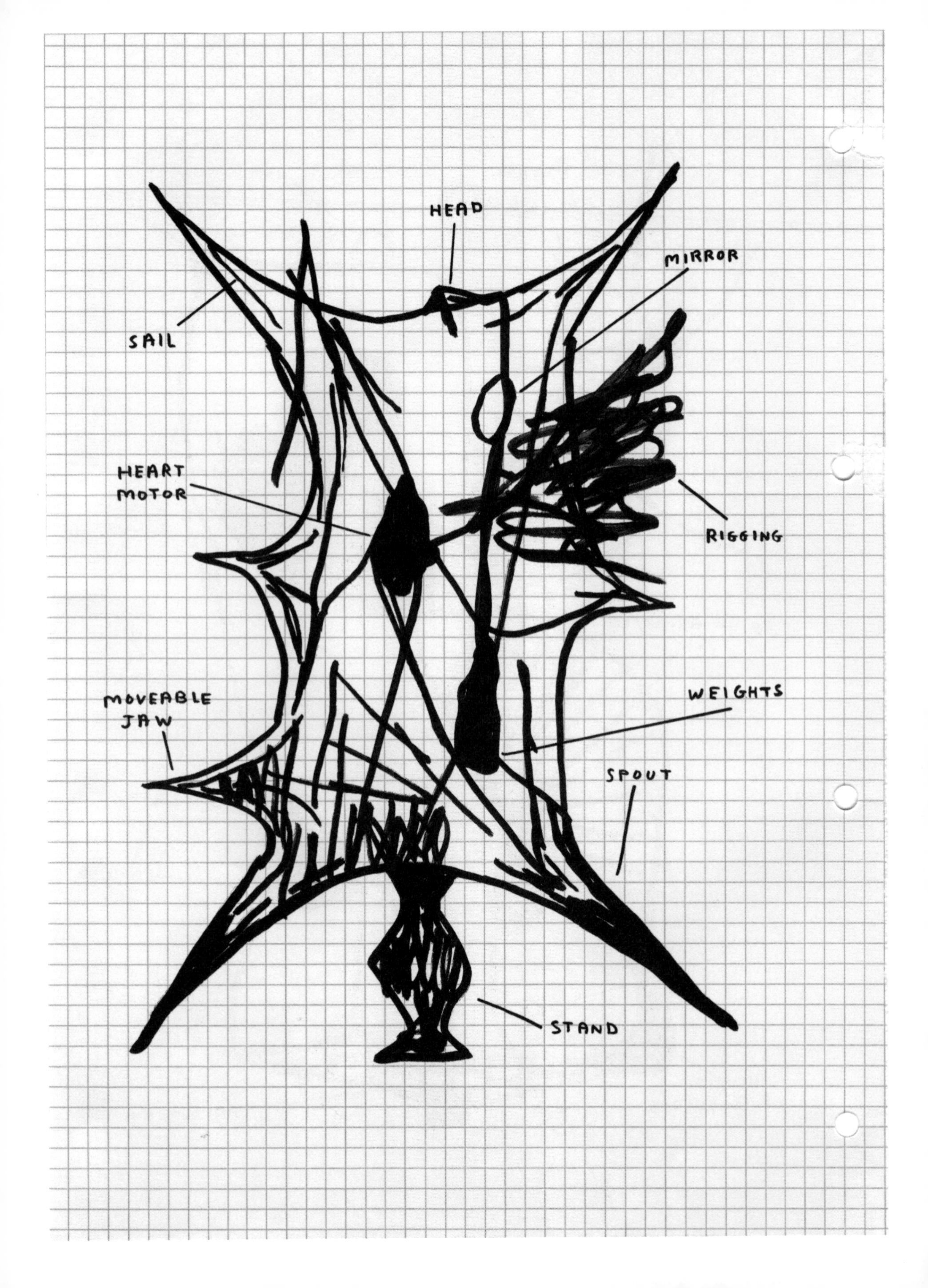
HEAD
MIRROR
SAIL
HEART
MOTOR
RIGGING
MOVEABLE
JAW
WEIGHTS
SPOUT
STAND

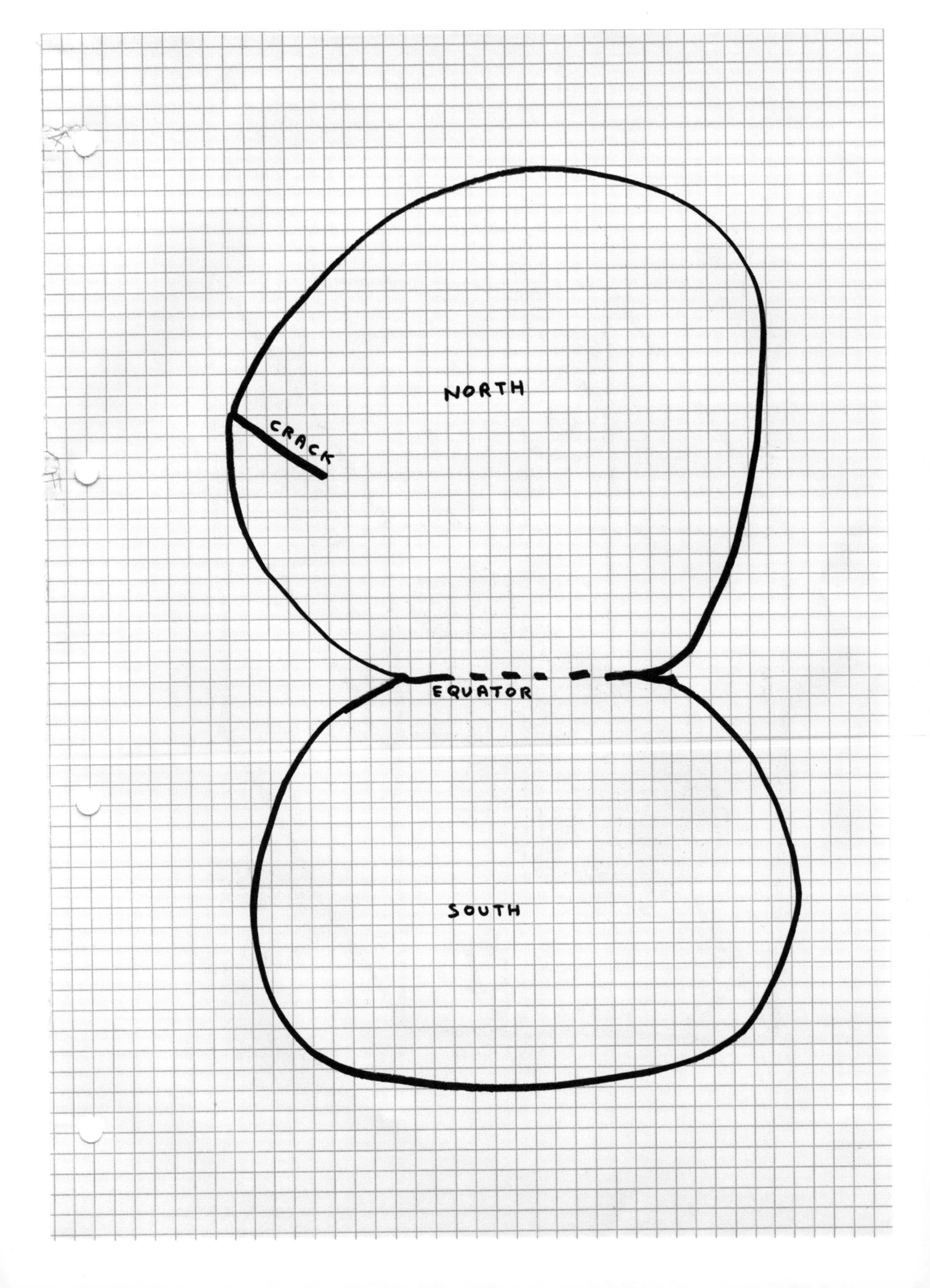
NORTH
CRACK
EQUATOR
SOUTH

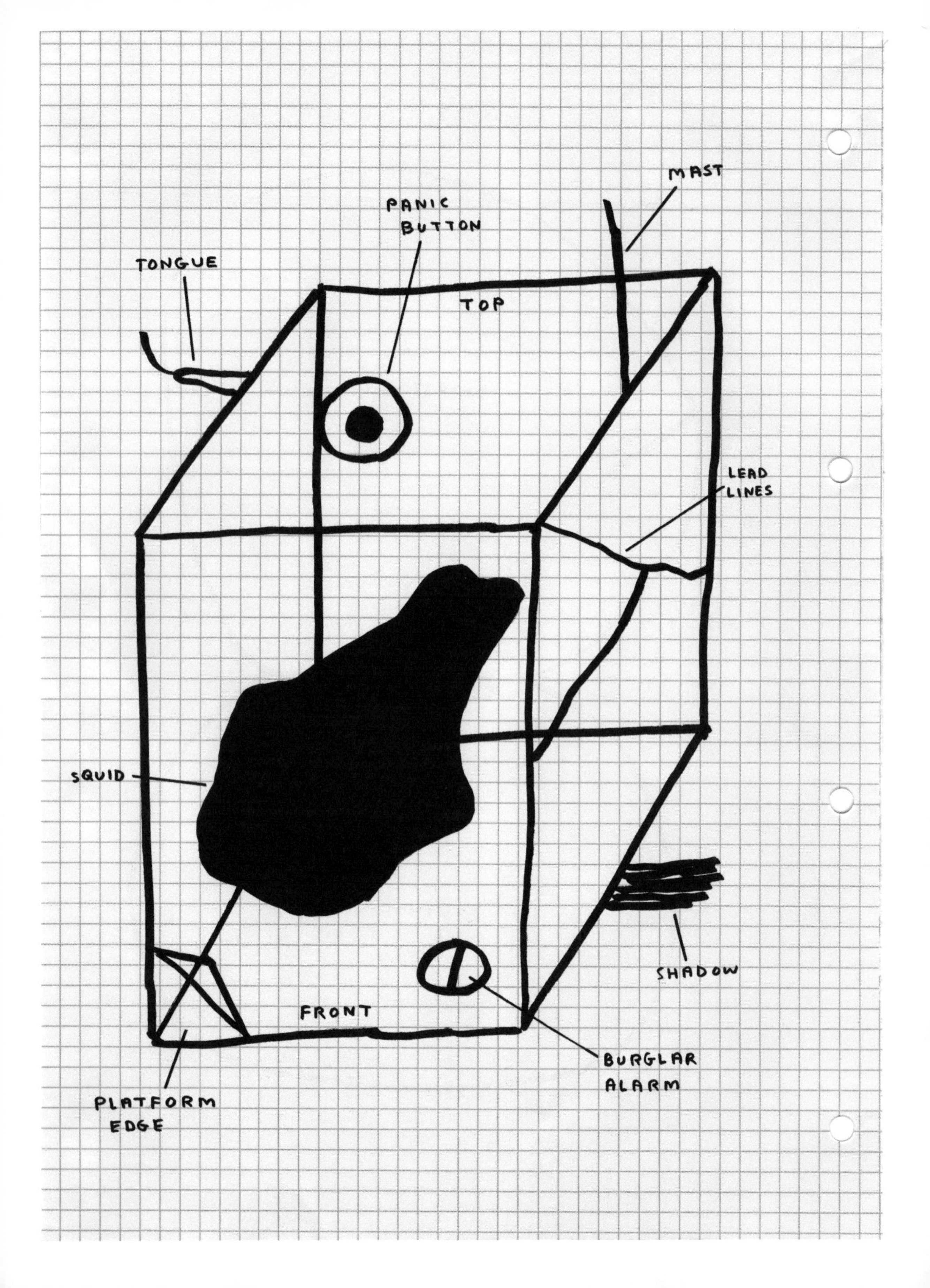

MAST
PANIC BUTTON
TONGUE
TOP
LEAD LINES
SQUID
SHADOW
FRONT
BURGLAR ALARM
PLATFORM EDGE

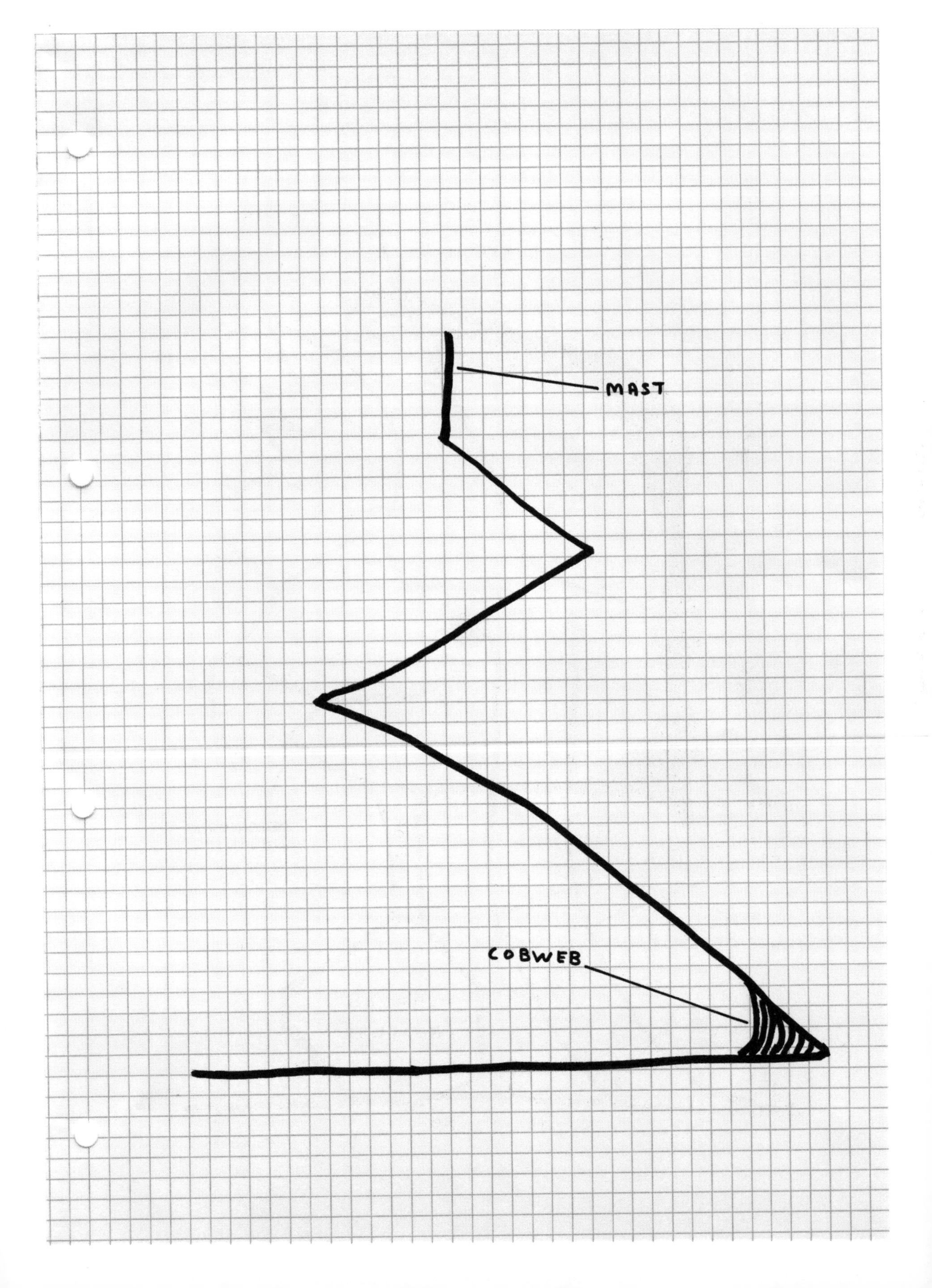
MAST
COBWEB

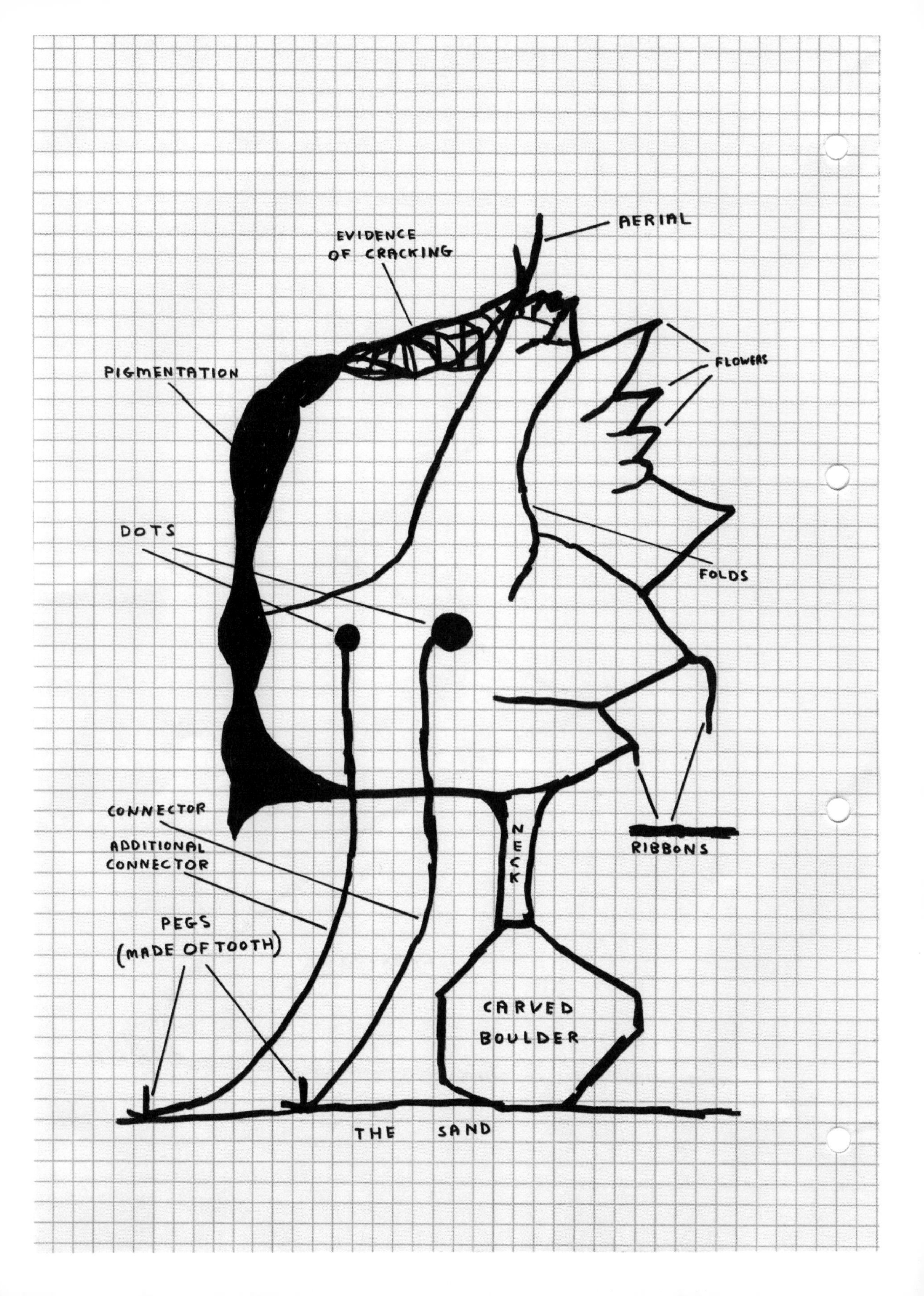
AERIAL
EVIDENCE
OF CRACKING
PIGMENTATION
FLOWERS
DOTS
FOLDS
CONNECTOR
ADDITIONAL
CONNECTOR
N
E
C
K
RIBBONS
PEGS
(MADE OF TOOTH)
CARVED
BOULDER
THE SAND

PLEASE
VISIT
OUR
DAMNED
SHOP

PLEASE
BUY
OUR
DAMNED
PRODUCTS

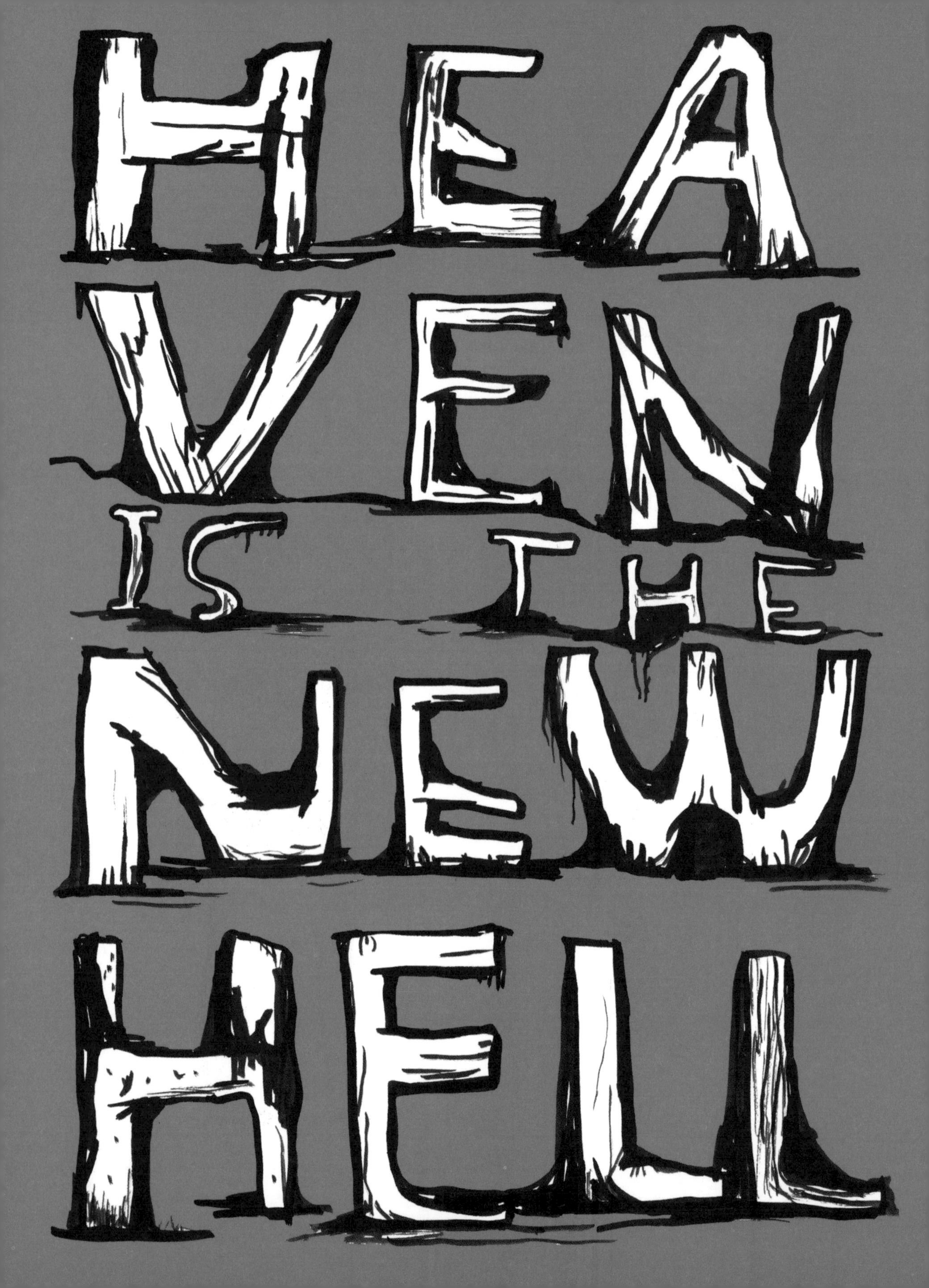
HEA
VEN
IS THE
NEW
HELL

EXAM
WHAT IS YOUR
NAME?
A. TED
B. BRIAN
C. DAVE
D. SUSAN

SMILE,
GOD
LOVES
YOU

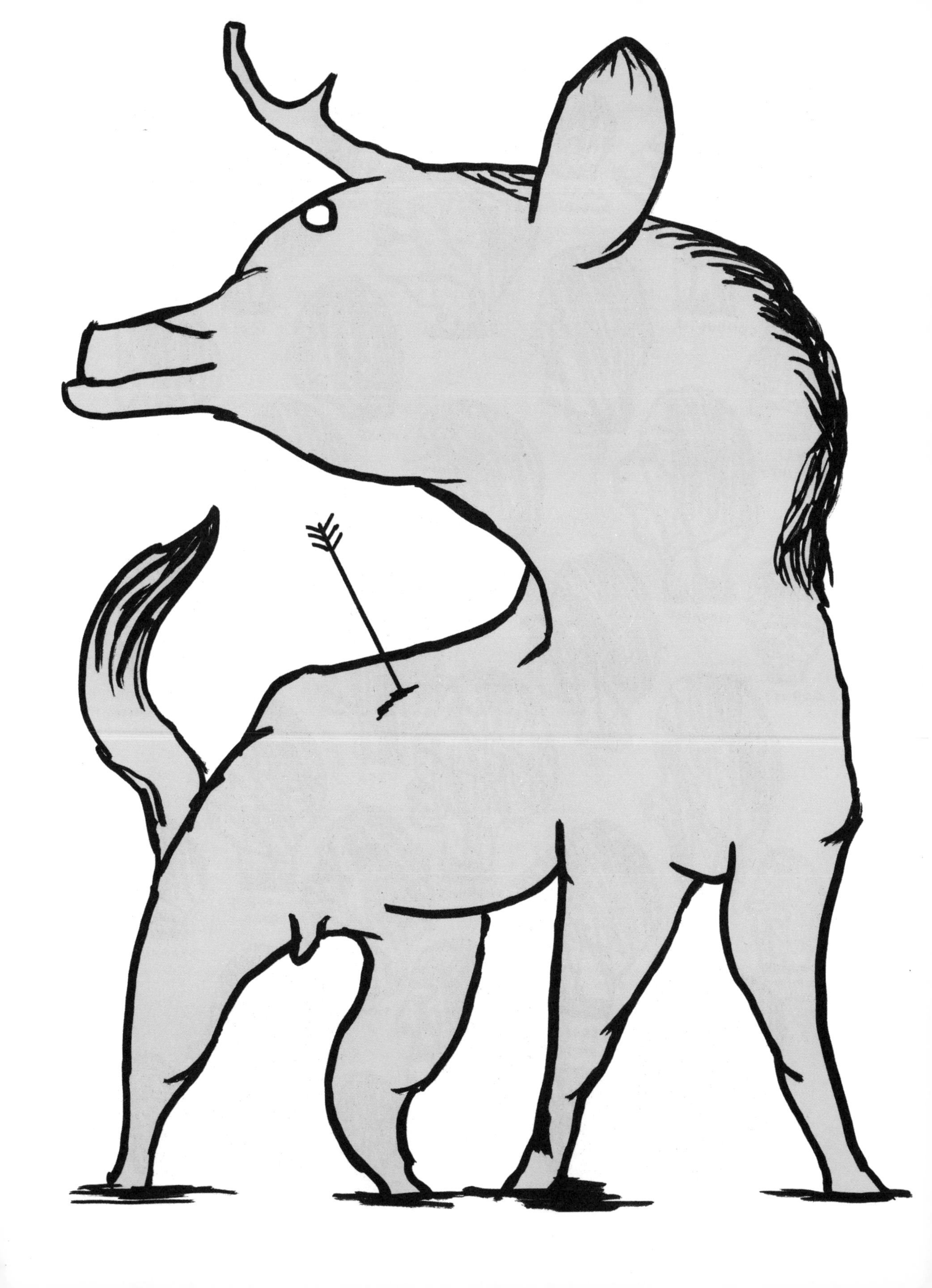

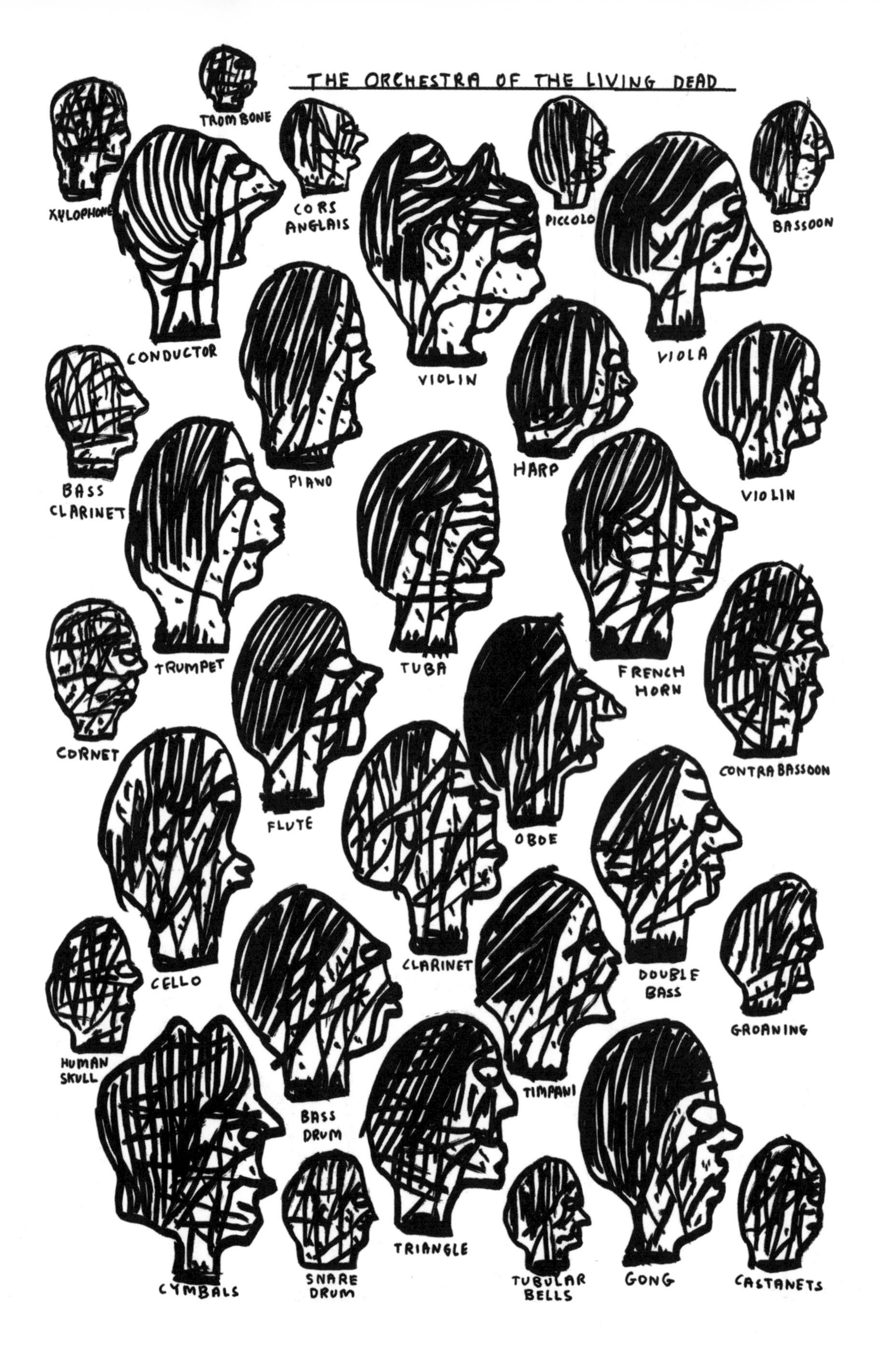

THE ORCHESTRA OF THE LIVING DEAD
TROMBONE
XYLOPHONE
CORS ANGLAIS
PICCOLO
BASSOON
CONDUCTOR
VIOLIN
VIOLA
BASS CLARINET
PIANO
HARP
VIOLIN
TRUMPET
TUBA
FRENCH HORN
CORNET
FLUTE
OBOE
CONTRA BASSOON
CELLO
CLARINET
DOUBLE BASS
GROANING
HUMAN SKULL
BASS DRUM
TIMPANI
CYMBALS
SNARE DRUM
TRIANGLE
TUBULAR BELLS
GONG
CASTANETS

LARGE INFLATABLE
BALL

I AM HAPPY
YOU ARE HAPPY
SKULL IS HAPPY
WE ARE ALL HAPPY

COCK

THE FIELD OF STRIPES

THE STRIPES INTERFOLD AND DISTRESS ME
I FEEL LIKE CRYING

SNIFFING GLUE REALLY IS THE MOST TERRIFIC FUN.

I LOVE IT AND AM GOING TO DO IT

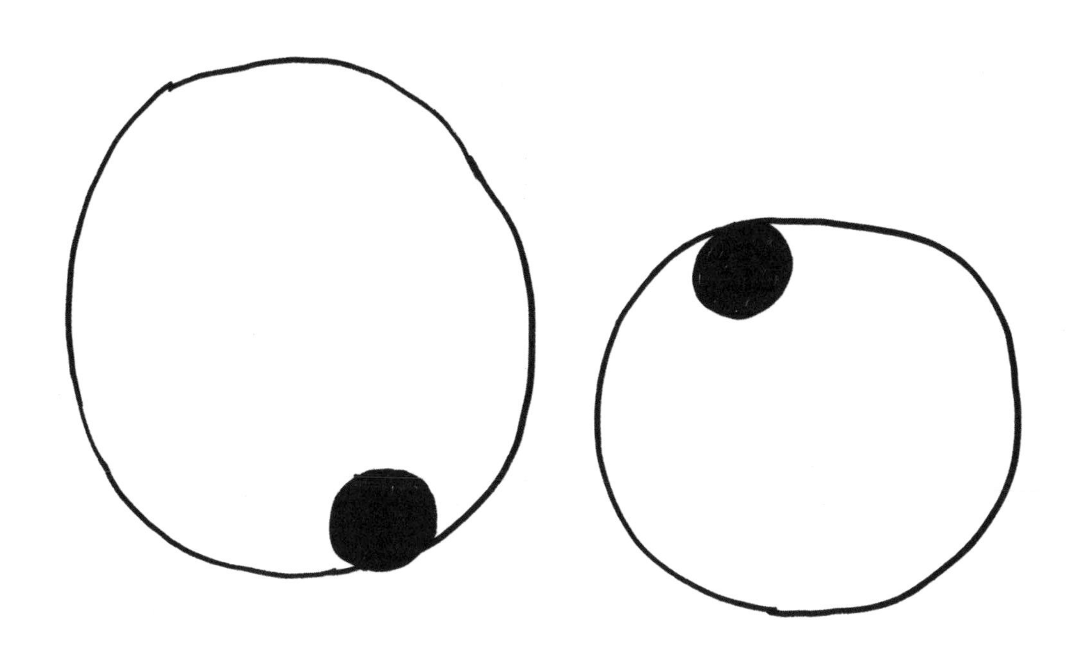

EVERYDAY FOR THE REST OF MY LIFE.

IF I HAD KNOWN HOW MUCH FUN IT WAS WHEN I WAS A YOUNGER MAN I WOULD NOT HAVE BOTHERED JOINING THE ARMY.

AVANT-GARDE FILMS DIRECT TO YOUR T.V.
VIA CABLE OR SATELLITE
UNLESS YOU STOP MASTURBATING

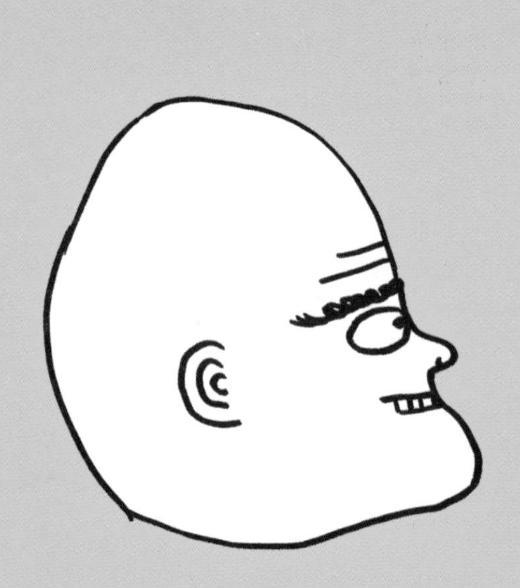

FRONT

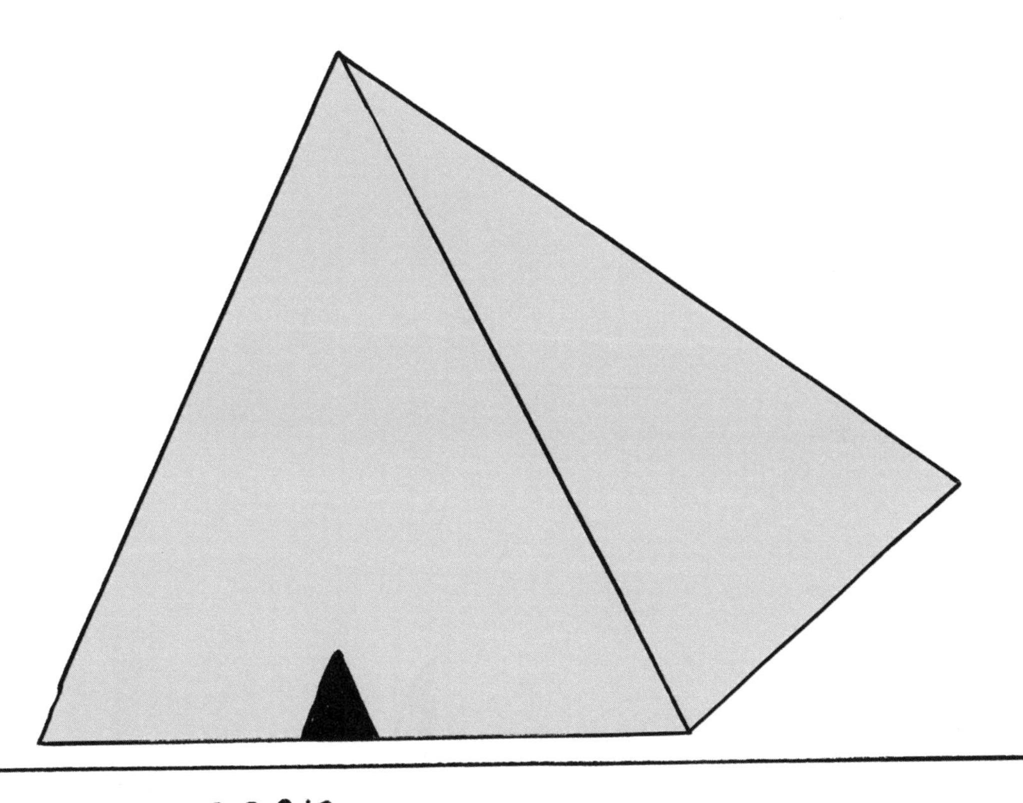

BACK

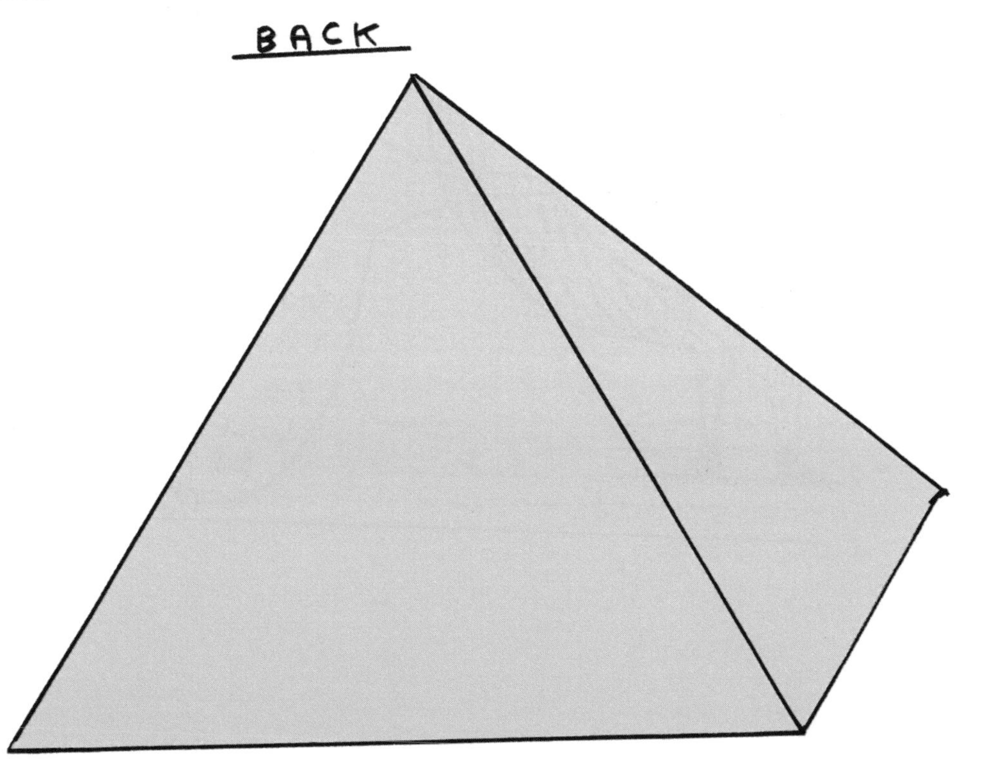

THE OTHER
BIRDS HAVE
BEEN BULLYING
ME SO I MUST
STAY ON THE
GROUND. THEY SAY
THAT IF I TAKE
TO THE AIR THEY
WILL PECK THE
BEJESUS OUT
OF ME.

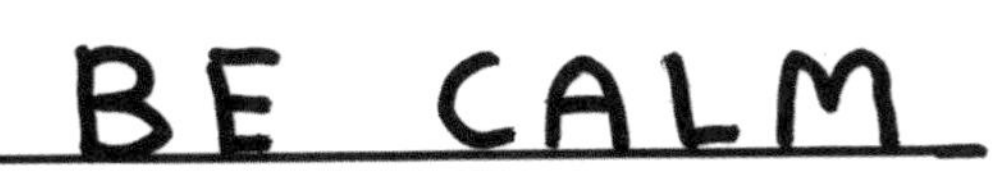
BE CALM

I WAS THE ONLY
ONE WHO OBEYED
HIM

HOW MUCH DOES IT COST ?
IT COSTS ONE HUNDRED MILLION POUNDS
IT'S AMAZING
IT'S VERY NICE
IT'S PROBABLY WORTH A LOT MORE

- HEY OLD PAL IT'S GOOD TO SEE YOU
- IT'S GOOD TO SEE YOU TOO. IT'S BEEN AGES
WHERE HAVE YOU BEEN?
- I'VE BEEN IN JAIL
- REALLY? SO HAVE I!
- WHAT A CO-INCIDENCE
- YES!
- HA HA HA HA
- HA HA HA HA

I'M TRAPPED

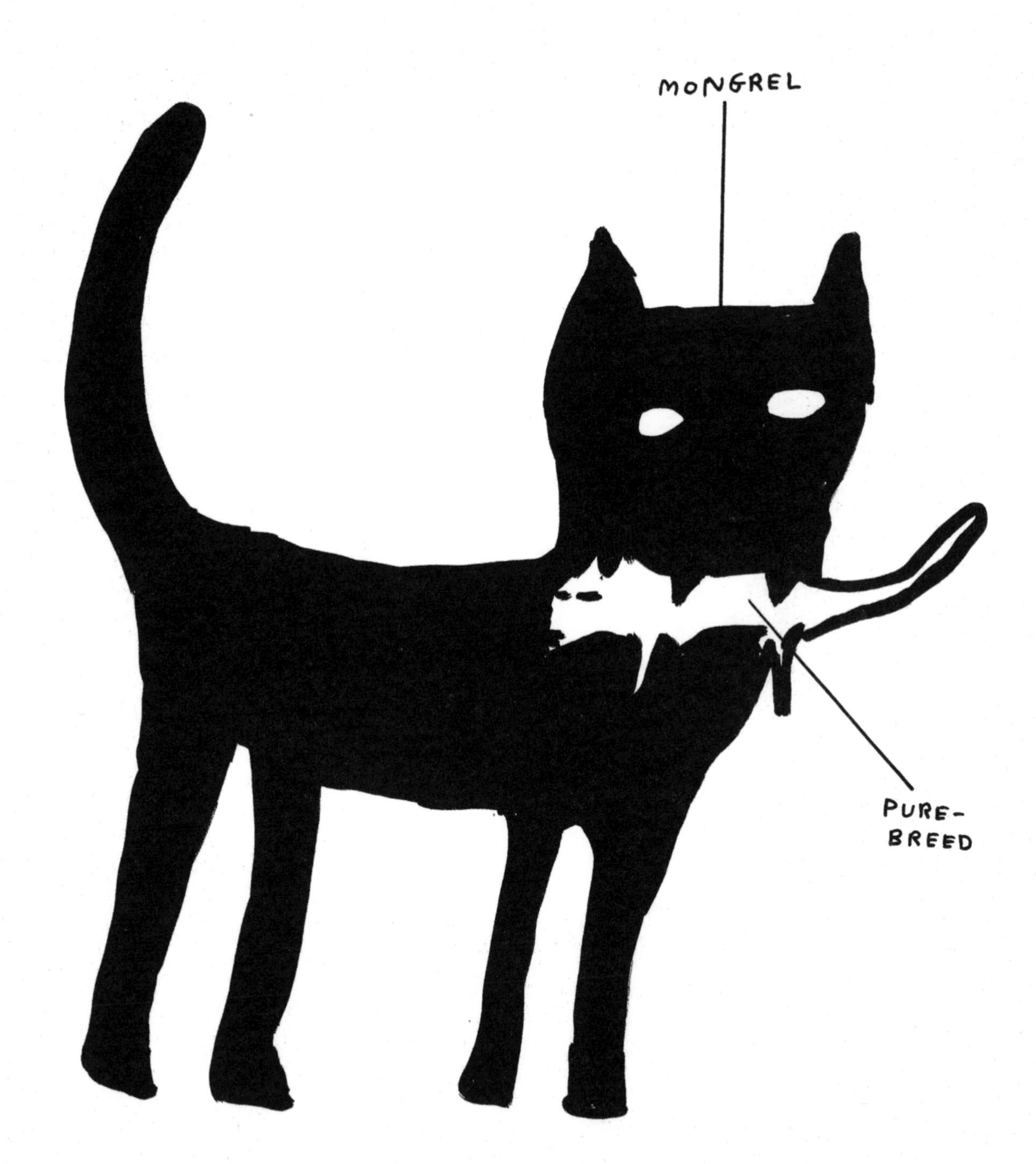
MONGREL
PURE-
BREED

PARTY

I WAS CHASED BY A WOLF
BUT THEN THE WOLF DIED OF A HEART ATTACK
AND THE POLICE CAME AND TRIED TO ARREST
ME. SO I RAN AND HID IN THE WOODS.

THAT WHICH IS NOT SAID

- WILL WE GO TO HEAVEN WHEN WE DIE?
- NO. HEAVEN IS ONLY FOR HUMANS. WE ARE WOODLAND FOLK AND OUR DESTINY IS THE SAME AS THAT OF APES AND MONKEYS. WE HAVE NO SOULS AND THEREFORE WE JUST DIE AND ROT.
- THAT SEEMS UNFAIR.
- YES. IT DOES SEEM VERY UNFAIR.

- WHERE IS THE EYE HOSPITAL ?
- IT'S RIGHT INFRONT OF YOU

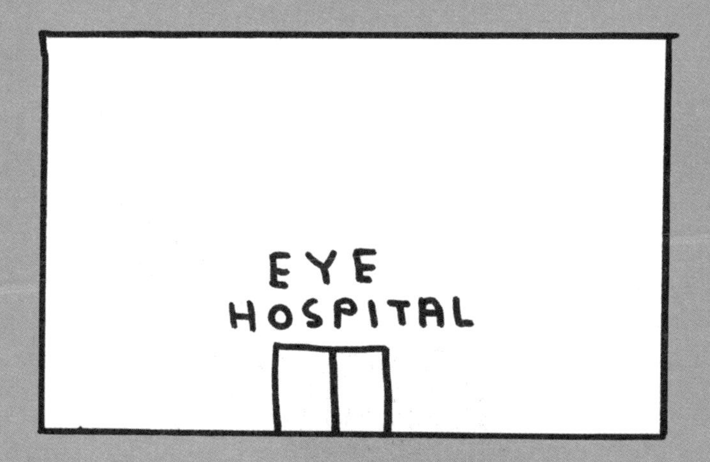

PORN

DIRTY, STINKING, HORRIBLE PORN RIGHT HERE, RIGHT NOW AND YOU ARE LOOKING AT IT. YOU WILL GO TO HELL FOR THIS.

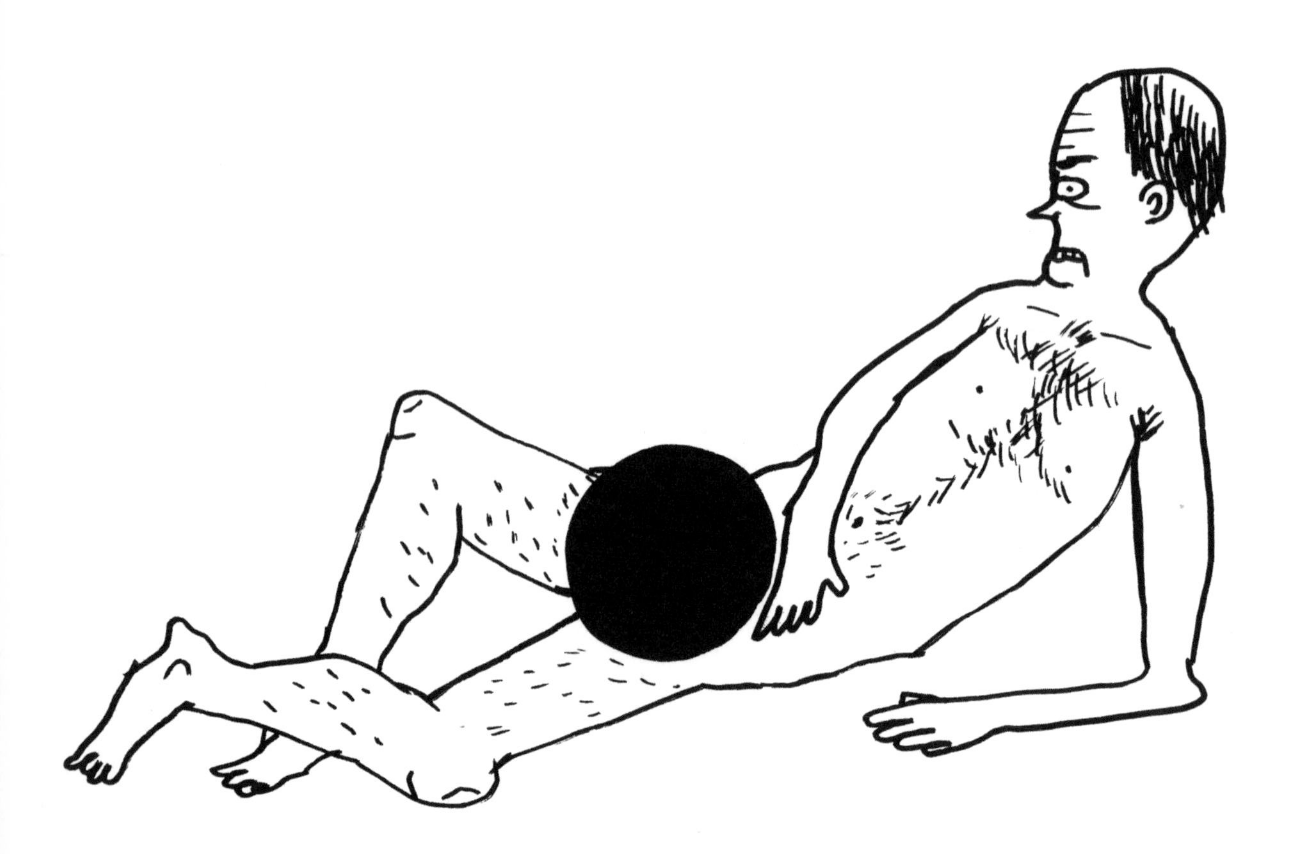

MISSING FROM YOUR
LIFE THUS FAR ;

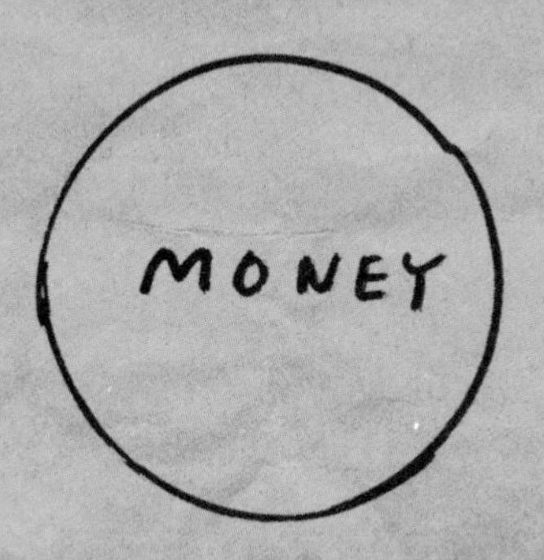

REASON

QUALIFICATIONS

YOU DON'T WANT TO END UP LIKE THIS DO YOU?

OF COURSE YOU DON'T

NO ONE DOES

IT WAS A SILLY QUESTION

AND I AM SORRY FOR ASKING IT

I AM A FRUIT

YOU CAN EAT ME

IF YOU WANT

SEXY

CHILD KEEPS ASKING FOR THE SWORD INCESSANTLY, OVER AND OVER.
"CAN I HAVE THE SWORD?"
"CAN I HAVE THE SWORD?"
GOD DAMN IT! JUST GIVE THE CHILD THE BLOODY SWORD AND THEN WE CAN ALL HAVE SOME PEACE!

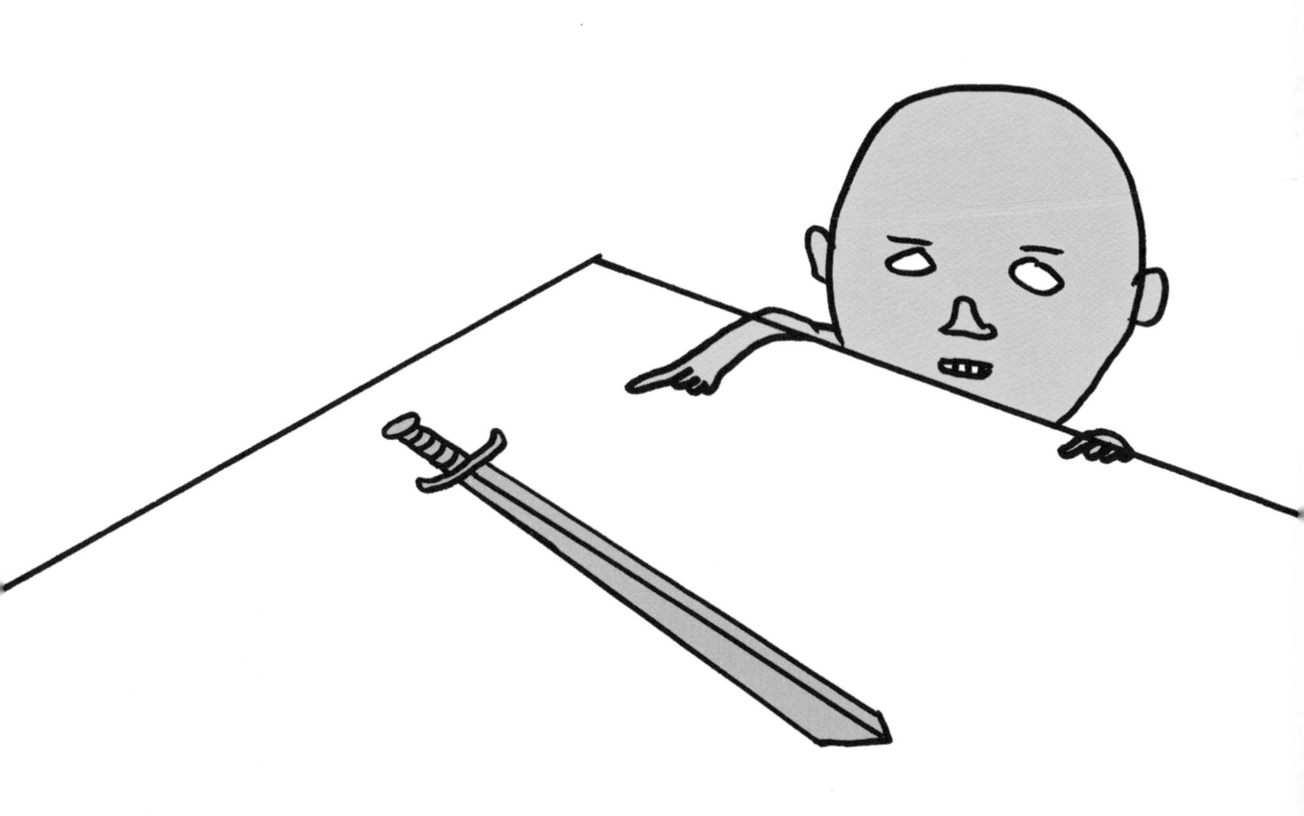

- WHICH ONE WOULD YOU LIKE TO BE SPEARED WITH?

- ARE THEY STERILE?

- NO. THIS ISN'T A HOSPITAL YOU KNOW

- I KNOW THAT. INCIDENTALLY, IS THERE A HOSPITAL NEAR HERE?

- THERE'S ONE 10 MINUTES WALK AWAY.

- WILL I BE ABLE TO WALK AFTER BEING SPEARED?

- PROBABLY NOT, BUT WE'LL GET SOMEONE TO DRAG YOU THERE. NOW HURRY UP AND DECIDE OR I'LL DECIDE FOR YOU.

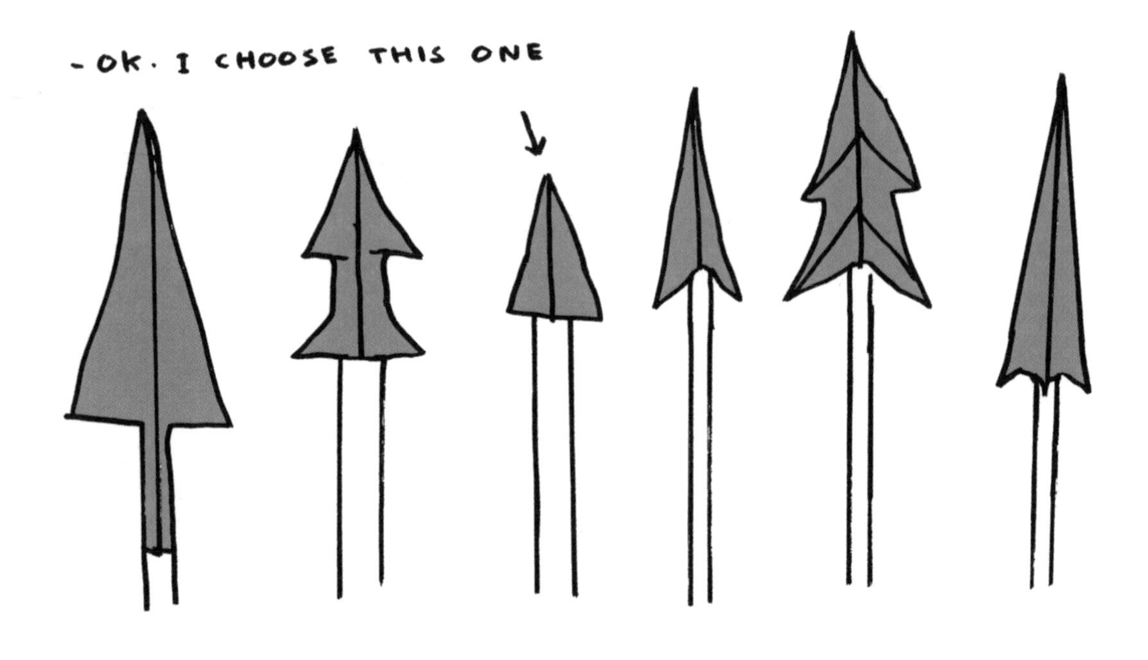

WE TOTALLY DON'T GIVE A SHIT ABOUT ANYTHING
WE REALLY ABSOLUTELY DON'T FUCKING CARE

BLOODY SWANS

MUSHROOMS
DEADLY POISON
DEADLY POISON
DEADLY POISON
DEADLY POISON
DEADLY POISON
DEADLY POISON
DEADLY POISON
DEADLY POISON
DEADLY POISON
DEADLY POISON
DEADLY POISON
CURE FOR ACUTE PARANOIA
DEADLY POISON
DEADLY POISON
DEADLY POISON
DEADLY POISON
DEADLY POISON
DEADLY POISON
DEADLY POISON
DEADLY POISON

I FOUND HIM IN
THE GARDEN
IN THE DIRT
THE URGE TO KILL HIM
IS IRRESISTIBLE

YOU ARE A BUCK-TOOTHED
SWINE THERE IS NO PLACE
FOR YOU IN THIS TOWN
IF IT WERE UP TO
ME I WOULD HAVE
YOU LEAVE THIS INSTANT
SUCH DOES YOUR PRESENCE
REPULSE AND TROUBLE
ME GO NOW YOU UGLY
FOOL IF YOU KNOW WHAT
IS GOOD FOR YOU AND IF
YOU KNOW WHAT IS RIGHT
WE WOULD RATHER BE WITH
OUT A DOCTOR THAN HAVE
ONE SUCH AS YOU

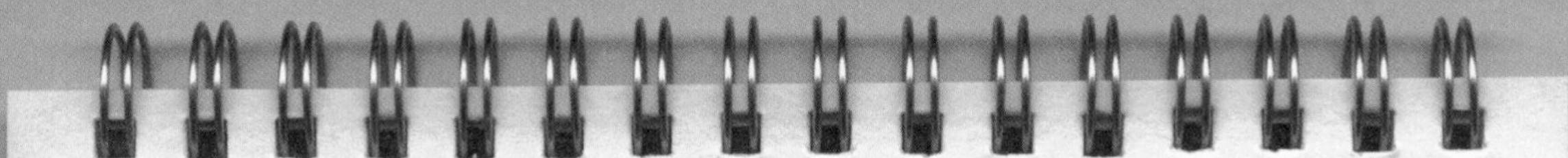

YOU WILL NEVER SEE IT

NOBODY
NOTHING
PEDESTAL

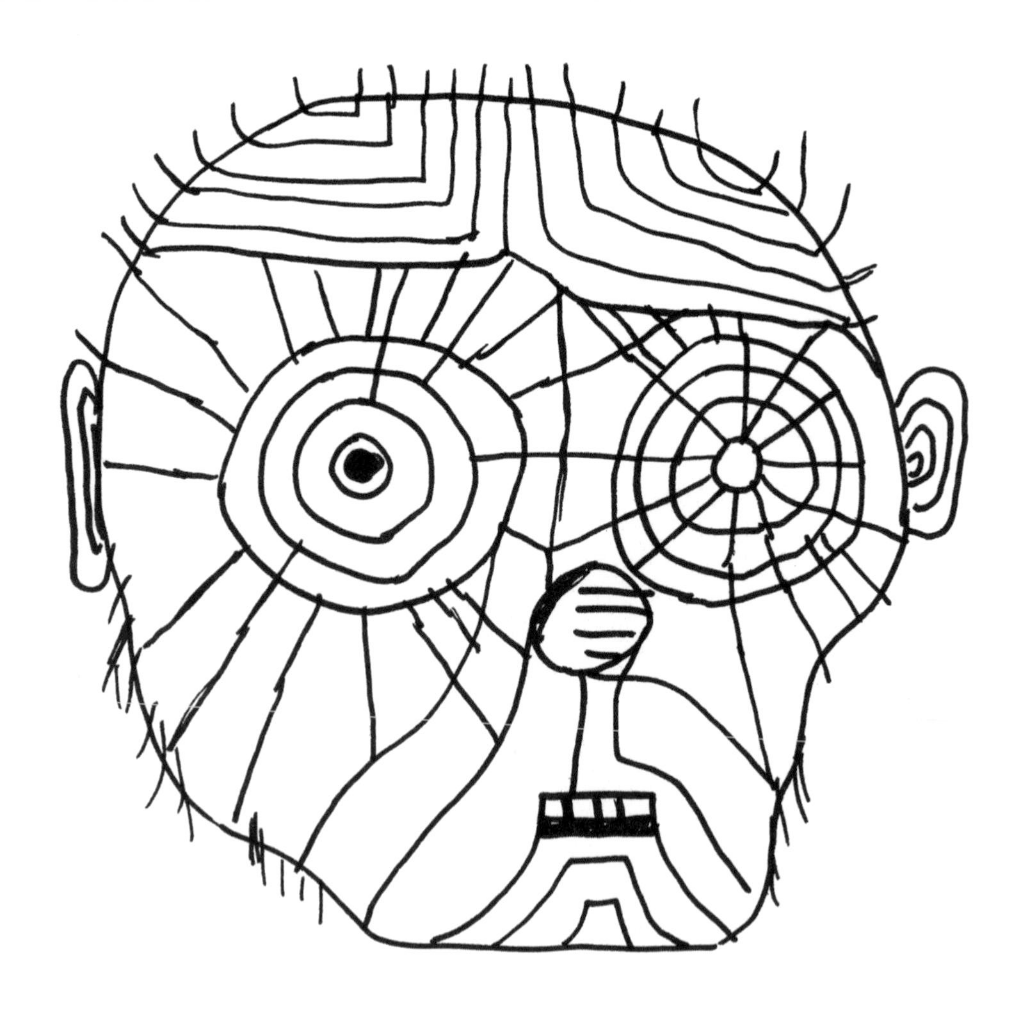

WHAT REALLY
TROUBLES ME
ABOUT HIM IS
THAT I ACTUALLY
THINK HE MIGHT
BE A BETTER
PERSON THAN I AM.

DEAR GOD,
PLEASE TAKE MY TWO EYES AND
MAKE THEM INTO ONE BIG EYE,
AMEN.

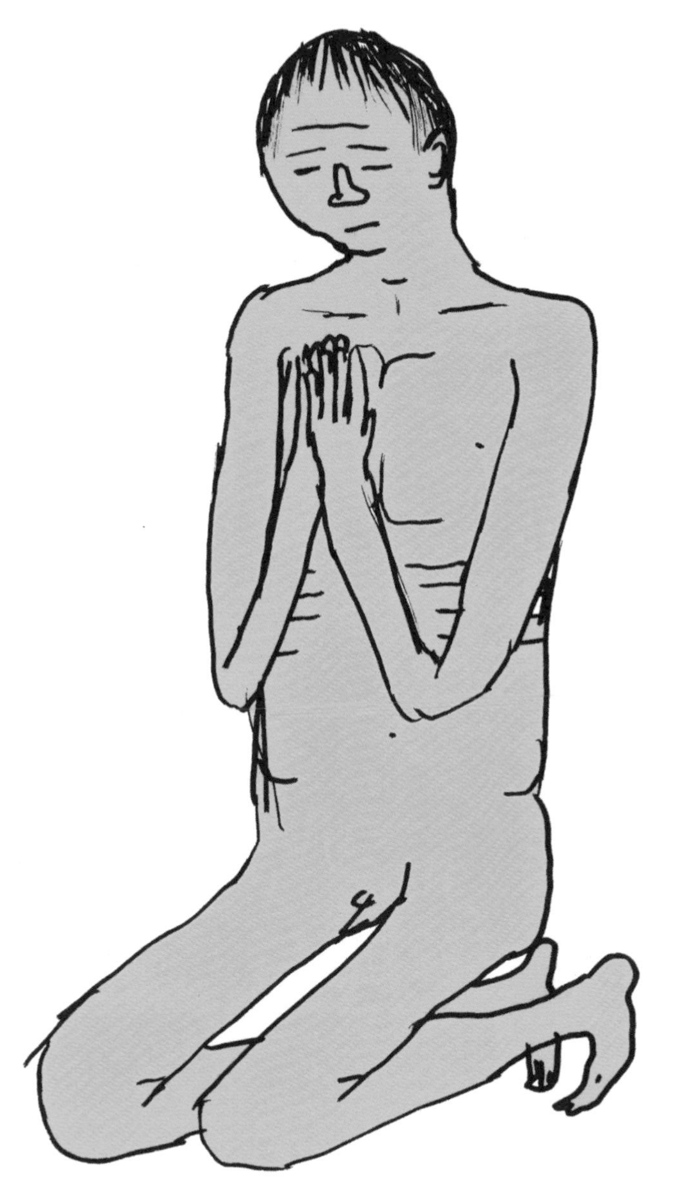

BOOZE
BOOZE
BOOZE
BOOZE

I'M
SO HUNGOVER
I WISH I
WAS
DEAD

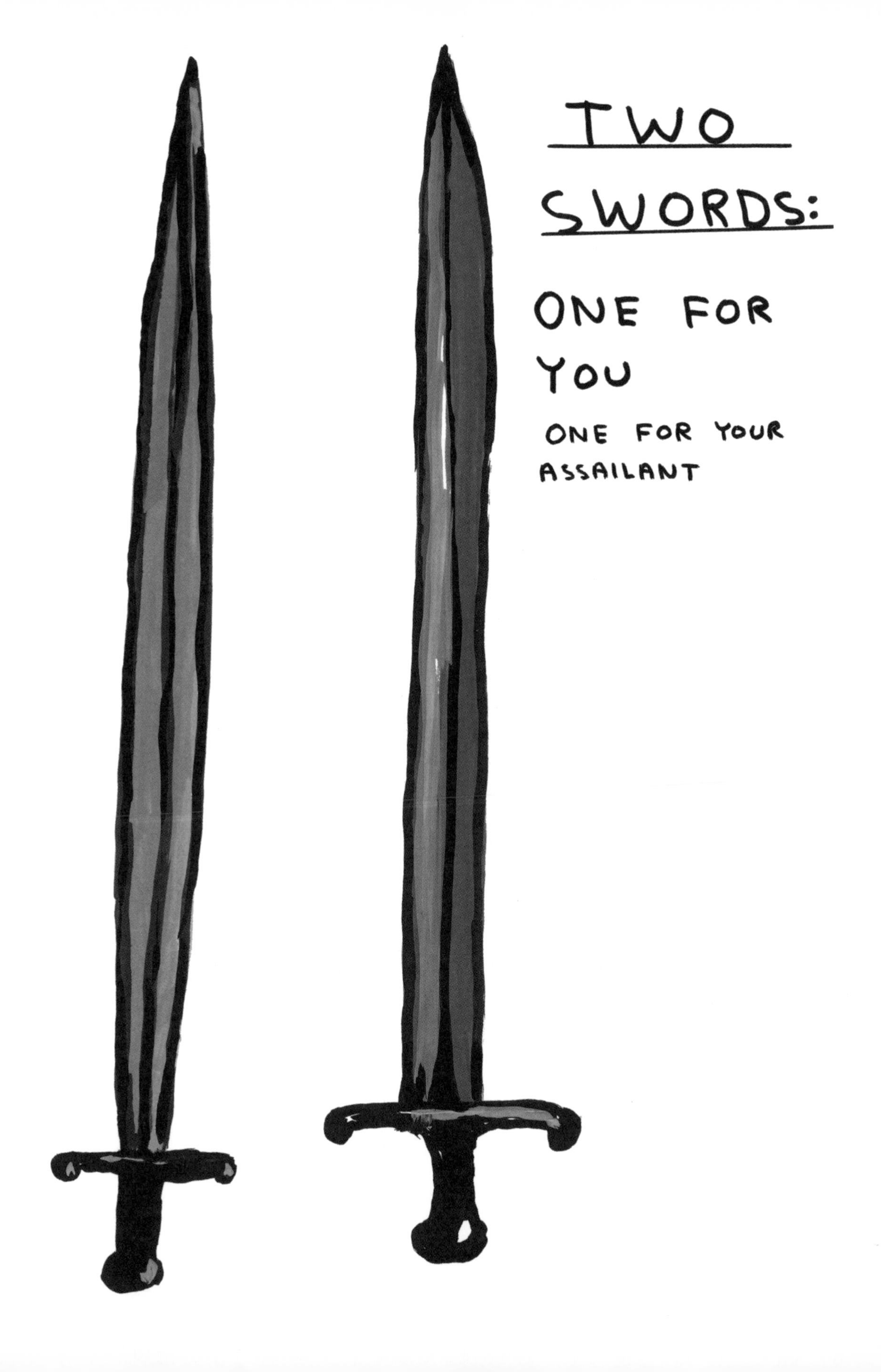
TWO
SWORDS:
ONE FOR
YOU
ONE FOR YOUR
ASSAILANT

YOU HAVE NO
FUCKING E-MAILS

ANTS

I WILL LIE HERE
UNTIL I AM
ASKED TO MOVE

H
A
T
E

CHEERS !

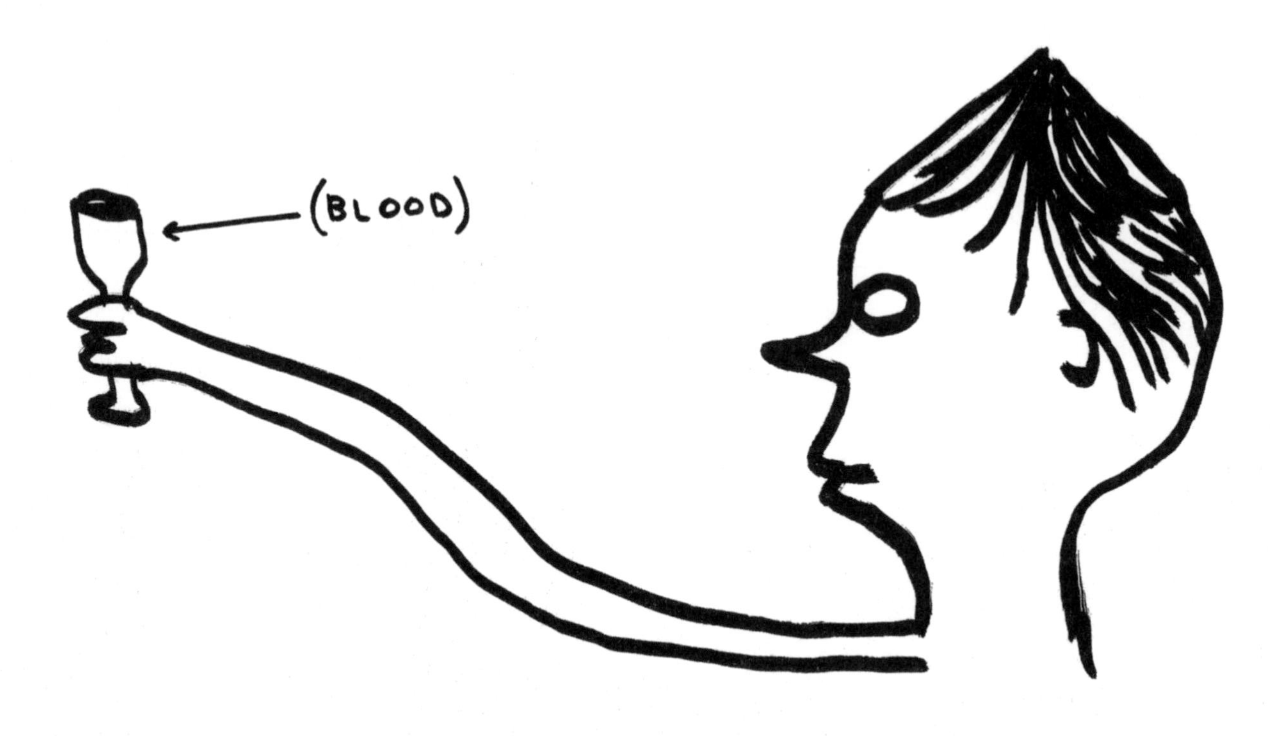

STOP IT! STOP IT!
STOP IT I SAY!
LEAVE ME ALONE
YOU HORRIBLE FREAKS!
STOP IT!
AAAAAAAHHHHHHHHHHH!

FLY HAS ESCAPED
IF YOU FIND THE FLY
PLEASE KILL IT
I WAS GOING
TO KILL IT MYSELF
BUT YOU CAN
DO IT FOR ME
IF YOU FIND IT
I DON'T MIND

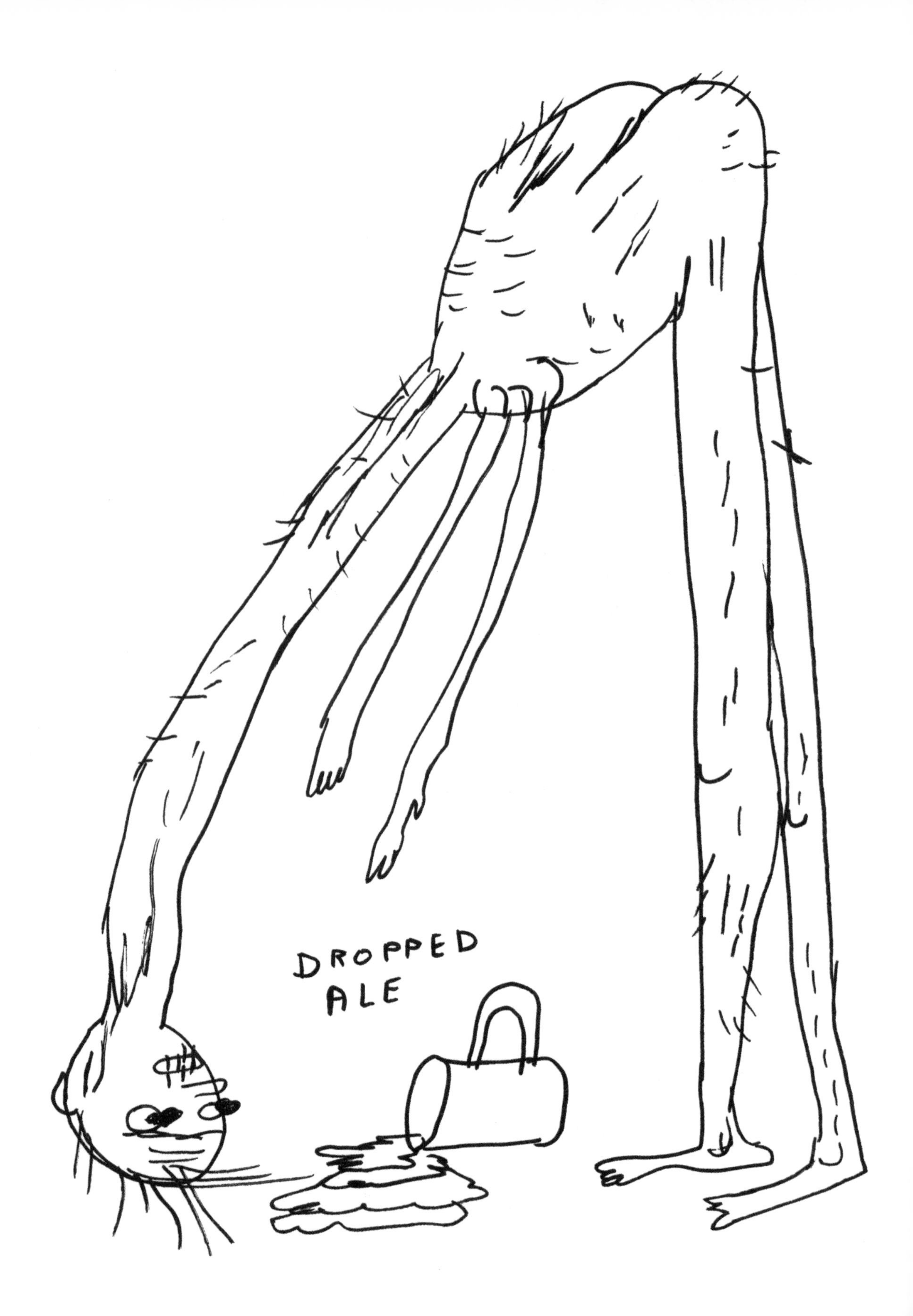
DROPPED
ALE

NO SPEED LIMIT ANYMORE

GO AS FAST AS YOU WANT
LIKE IN GERMANY

THINGS WHICH ARE AVAILABLE
WITH WHICH TO POKE THE
WITCH IN THE EYE
1. PRONG
2. STICK
3. SCREWDRIVER
4. COCK
5. PENCIL
6. PAINTBRUSH
7. CIGARETTE
8. POLE
9. SHAFT
10. SPIKE
11. POINT
12. NEEDLE
13. SPINE
14. ARROW
15. SPEAR
16. BAYONET
17. SWORD
18. DAGGER
19. BARB
20. HORN
21. ANTLER
22. BRIER
23. TUSK
24. SPIRE
25. TOOTH
26. NIB
27. PIKE
28. REAPING-HOOK
29. SECATEURS
30. HEDGEHOG

THE PAPER SCULPTURE

1. FOLD THE PAPER LENGTHWAYS WITH THE SHEEN OUTER
2. EARMARK THE WESTERNMOST CORNER OF THE STARBOARD HALF
3. TEAR THE REMAINING (PORT) HALF SLIGHTLY TO THE RIGHT AND
CURVE THE THUS-CREATED RIDGE BETWEEN THE HEEL OF YOUR
OTHER HAND (REVERSE IF YOU ARE EAST-HANDED) AND FOREFINGER
4. FOLD BOTH HEMISPHERES AGAIN QUICKLY AND THEN ONCE AGAIN
AND THEN FLATTEN IT OUT
5. TURN THE PAPER OVER
6. REPEAT
7. YOU SHOULD NOW HAVE AN EVENLY DIVIDED PLANE OF TIGHT FOLDS
POINTING UPWARDS. WHILST PRESSING ON THE NETHER-SIDE CORNER
WITH THUMB AND/OR INDEX FINGER OF YOUR DOMINANT HAND,
LIGHTLY BRUSH YOUR WEAKER INNER WRIST OVER THE PUCKERINGS
IN A FORWARD MOTION UNTIL THEY ARE FLAT AGAIN
8. TAKE THE FAR CORNER OF THE PAPER UNDER YOUR LEFT OR RIGHT
THUMB AND WITH YOUR OTHER THUMBNAIL, PARTLY SCORE A LINE
FROM MIDDLE TO TOP, APPROXIMATELY TWO THIRDS FROM THE
NEGATIVE EDGE.
9. GENTLY CURL THE UNINVOLVED PORTION UNTIL JUST BEFORE ITS
NATURAL CREASING POINT, TAKING CARE NOT TO ACTUALLY GO
OVER THE MARK
10. TAKE THE NORTH EDGE IN A SCISSOR-LIKE FASHION BETWEEN
THE INDEX AND MIDDLE FINGER OF YOUR SUBORDINATE HAND,
AND WITH YOUR OTHER ELBOW LOCATE AND FLATTEN THE
APEX YOU HAVE PREVIOUSLY MADE.
11. MAKE A FIST ON YOUR LOWER SIDE AND SLOT THE MOST GAUNT
EDGE INTO THE WIDEST TUCK BETWEEN YOUR FINGERS AND
WITH THE BALL OF YOUR UN-USED FIST, DULL EACH EXTREMITY IN
TURN UNTIL 'SPIT WILL NOT RUN-OFF IT'.
12. FOLD THE PAPER DIAGONALLY SEVERAL TIMES SO THAT THE CORNERS
DON'T TOUCH, FLATTEN, REPEAT AND FLATTEN AGAIN
13. TAKING ADJACENT CORNERS BETWEEN THUMB AND SMALLEST FINGER,
DRAW THE SHEET TOGETHER AND HOLD IT FOR 2-5 MINUTES
14. TURN THE SHEET OVER AND REPEAT
15. FIND A CYLINDER WITH A CIRCUMFERANCE NEAR AS DAMN IT EQUAL
TO THE LONGEST EDGE OF THE PAPER (IF NO CYLINDER IS
AVAILABLE YOU MAY USE ONE OF YOUR LIMBS)
16. FASTEN THE SHEET AROUND THE CYLINDER/LIMB WITH A PIECE
OF TAPE.
17. WRITE THE NAMES OF THINGS WHICH YOU LIKE ON THE PAPER
18. UNFASTEN
19. MAKE THE PAGE INTO WHAT YOU CONSIDER TO BE A NONAGON,
WITH THE FLAPS POINTING DOWN
20. WITH YOUR RIGHT HAND MANIPULATE THE SHEET SLIGHTLY WITH
A FLATTENED PALM UNTIL THE FACING SIDE LOOKS LIKE (WHAT
YOU UNDERSTAND TO BE) A ROUGH TRAPEZOID FROM WHERE YOU
ARE SITTING / STANDING
21. THEN MOVE YOUR OTHER HAND AROUND THE PIECE AND
APPROXIMATE THE EXACT OPPOSITE ACTION (AGAIN WITH A
FLATTENED PALM) WHICH YOU HAVE JUST UNDERTAKEN
WITH YOUR RIGHT HAND UNTIL THE SHEET TAKES BACK
(WHAT YOU REMEMBER AS) ITS FORMER SHAPE
22. UNFOLD.

TIME TO REFLECT

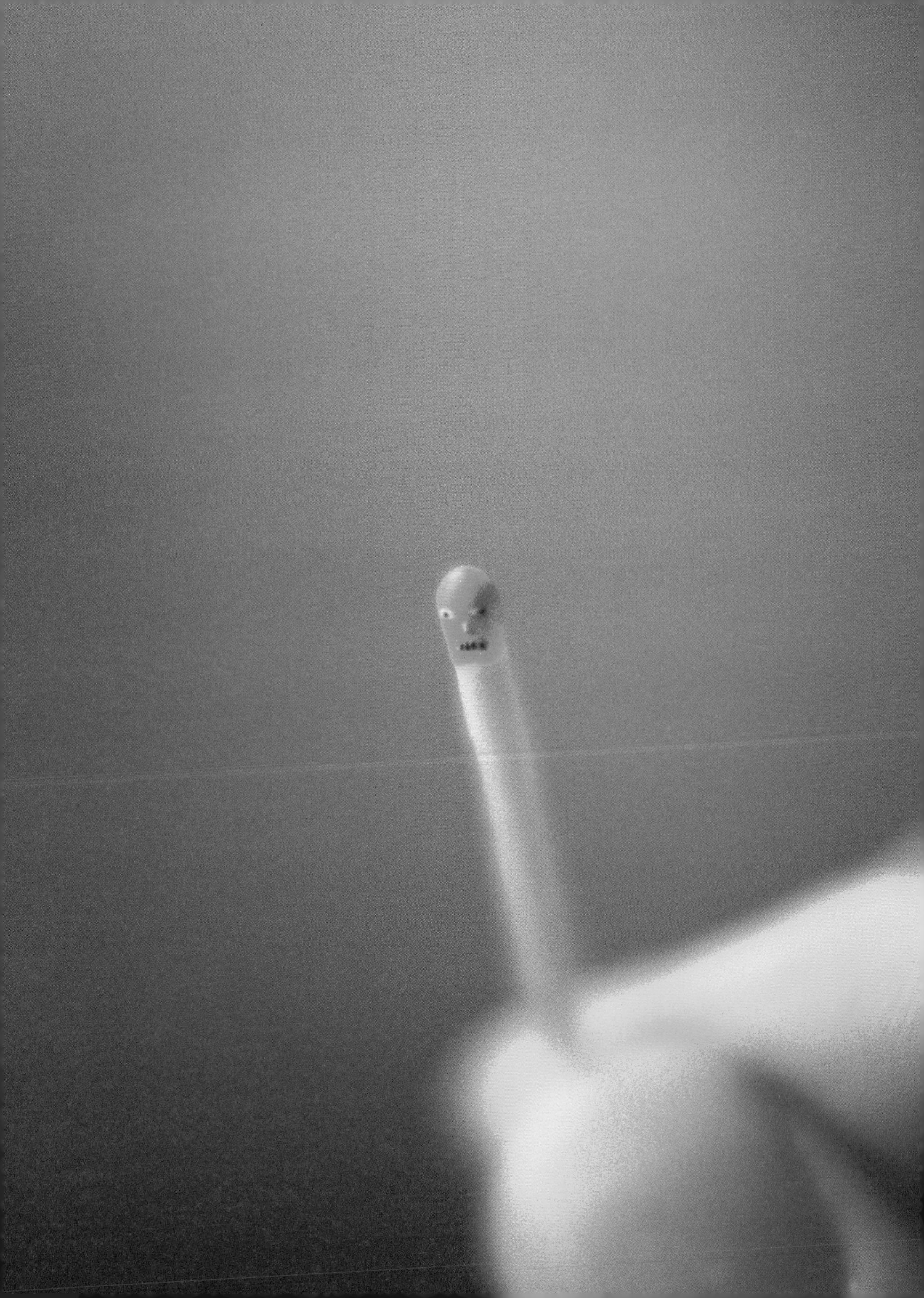

EVIL

DEVIL: FOR WHAT WOULD YOU TRADE YOUR SOUL ?

ARCHITECTURE STUDENT: FOR A METAL RULER

(DEVIL DEPARTS TO HARDWARE OUTLET)
(DEVIL RETURNS)

DEVIL: HERE YOU ARE...

(DEVIL GIVES ARCHITECTURE STUDENT A METAL RULER)

DEVIL: NOW LET ME HAVE YOUR SOUL

STUDENT: THIS ISN'T LONG ENOUGH

DEVIL: HOW LONG DOES IT HAVE TO BE ?

STUDENT: IT HAS TO BE A METRE LONG. THIS ONE IS ONLY 30 cm.

(DEVIL DEPARTS AGAIN)
(DEVIL RETURNS)

DEVIL: THEY DON'T HAVE ANY METRE-LONG METAL RULERS IN STOCK

STUDENT: WELL YOU CAN'T HAVE MY SOUL THEN.

DEVIL: OH WELL. MAYBE AFTER YOU GRADUATE.

IN I GO

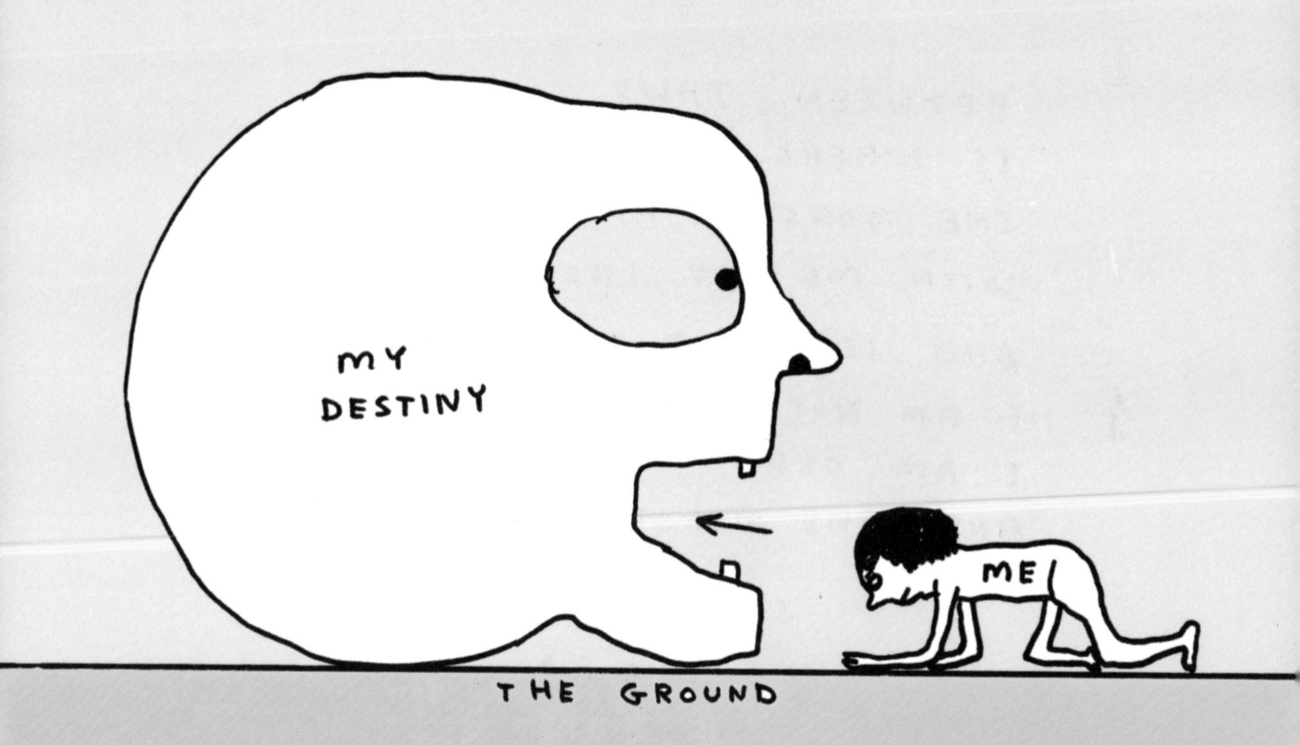

BETWEEN JAWS
IS WHERE I CURRENTLY RESIDE
THE MONSTER HAS CAUGHT UP
WITH ME AT LAST
AND IS ABOUT TO EAT ME
I AM NOT UNHAPPY ABOUT THIS
I AM OLD
AND THE MONSTER IS STARVING

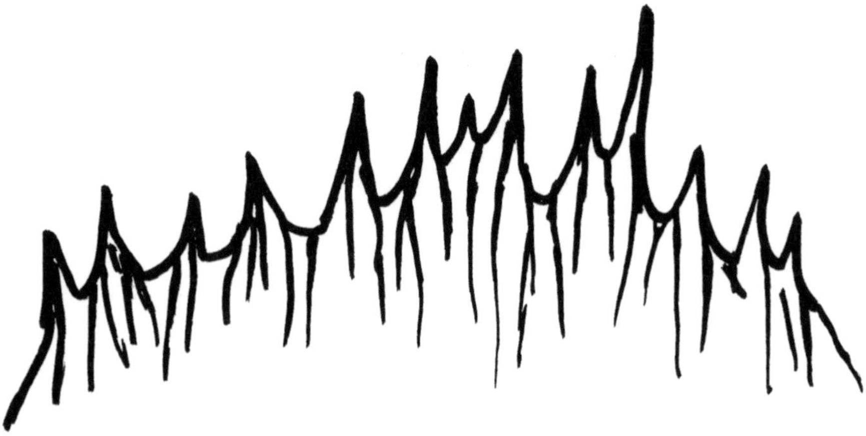

PLEASE DON'T
DROP BOMBS
ON ME

THE MOON SHINES DOWN ON US
AND SENDS US ALL MAD
WE DANCE AND SING AND FORNICATE
AND THEN WE SET THINGS ON FIRE
AND TRY TO KILL EACH OTHER
THIS IS WHERE THE WORD LUNATIC
COMES FROM
LUNA MEANING MOON

DING DONG
DONG
DING DONG

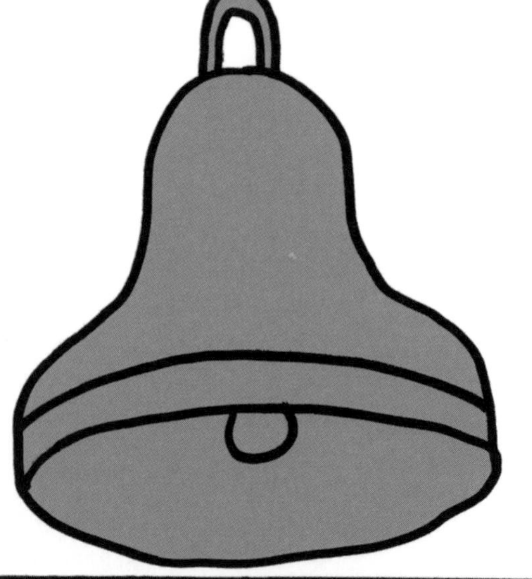

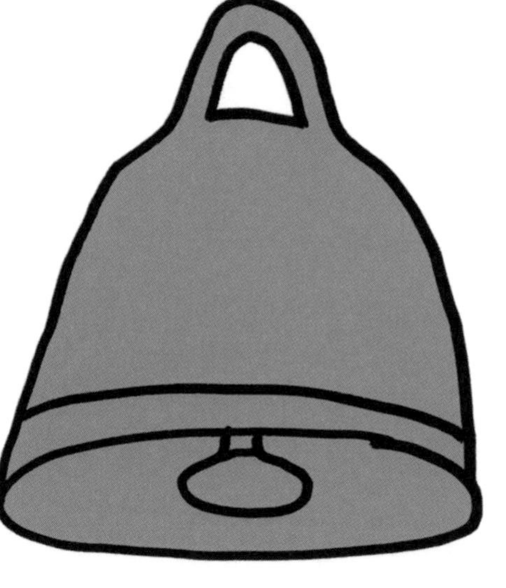

DAMN IT!
I WILL NEVER
BE ABLE TO
GET ONE OF
THE SKULLS
THE MACHINE
IS TOO DIFFICULT
TO OPERATE

THE WIND

←

THE
WIND IS
BLOWING
FROM THIS
DIRECTION

WHAT IS IT DADDY?
IT'S BLOODY BRILLIANT SON, THAT'S WHAT IT IS.

DELIVERED TO YOUR DOOR

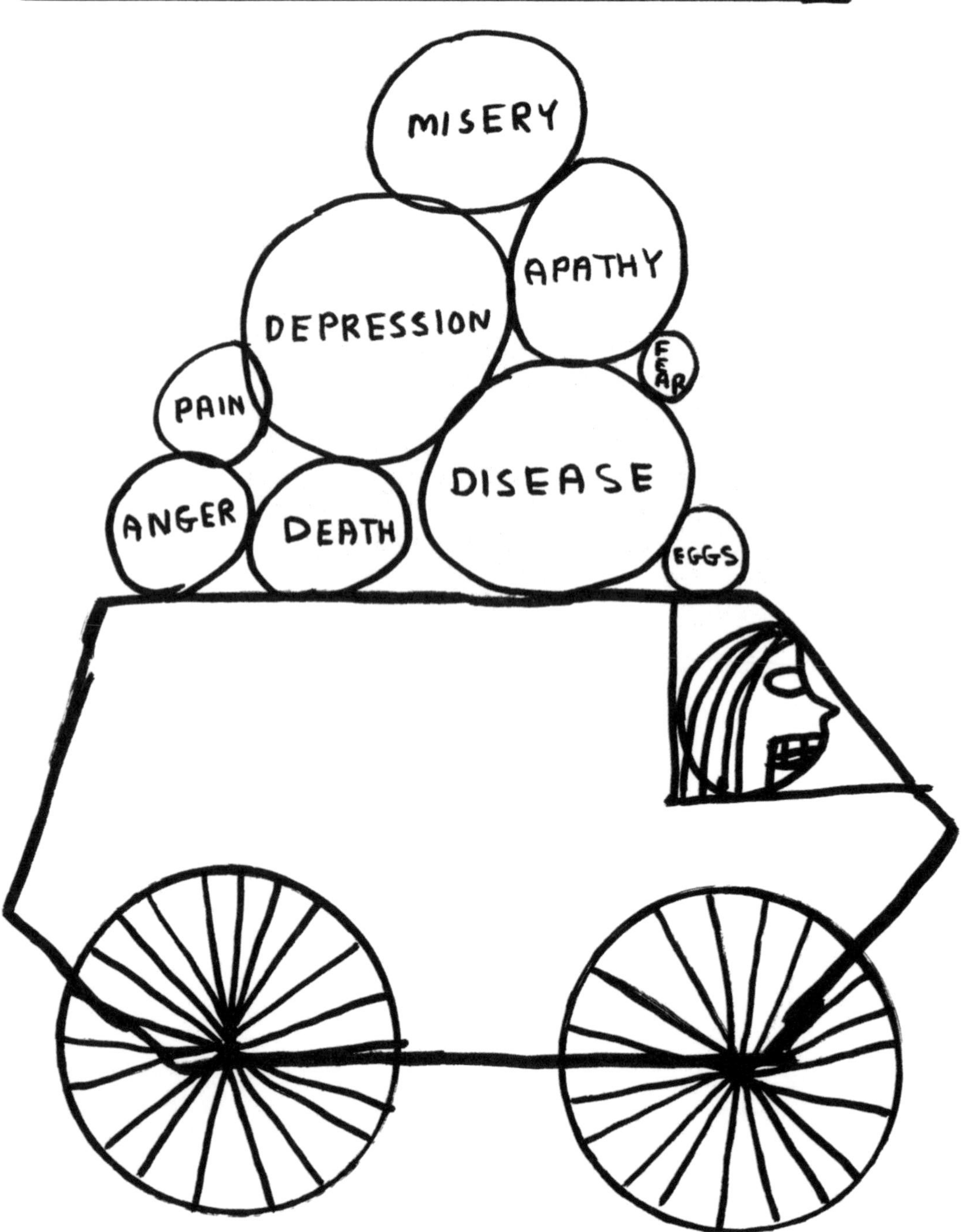

ARE YOU EMBARRASSED BY YOUR BALDNESS?
YES I AM
WE CAN HELP YOU

AND THEY SAID THAT HE WAS A FOOL

BUT I DID NOT THINK HE WAS A FOOL

BUT IT WAS LATER PROVEN THAT HE WAS A FOOL

BABIES

THERE IS LIGHT AT
THE END OF THE TUNNEL.
PETE IS ALSO AT THE END OF
THE TUNNEL.

A BRICK

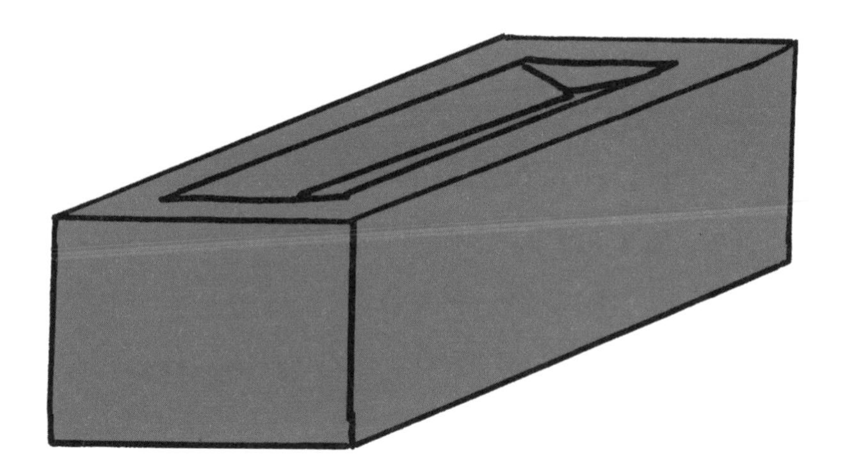

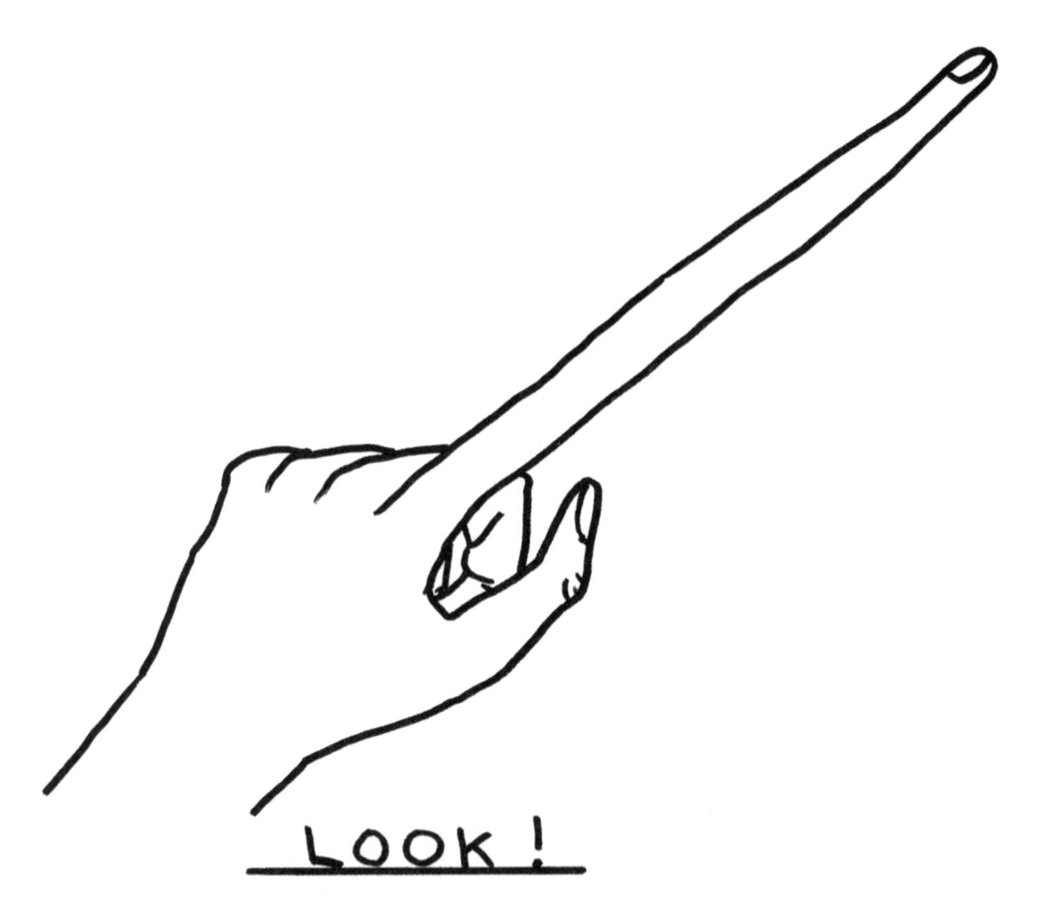

LOOK!

- IT'S TWO MONKEYS PLAYING CONKERS!
- THEY'RE NOT PLAYING CONKERS, THEY'RE GROOMING EACH OTHER.
- GROOMING EACH OTHER?
- YES, PICKING THE FLEAS OFF EACH OTHER AND EATING THEM
- OH DEAR. DO THEY SWALLOW THE FLEAS OR SPIT THEM OUT?
- I DON'T KNOW. I PRESUME THEY SWALLOW THEM. THEY'RE NUTRITIOUS.
- OH DEAR, THAT'S DIRTY.

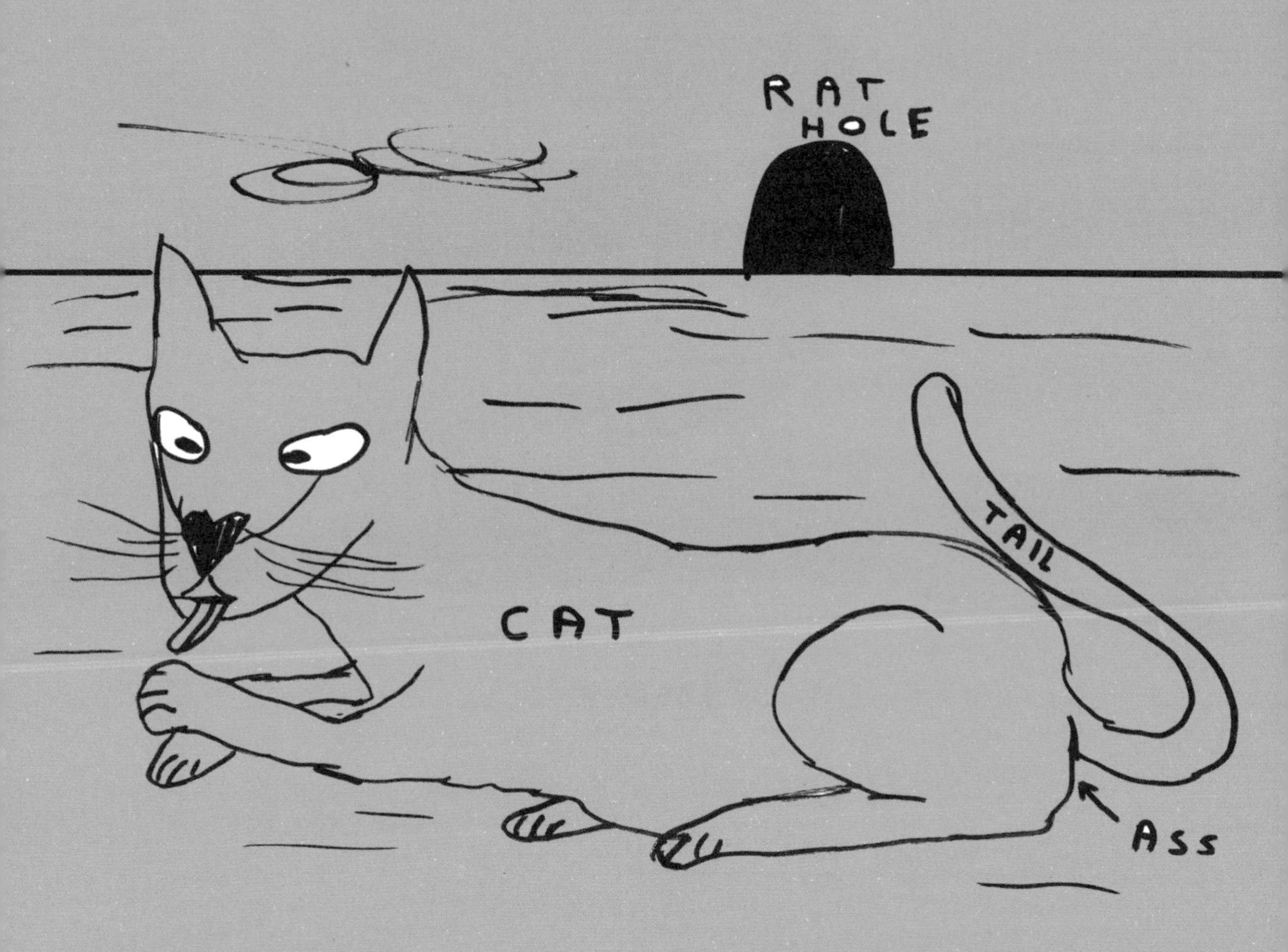
RAT
HOLE
TAIL
CAT
ASS

"TIMMY"

PIGEONS TIMMY HAS FUCKED:

"SPAM"

"FUCKWING"

"ELAINE"

"BERNARD"

"LITTLE-MISS TURD-EATER"

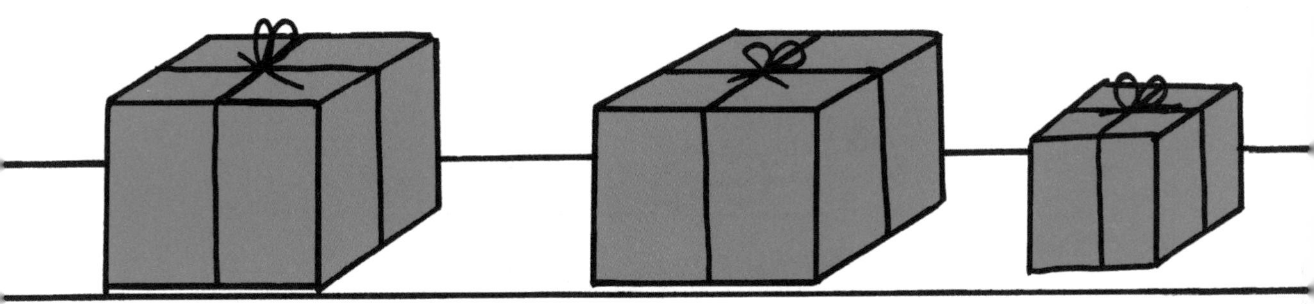

- I KNOW WHAT YOU'RE GETTING FOR CHRISTMAS
- WHAT ?
- YOUR GIFTS ARE HIDDEN ON A SHELF IN THE CLOSET
- WHAT ARE THEY ?
- THEY ARE IN BOXES TIED UP WITH STRING
- WHAT'S IN THE BOXES ?
- I KNOW BUT YOU DON'T KNOW
- I THINK WE'VE ESTABLISHED THAT. NOW ARE YOU GOING TO TELL ME OR NOT ?
- I'M NOT GOING TO TELL
- WELL WHY DID YOU CALL ME AT WORK THEN ? I'M VERY BUSY AT THE MOMENT, I'M WITH A PATIENT SO I'LL HAVE TO GO NOW, I'LL SEE YOU AT DINNER.
- I KNOW WHAT YOU'RE HAVING FOR DINNER (HANGS UP)

GOING

NOWHERE

WHOPPER

I TOOK YOUR LOVE AND I MADE IT INTO CHEESE. I SPRINKLED THE CHEESE ON TOAST SO THAT IT MELTED AND I MADE THEM INTO SANDWICHES. WHEN THEY HAD COOLED I PUT THEM IN A BAG TO KEEP THEM FRESH UNTIL LUNCHTIME. NOW I AM AT WORK. I JUST LOOKED IN MY BREIFCASE AND I REALISED THAT I LEFT THE SANDWICHES AT HOME ON THE KITCHEN TABLE. DAMN, DAMN, DAMN, THAT MEANS I'LL HAVE TO GO TO BURGER KING AGAIN AND I HATE BURGER KING.

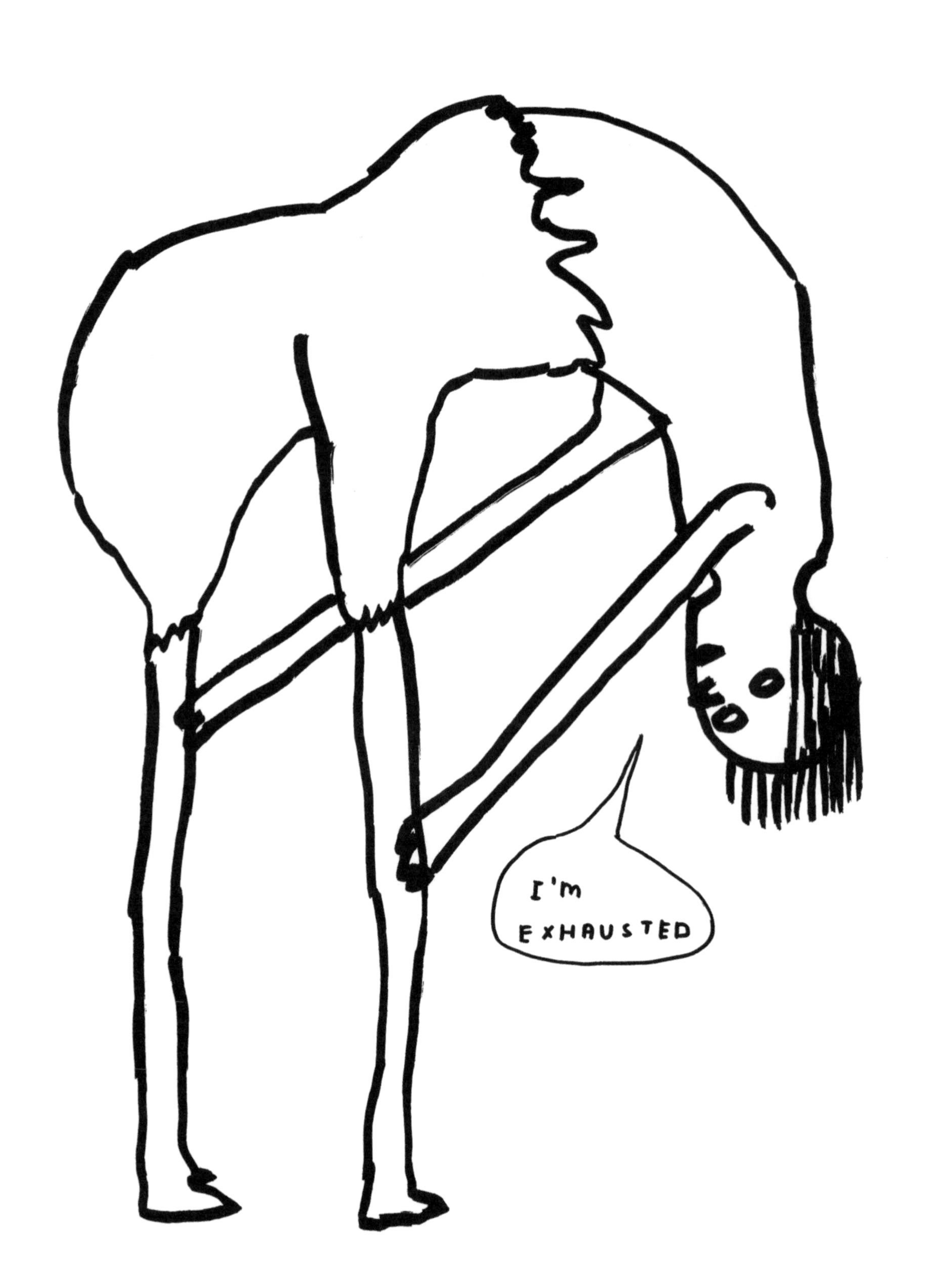
I'm EXHAUSTED

MAN AND WOMAN

I LIKE THE
DRIVING GAME
I WOULD PLAY
IT ALL DAY
IF I COULD
BUT IT COSTS
2 POUNDS PER
GAME
AND I AM
UNEMPLOYED

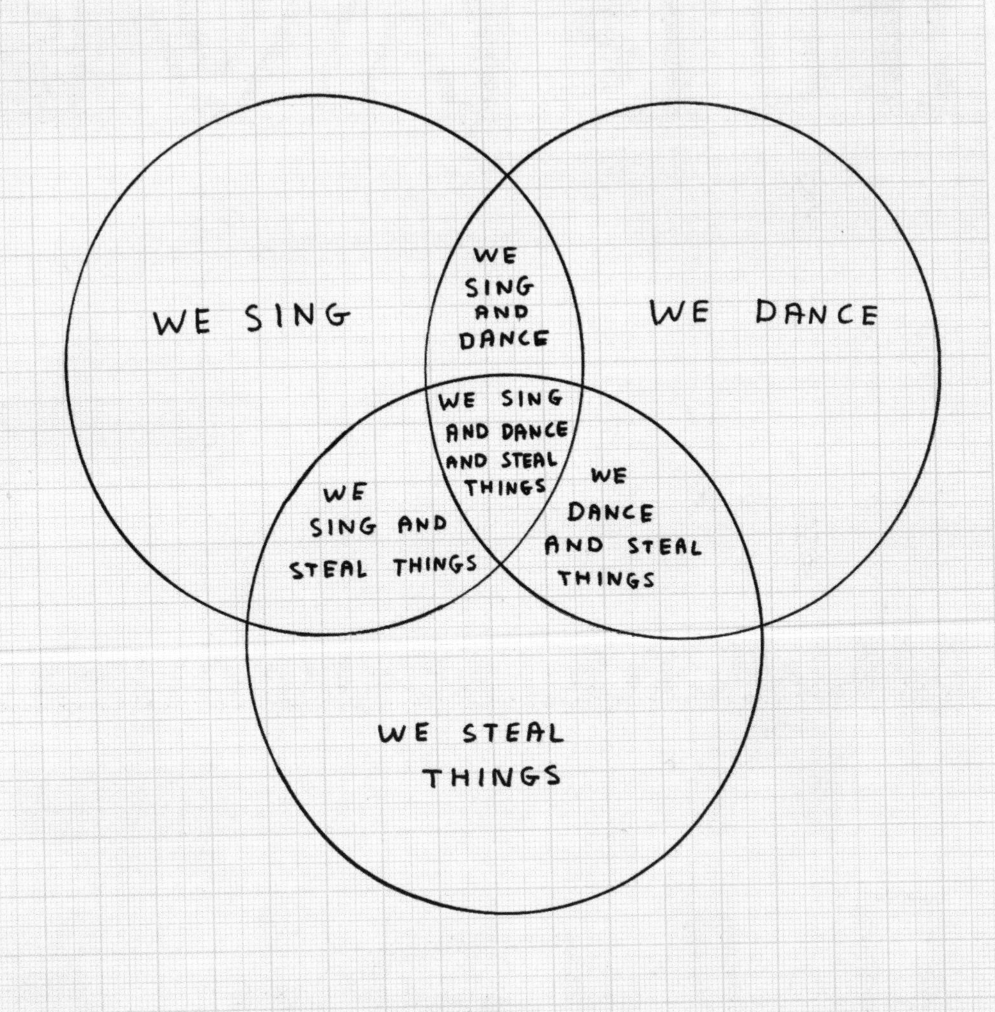
WE SING
WE SING AND DANCE
WE DANCE
WE SING AND DANCE AND STEAL THINGS
WE SING AND STEAL THINGS
WE DANCE AND STEAL THINGS
WE STEAL THINGS

HEAVEN

NEWCASTLE-UPON-TYNE

HELL

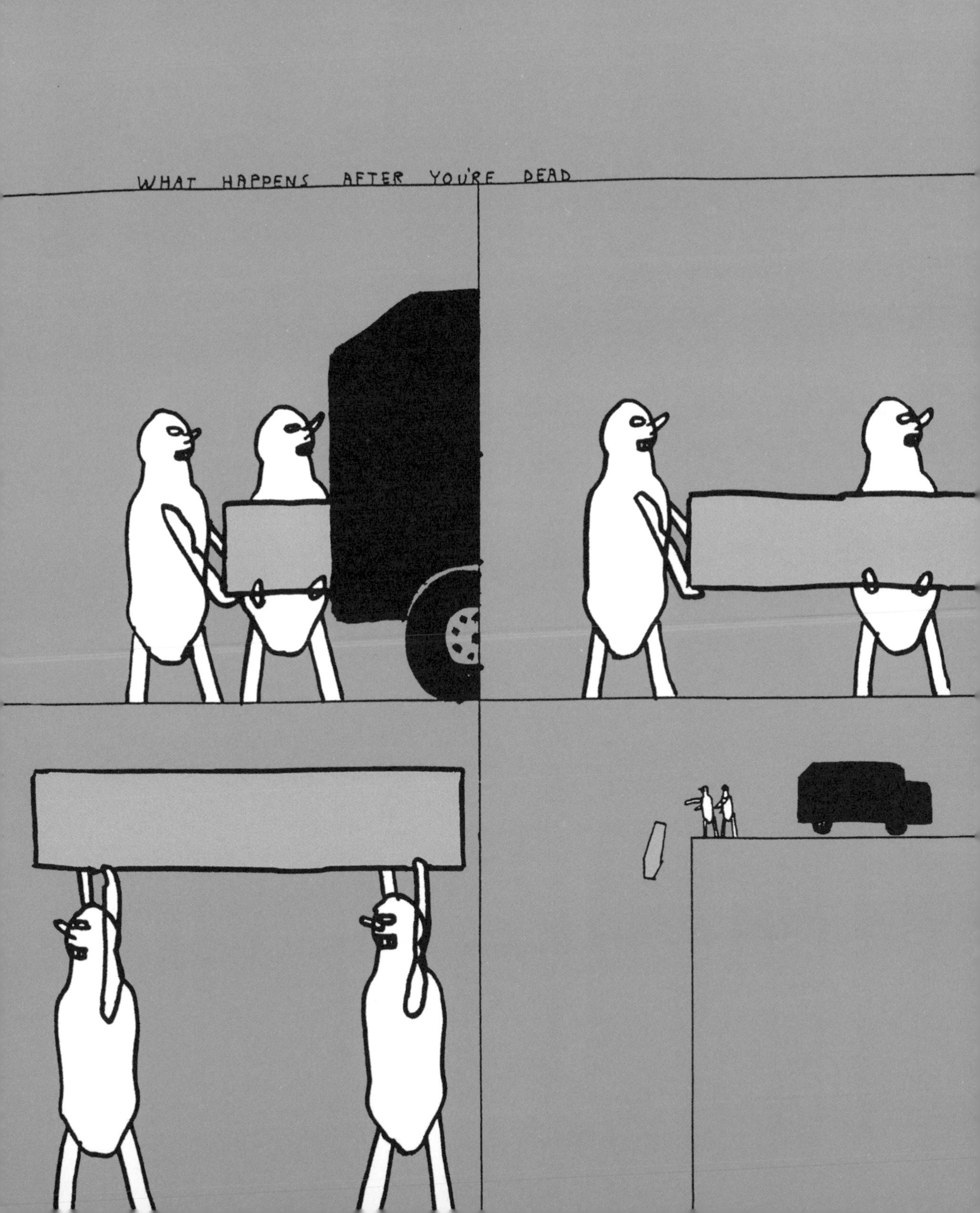
WHAT HAPPENS AFTER YOU'RE DEAD

DEAR NEIGHBOURS,
PLEASE KEEP THE FUCKING
NOISE DOWN YOU INCONSID-
ERATE BUNCH OF STUPID
CUNTS

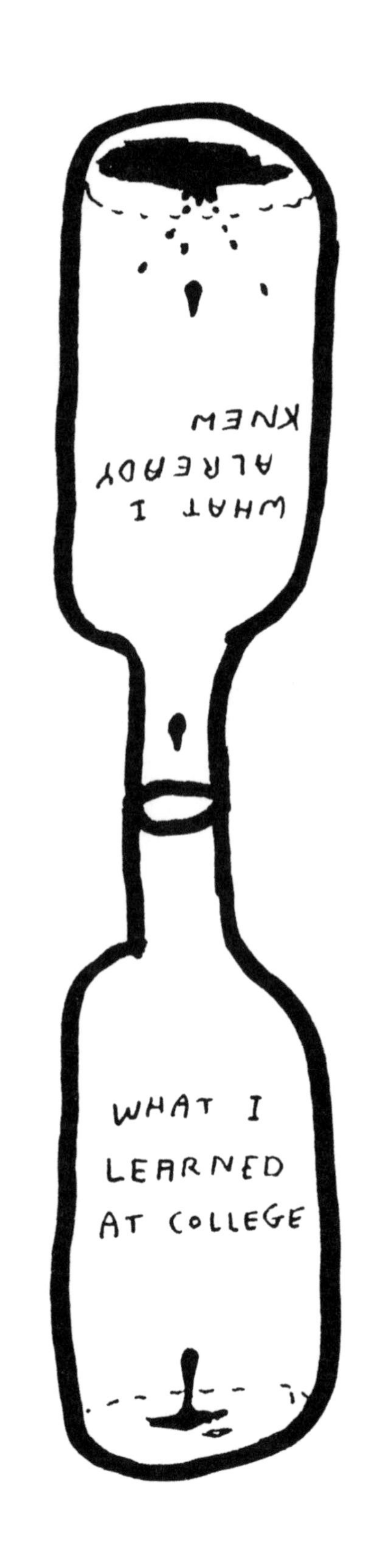
WHAT I ALREADY KNEW
WHAT I LEARNED AT COLLEGE

A STORY TOLD IN FOUR PARTS

THE FIRST PART CONCERNS THE INTRODUCTION OF THE CENTRAL CHARACTER; WHO HE IS, ETC.
THE SECOND PART CONCERNS AN EXTRAORDINARY EVENT THAT BEFALLS THE CENTRAL CHARACTER.
THE THIRD PART CONCERNS HOW THE CENTRAL CHARACTER DEALS WITH THE EXTRAORDINARY EVENT THROUGH SUBSTANCE ABUSE.
THE FORTH PART IS THE CONCLUSION WHICH, WHILST IT PROVIDES CLOSURE, LEAVES ROOM FOR A CONTINUATION OF THE STORY.

DEATH

I DON'T
LIKE IT

DIGGING LESSONS

AND I FOLLOWED HIM
AND YOU CAN COMPLETE
THE STORY ▬ YOURSELF

FOETUSES PLAYING CARDS

WHOEVER WINS GETS BORN

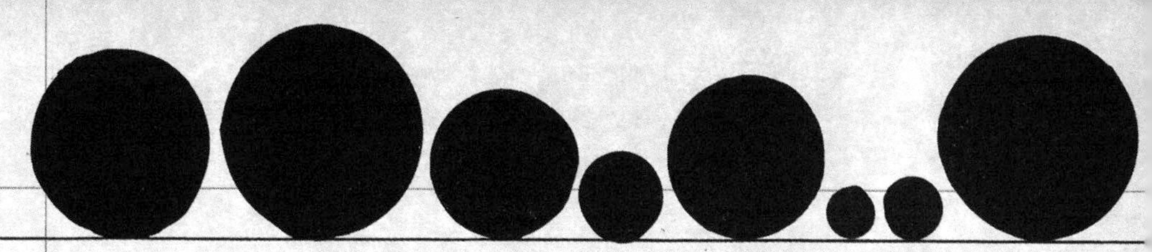

WITH THESE I CONTROL THEE
THOU ART SCARED OF THEM
AND THUS OF ME
THEY PUTS THE FEAR OF GOD IN THEE
THOU DREAMS NIGHTMARES ABOUT THEM
AND AWFUL THINGS HAPPENING TO THEE DONE BY THEM
THOU WILL NOT GET OUT OF HAND AS LONG
AS THESE ARE ON THE SHELF
WHERE THOU CAN SEE THEM
THEY HAVE COME AS A GODSEND TO ME
THIS LAST WHILE
I WAS STRUGGLING TO COPE WITH THEE

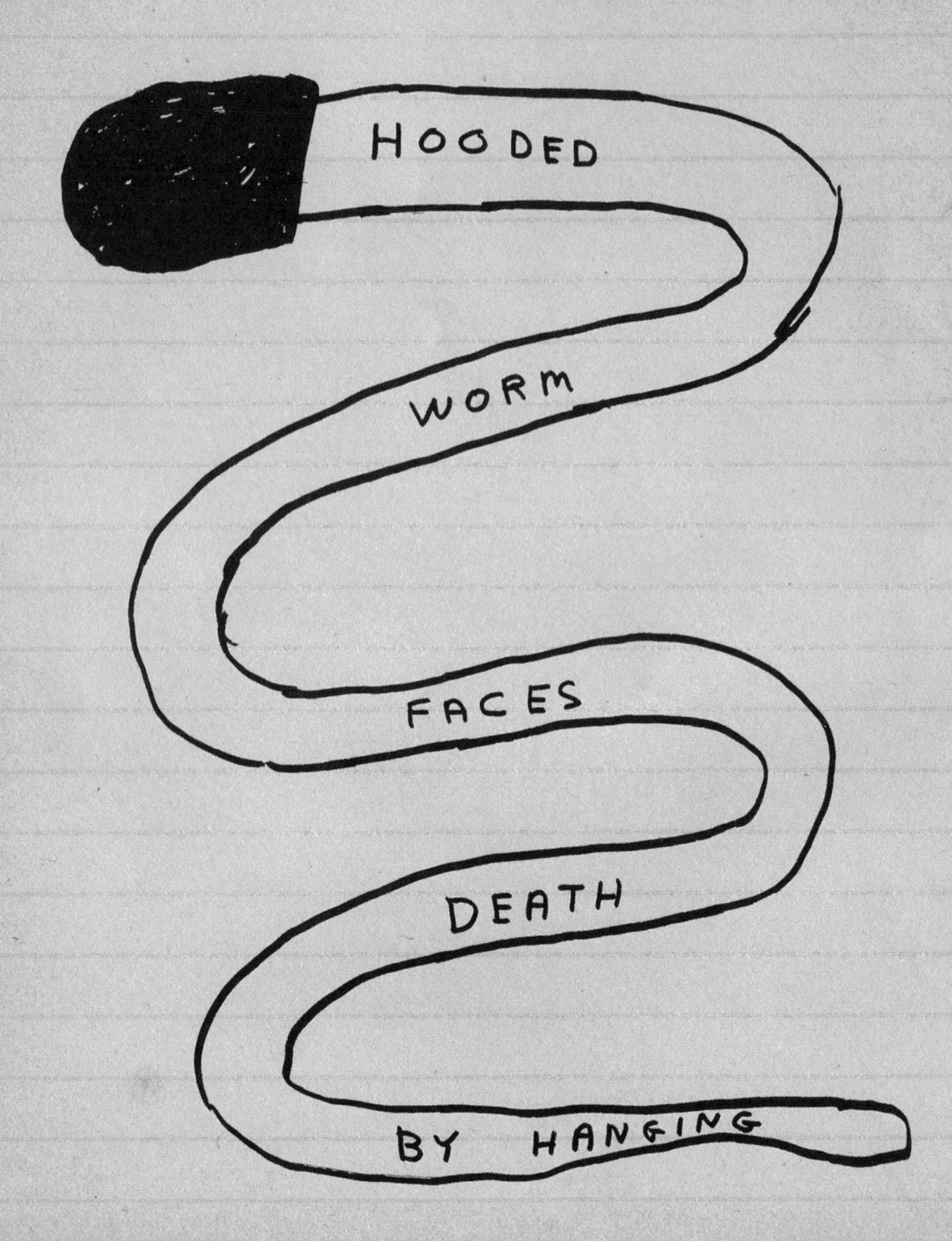
HOODED
WORM
FACES
DEATH
BY HANGING

EYE OF GOD

TASTES HOLY

VOICING VARIOUS CONCERNS

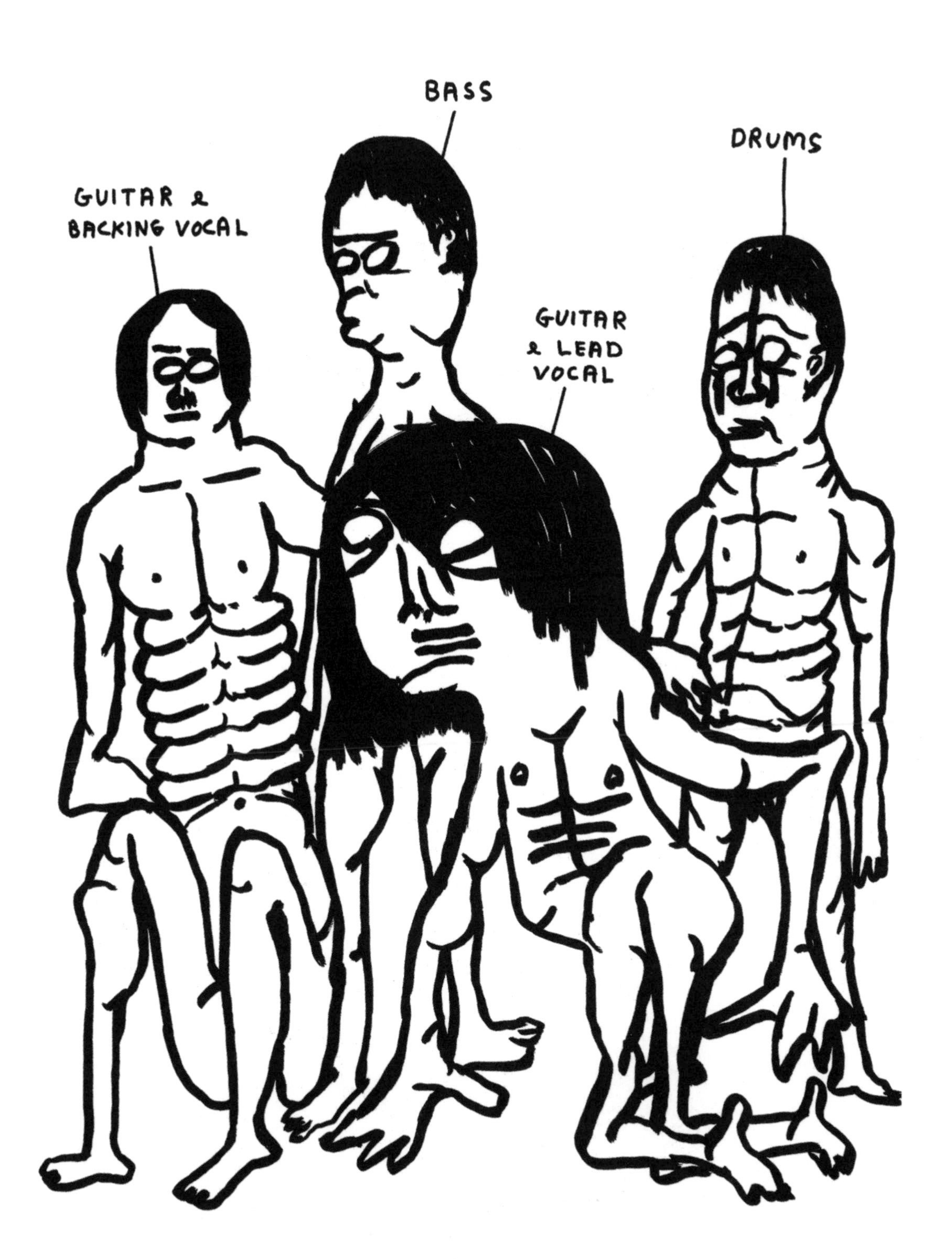
BASS
DRUMS
GUITAR & BACKING VOCAL
GUITAR & LEAD VOCAL

CAN'T SEEM TO
FOCUS ON THE
PACK OF DOGS

THE FOREIGN MEAT

I WILL EAT THE FOREIGN MEAT
YES, I WILL EAT THE FOREIGN MEAT
I WILL EAT IT WITH MY HANDS
I WILL EAT IT WITH MY FEET

I WILL EAT THE FLAME-GRILLED WHOPPER
YES, I WILL EAT THE FLAME-GRILLED WHOPPER
I WILL EAT IT FOR MY BREAKFAST
I WILL EAT IT FOR MY SUPPER

I WILL EAT THE STICKY PUDDING
YES, I WILL EAT THE STICKY PUDDING
I WILL EAT IT AT YOUR FUNERAL
I WILL EAT IT AT MY WEDDING

I WILL EAT THE ELEPHANT POO
YES, I WILL EAT THE ELEPHANT POO
I WILL EAT IT IN THE WILD
I WILL EAT IT AT THE ZOO

I WILL EAT THE HUMAN CORPSE
YES, I WILL EAT THE HUMAN CORPSE
I WILL EAT IT WITH A SPOON
I WILL EAT IT WITH A FORK

I WILL EAT THE BAR OF SOAP
YES, I WILL EAT THE BAR OF SOAP
I WILL PUT IT IN MY MOUTH
I WILL SWALLOW IT DOWN MY THROAT

OH DEAR
YOU'VE BEEN SLAIN

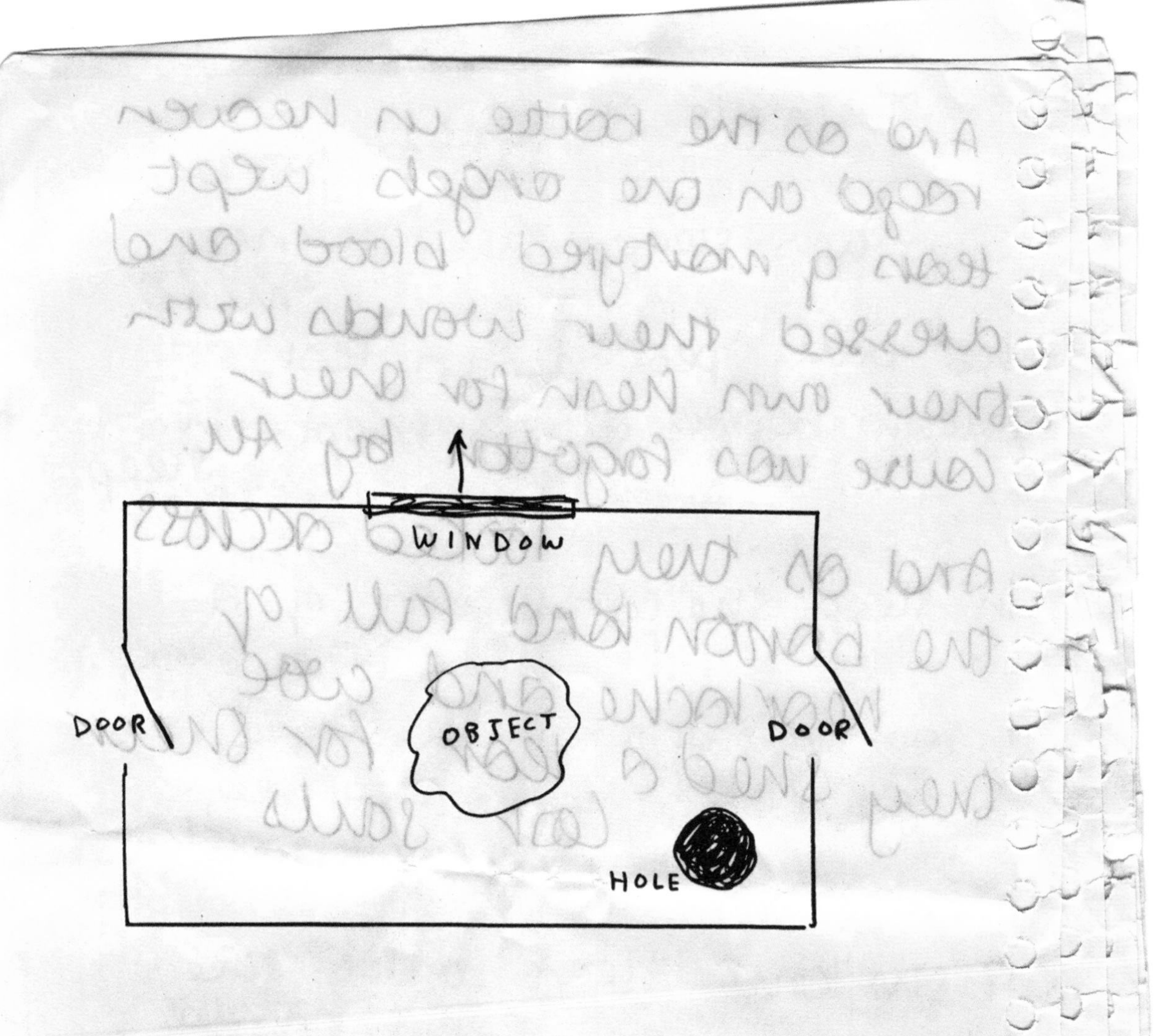

I WALKED INTO A ROOM
AND I LOOKED AT THE THINGS IN THE ROOM
AND THEN I WALKED OUT
AND THEN I WALKED INTO ANOTHER ROOM
BUT THERE WASN'T ANYTHING THERE
SO I PASSED STRAIGHT THROUGH
AND INTO ANOTHER ROOM
BUT THERE WASN'T MUCH IN THERE EITHER
EXCEPT SOME BITS AND BOBS
SO I WENT INTO ANOTHER ROOM
WHERE THERE WAS A BIG WINDOW
SO I LOOKED OUT OF THE WINDOW
AND THERE WAS A MAN OUTSIDE FIXING HIS CAR
SO I WATCHED HIM FOR ABOUT TWENTY MINUTES
AND IT WAS QUITE INTERESTING

ABOUT THE BUILDING

- THE ILLUSION OF SPACE IS CREATED BY **THE WALLS**

- THEY WANTED TO REMOVE THE FIRE ALARM AND THE **EXIT SIGNS** BUT THEY COULDN'T BECAUSE IT IS AGAINST THE LAW

- THE DOORS OPEN AND **SHUT** BY THEMSELVES

- THE COLUMNS ARE PURELY **DECORATIVE**

- THE **ROOF** IS THATCHED

- THE FLOOR IS **HARD**

- THE LIGHTS ON THE **CEILING** KILL FLIES

- THE STEEPLE IS A KIND OF **CHIMNEY**

- THE **COLOURS** WERE CHOSEN AT RANDOM

- THE WATER FEATURE IS CONTROLLED BY YOUR **THOUGHTS**

- THE MAZE IS UNCHALLENGING FOR SAFETY REASONS. FEW REALISE IT **IS** A MAZE

- I ONCE FELL DOWN SOME STEPS AND LANDED IN A HEAP AT THE BOTTOM. I LAY THERE FOR SOME TIME BEFORE I WAS DISCOVERED

i have
swallowed
a piece
of lego
Early
Learning
Centre

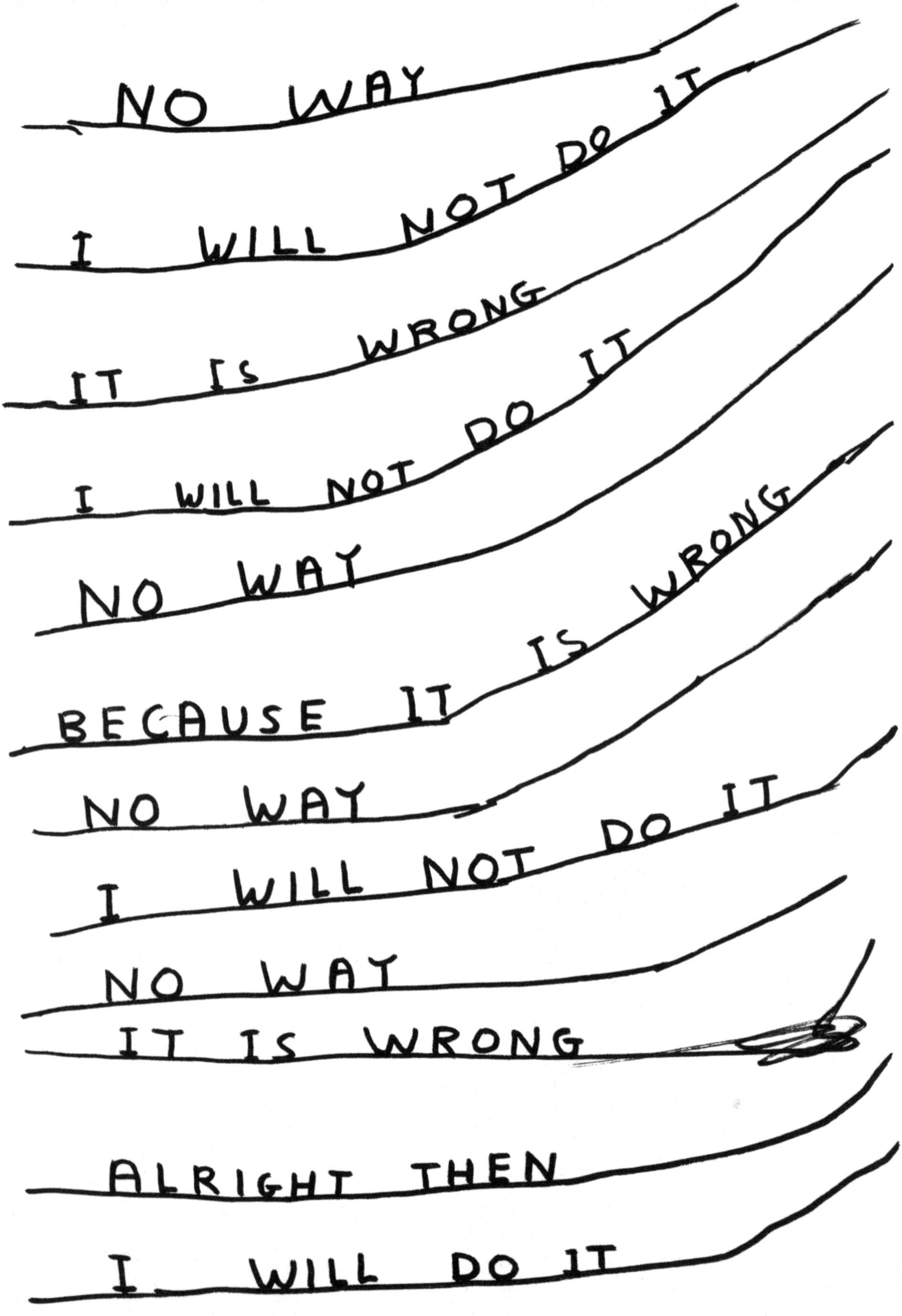

NO WAY

I WILL NOT DO IT

IT IS WRONG

I WILL NOT DO IT

NO WAY

BECAUSE IT IS WRONG

NO WAY

I WILL NOT DO IT

NO WAY

IT IS WRONG

ALRIGHT THEN

I WILL DO IT

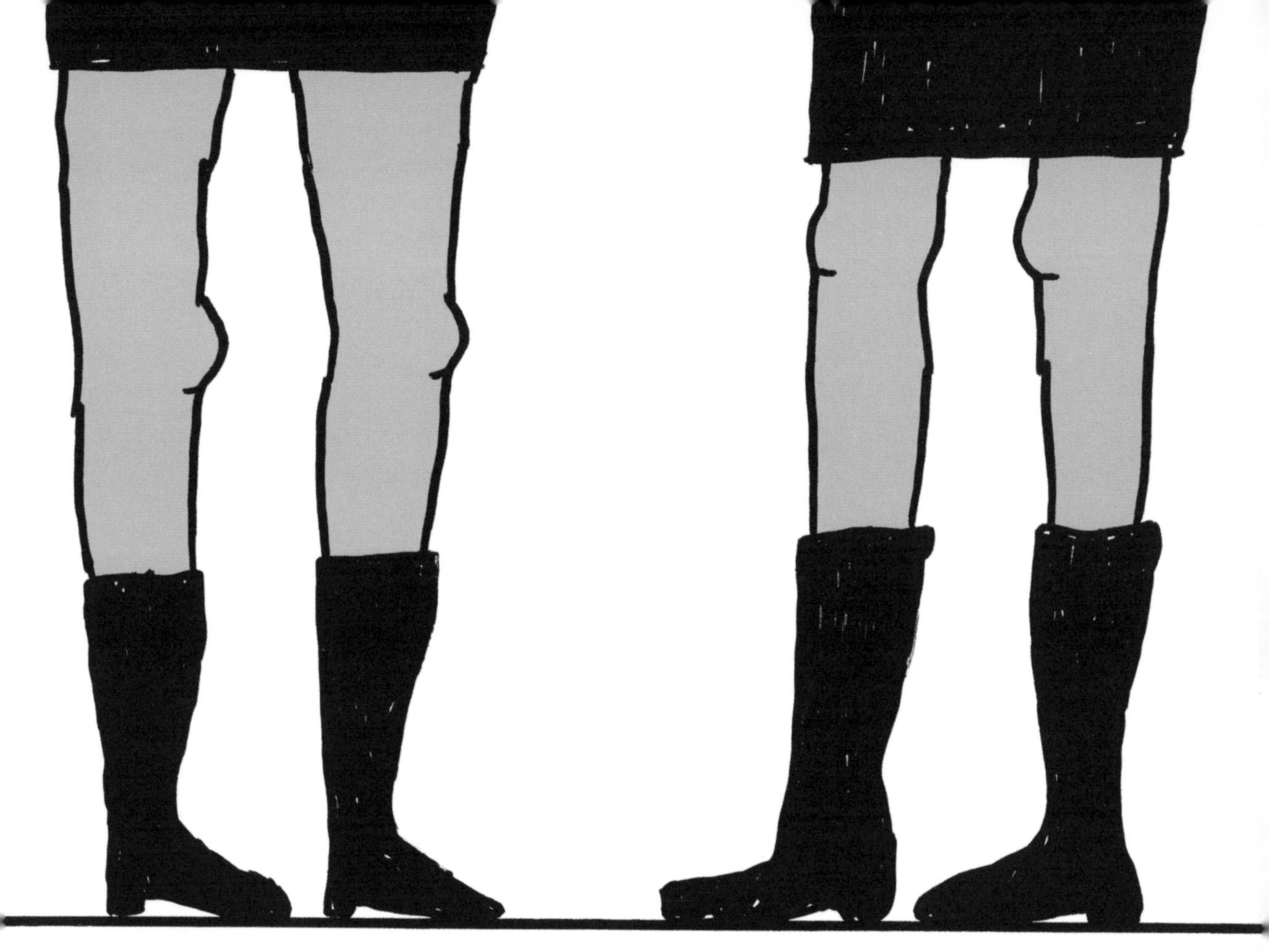

PROSTITUTES PROSTITUTES
PROSTITUTES PROSTITUTES
PROSTITUTES PROSTITUTES
PROSTITUTES PROSTITUTES
PROSTITUTES PROSTITUTES
PROSTITUTES EVERYWHERE
APPEALING FOR OUR
SUPPORT. I'M NOT VOTING
FOR THE PROSTITUTES.
I DON'T WANT THEM RUNNING
THE COUNTRY

DRINK
ME

I WANT GOD TO COLLECT ME FROM SCHOOL IN AN AEROPLANE
IN ORDER TO PROVE HIS EXISTENCE

BIG
NOSE

YAK
YAK

YAK
YAK

YAK
YAK

YAK

YAK

SUNSHINE
RAIN
SUNSHINE
RAIN
SUNSHINE
RAIN
SUNSHINE
RAIN
SUNSHINE

INSECTS
CRAWLING
ON THE
WALL
HOW DO
YOU STICK
THERE ?
WHY DON'T
YOU FALL?

LET'S
PLAY
LEAPFROG

PISS
ACID

MICHAEL JACKSON

HIDING FROM THE AUTHORITIES

AND FROM MY WIFE
AND FROM RESPONSIBILITY

MATCHSTICKS
FIREWOOD

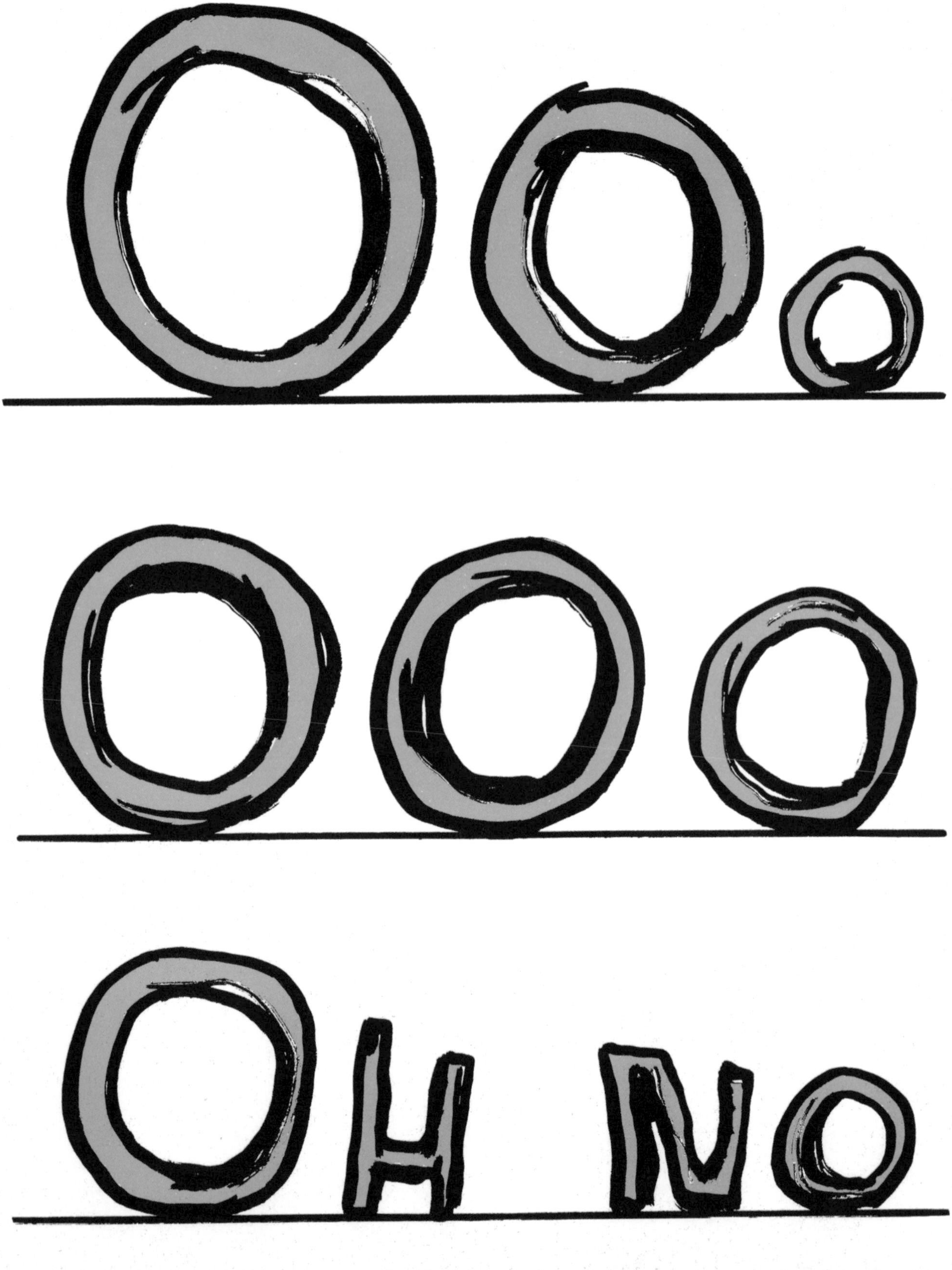

Ooo

OOO

OH NO

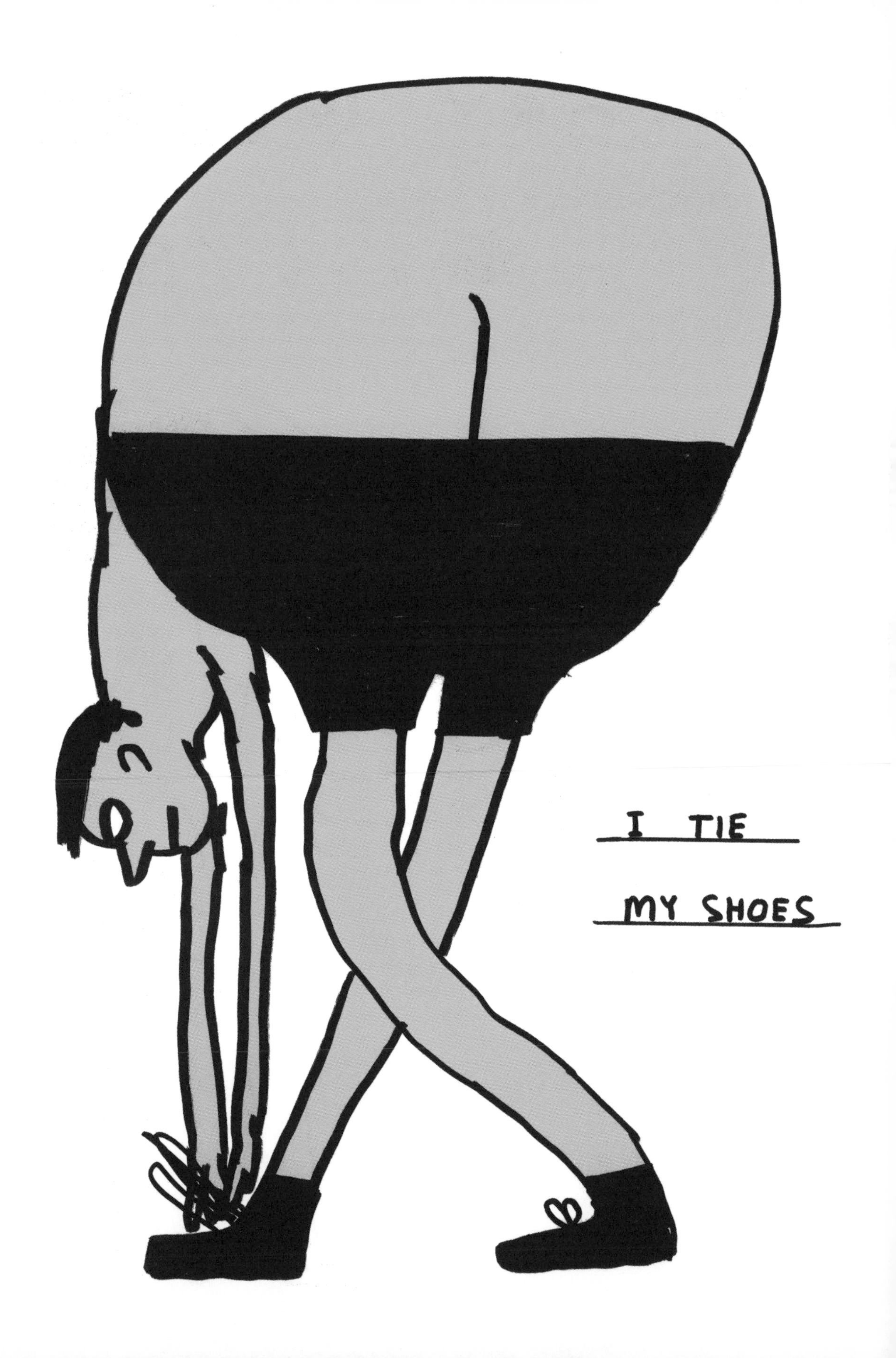
I TIE
MY SHOES

GLORY GLORY

HALL■ELUJAH

IMAGINE
THE GREEN
IS RED

THE

SWAMP SCHOOL

A SCHOOL LOCATED AT THE SWAMP

THE

SCHOOL SWAMP

A SWAMP LOCATED AT THE SCHOOL

YIELD

DO
IT
NOW

OBEY
THE
SIGNS

HESITATE

SPIRIT DEPARTS

FLIES ARRIVE

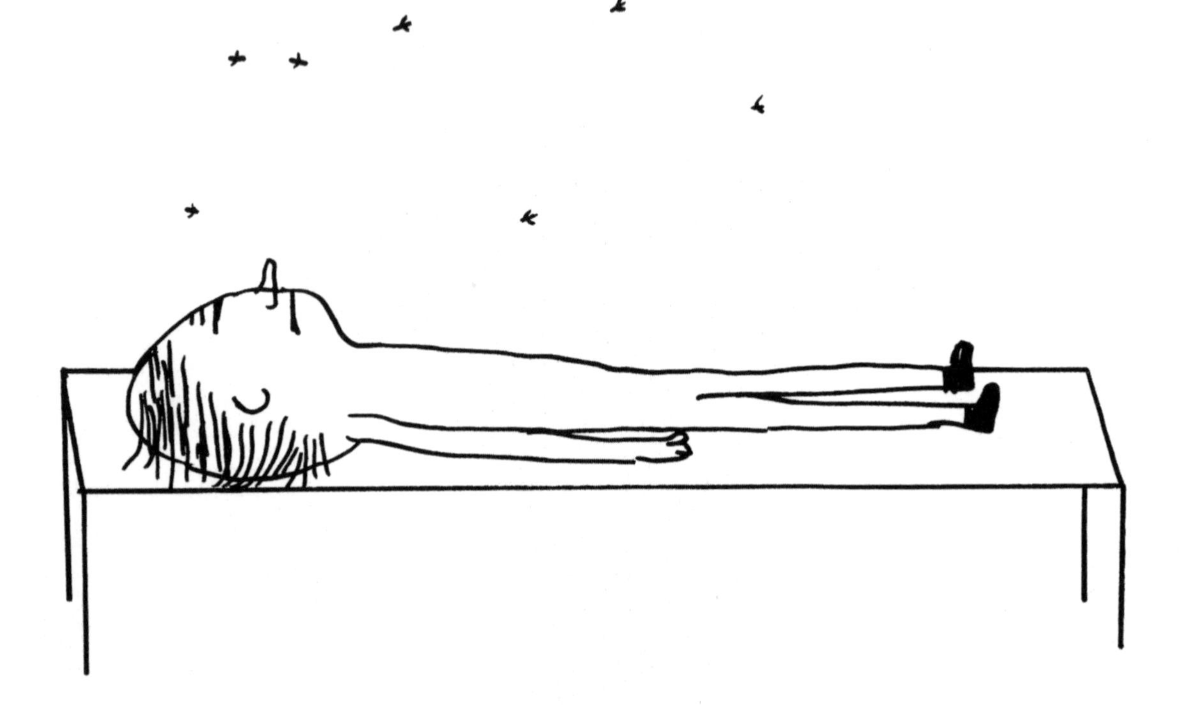

LEISURE CENTRE

85 EUROS

80 €

70 €

100 EUROS

150 EUROS

THEY ARE BEAUTIFUL
BUT THEY ARE NOT WORTH
THE PRICES THEY ARE CHARGING
BUT OH, I DO SO WANT ONE!
IF I HAD THE COURAGE
I WOULD STEAL ONE
PERHAPS I COULD HIDE IT
BENEATH MY DRESS
AND WALK OUT OF THE SHOP

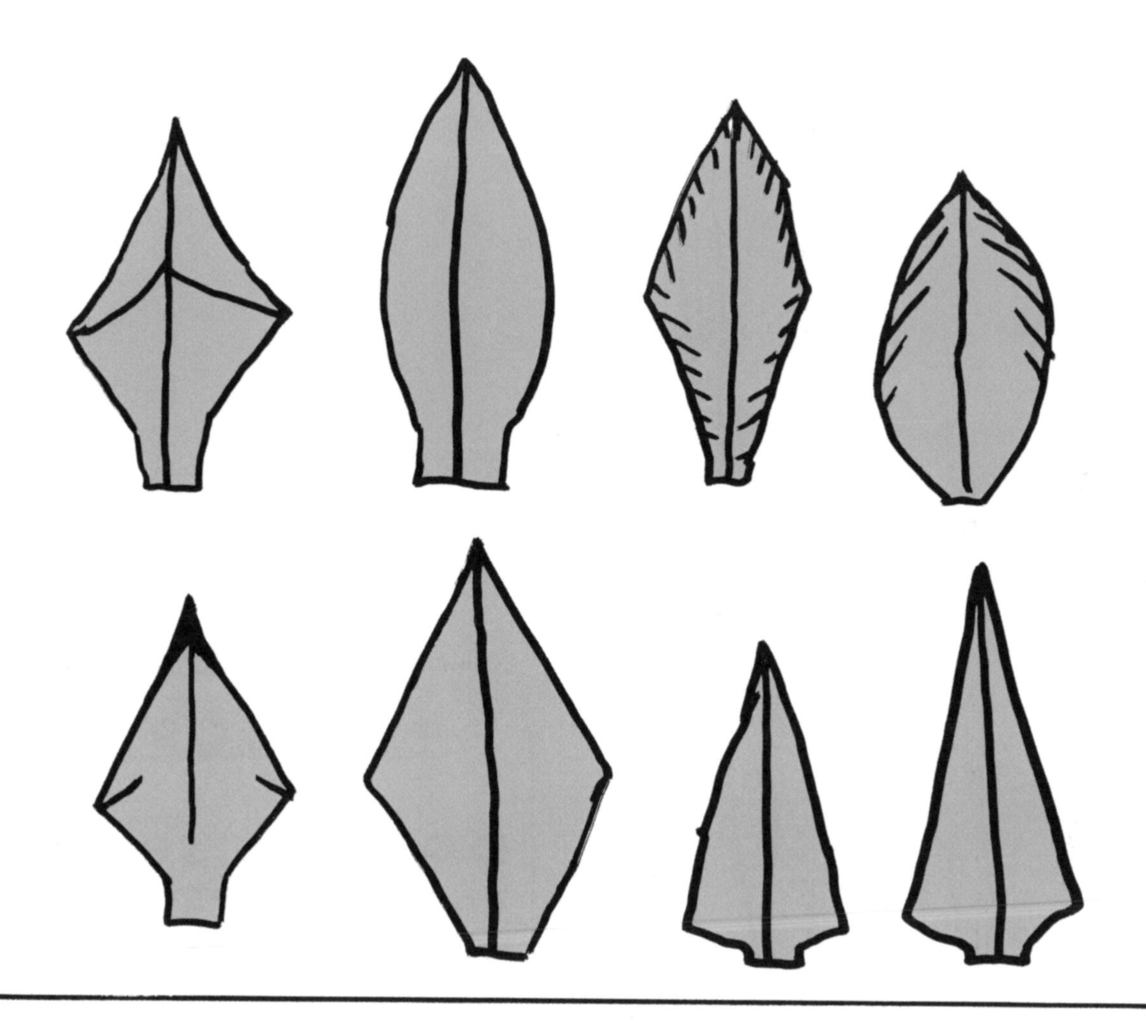

THEY USED TO HUNT WITH SPEARS

THEY CARVED THE SPEARHEADS FROM QUARTZ

THEY USED TO HUNT BISON

WHEN THE BISON WERE GONE

THEY HUNTED PEOPLE

NOW THEY ARE IN JAIL

AWAITING EXECUTION

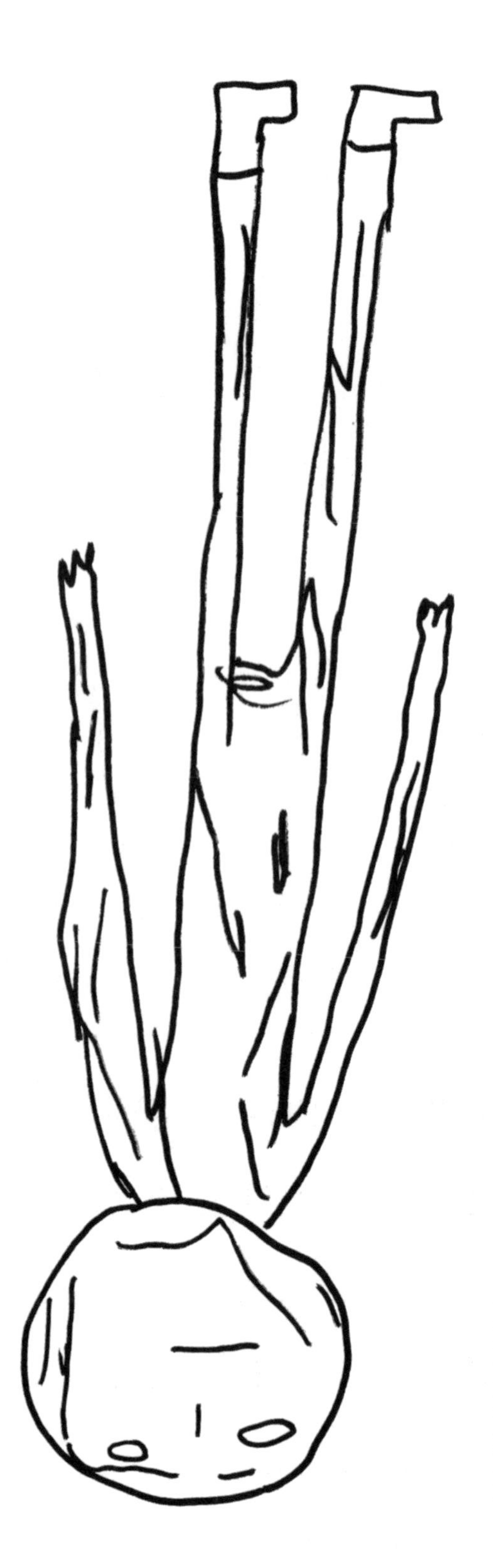
NOTICE
DO NOT SPEAK TO THE UPSIDE-DOWN MAN
DO NOT TOUCH THE UPSIDE-DOWN MAN
THE UPSIDE-DOWN MAN IS NOT FOR SALE

A PROSTITUTE

TODAY I PERFORMED
2 KNEE OPERATIONS

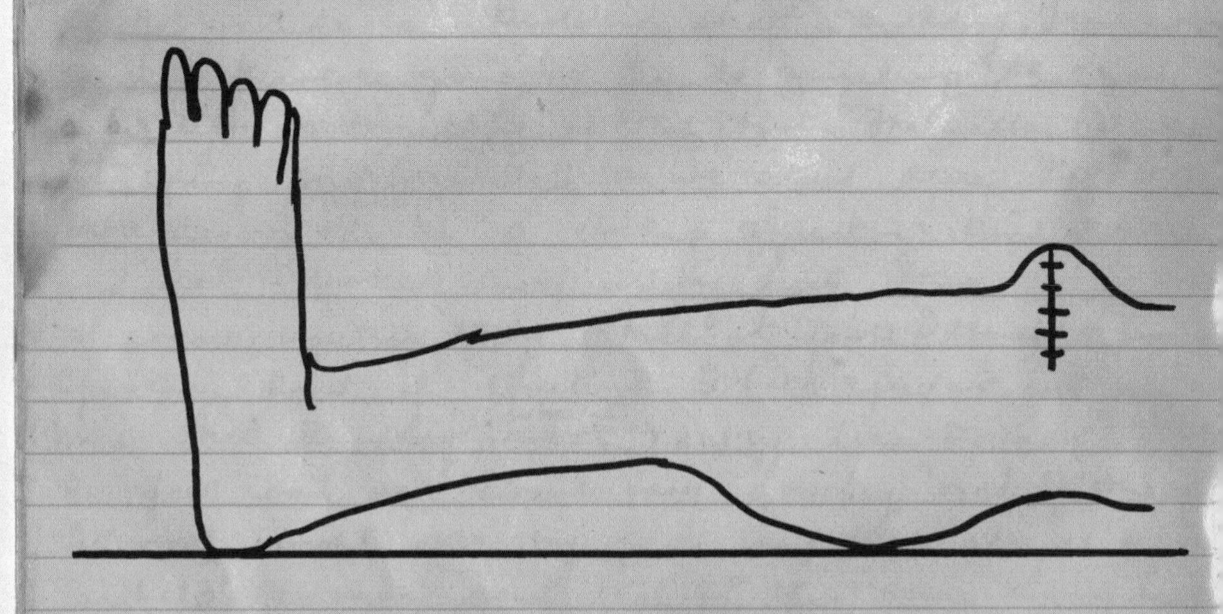

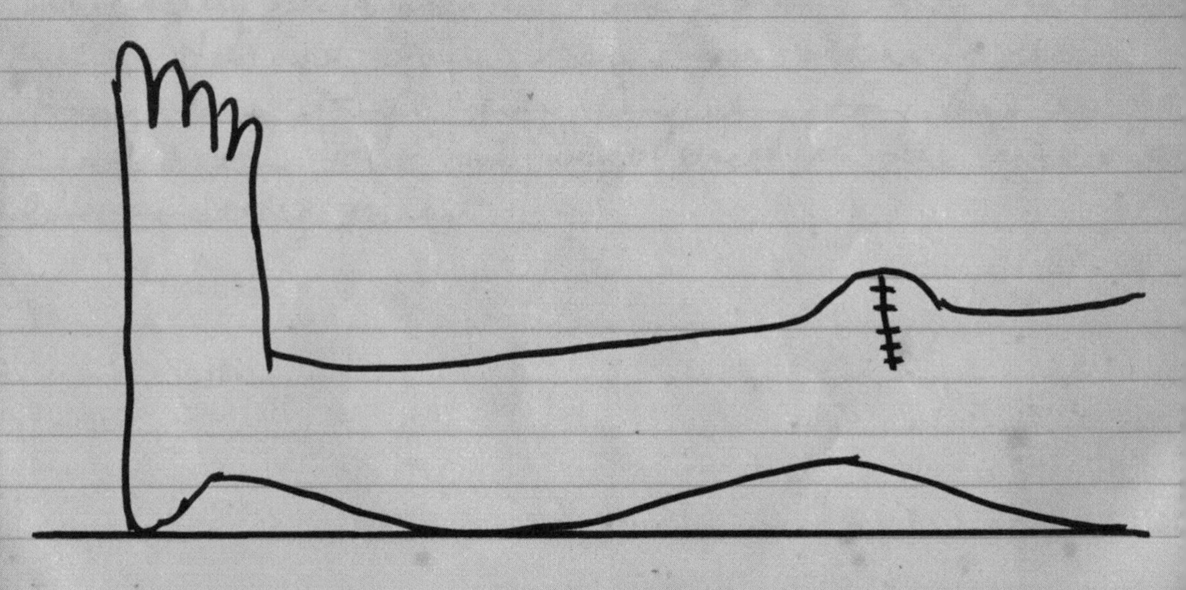

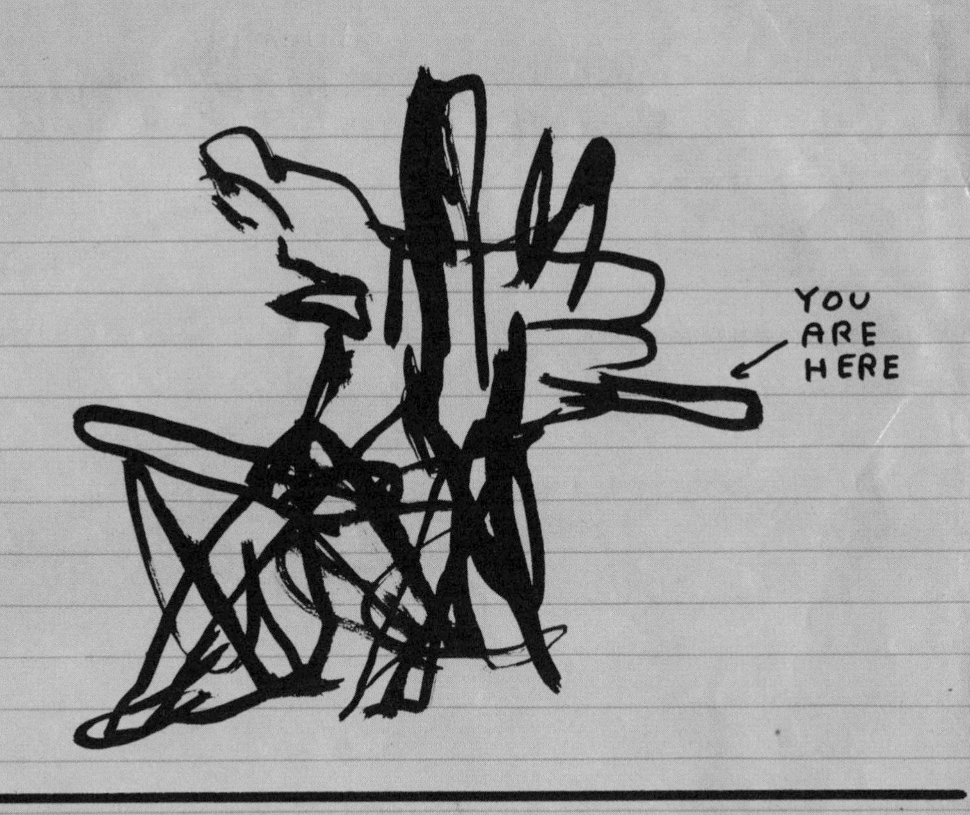
YOU
ARE
HERE

AND
YOU
ARE
HERE

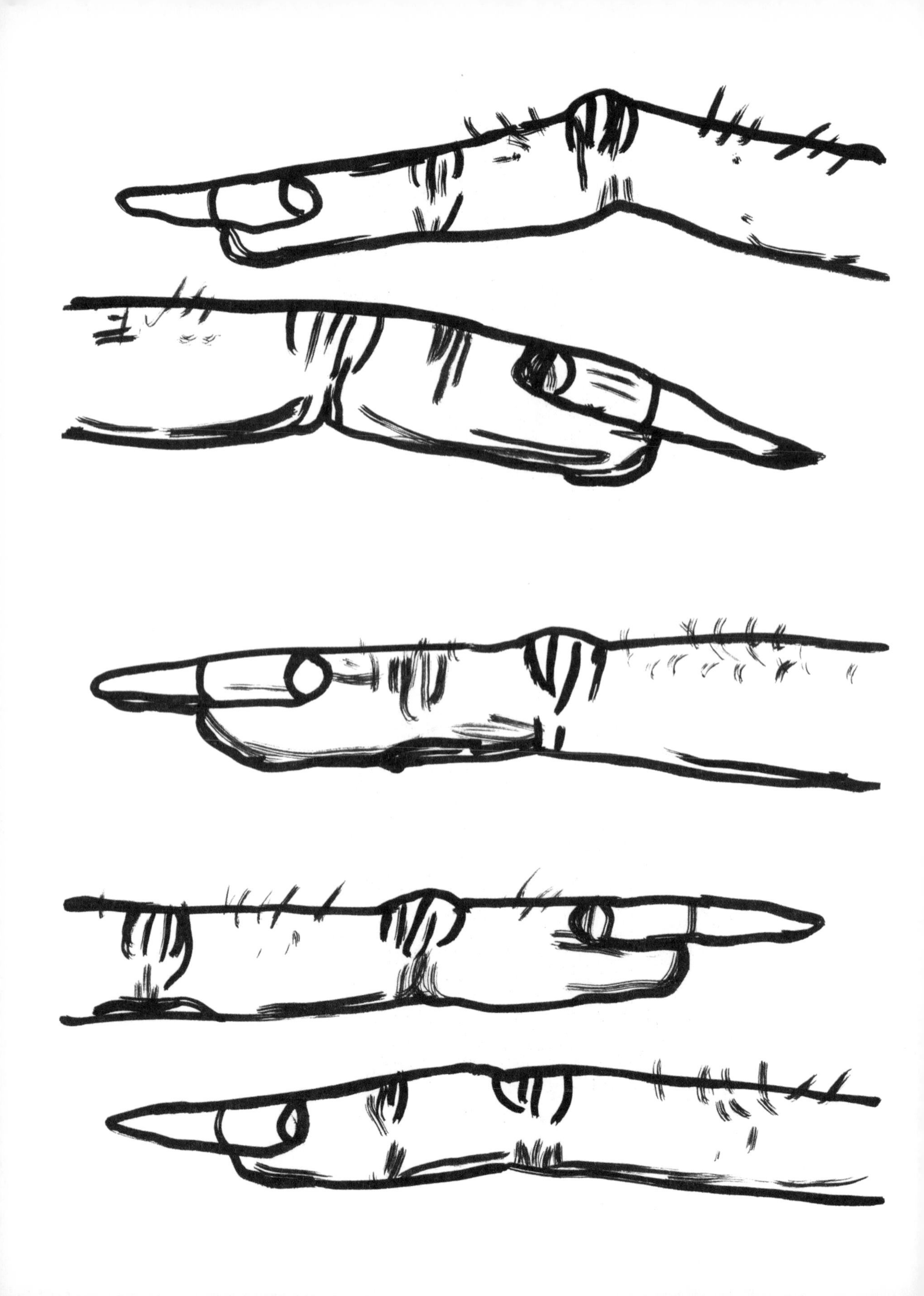

PLEASE
DO NOT
RETURN
THIS TO
ME AS
I DO NOT
WANT IT
BACK.
THANK.
YOU

MY ONLY

TASK IS

TO FILL THE

PAGE

YOU HAVE NOT

BEEN GIVEN A TASK

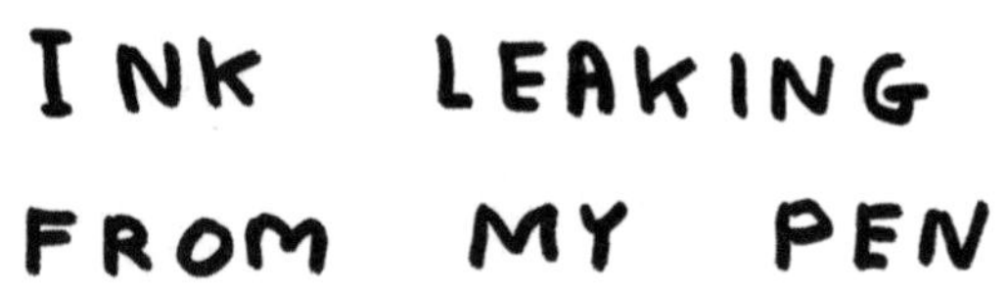
INK LEAKING
FROM MY PEN

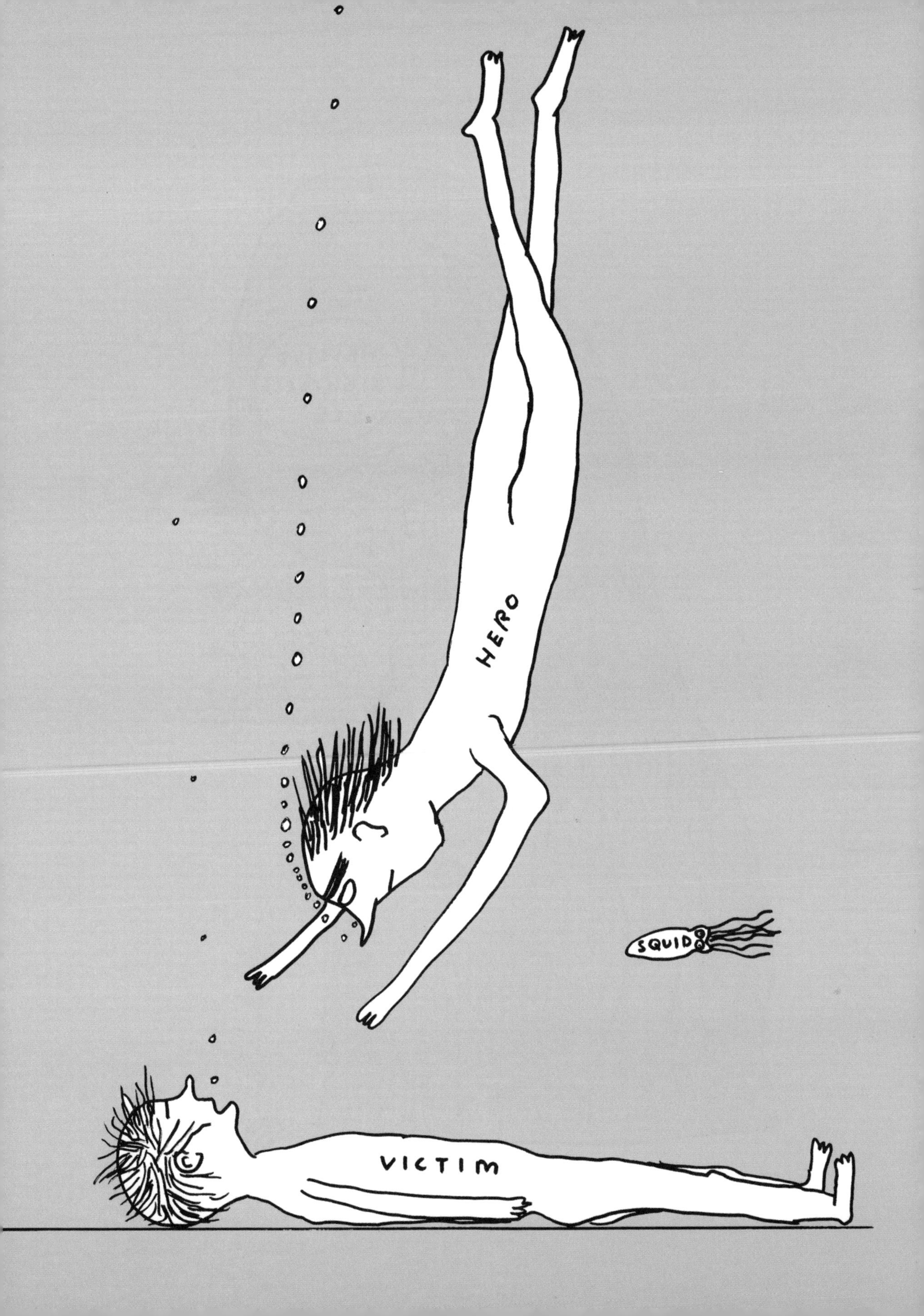
HERO
SQUID
VICTIM

MASSIVE
SIGHTLESS
EYE

UDDER

NOTICE
WHILE YOU ARE READING
THIS THERE IS A MAN IN
ONE OF THE WINDOWS
HIGH ABOVE YOU WHO IS
TAKING YOUR PHOTOGRAPH.
HE WILL THEN MAKE A WEE
MODEL OF YOU AND PUT
IT WITH OTHER WEE
MODELS OF OTHER PEOPLE.
THEN HE PLAYS WEIRD
GAMES WITH THEM.

- WHAT ARE WE WAITING FOR ?

- WE ARE WAITING FOR THEM TO TURN IN TO BUTTERFLIES.

- BUT THEY WILL NOT TURN INTO BUTTERFLIES.

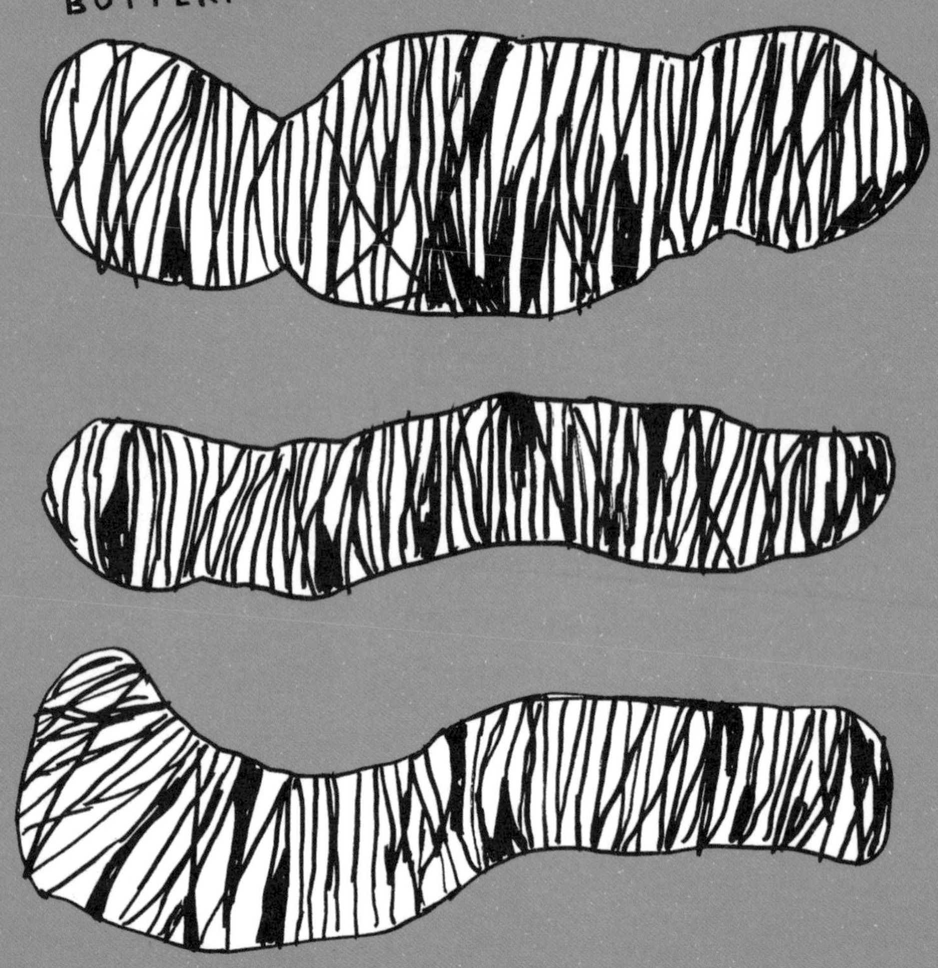

- WHY NOT ?

- BECAUSE THEY ARE WORMS

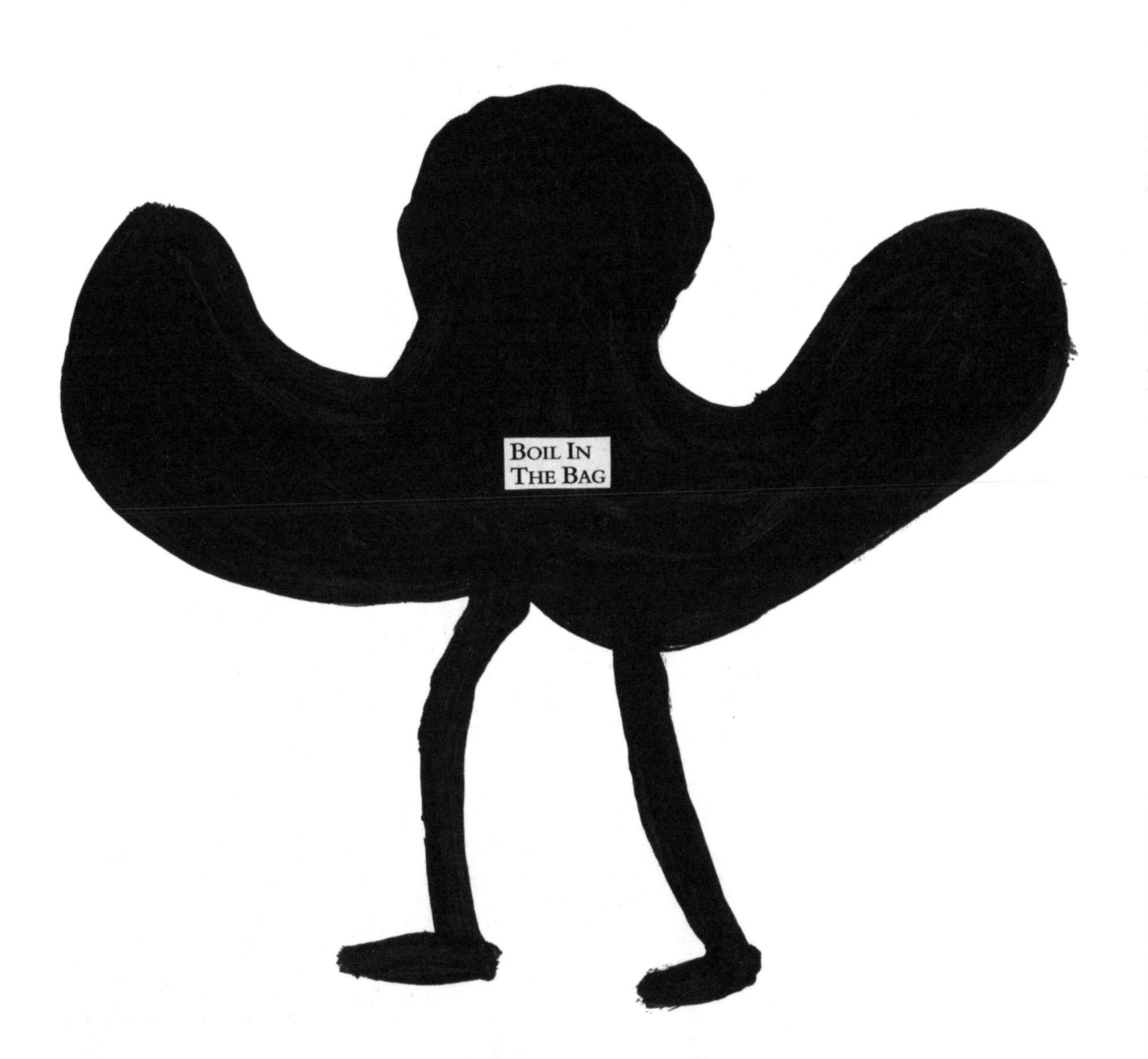
BOIL IN
THE BAG

OLD BIRD

SHUT YOUR BAG
DON'T LET THEM STEAL YOUR MAN

SCULPTURE

WHERE THE FUCK IS IT ?

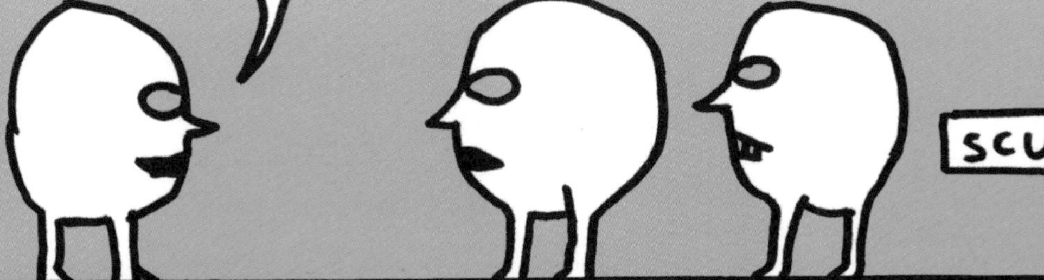
WE COULDN'T FIND THE SCULPTURE
IT ISN'T BUILT YET
SCULPTURE

A PHOTOGRAPH

A

a *or* **A** (eɪ) *n., pl.* **a's, A's,** *or* **As. 1.** the first letter and first vowel of the English alphabet. **2.** any of several speech sounds represented by this letter, as in *take, bag,* or *calm.* **3.** Also called: **alpha.** the first in a series, esp. the highest mark. **4. from A to Z.** from start to finish.

a[1] (ə; *emphatic* eɪ) *determiner.* (*indefinite article;* used before an initial consonant. Cf. **an**[1]) **1.** used preceding a singular countable noun, not previously specified: *a dog; a great pity.* **2.** used preceding a noun or determiner of quantity: *a dozen eggs; a great many; to read a lot.* **3.** (preceded by *once, twice, several times,* etc.) each or every; per: *once a day.* **4.** a certain; one: *a Mr Jones called.* **5.** (preceded by *not*) any at all: *not a hope.* – Cf. **the**[1].

a[2] *symbol for:* **1.** acceleration. **2.** are(s) (metric measure of area). **3.** alto-

A *symbol for:* **1.** *Music.* **a.** the sixth note of the scale of C major. **b.** the major or minor key having this note as its tonic. **2.** a human blood type of the ABO group, containing the A antigen. **3.** (in Britain) a major arterial road. **4.** ampere(s). **5.** absolute (temperature). **6.** area. **7.** (*in combination*) atomic: *an A-bomb; an A-plant.* **8. a.** a person whose job is in top management, or who holds a senior administrative or professional position. **b.** (*as modifier*): *an A worker.* – See also **occupation groupings.**

Å *symbol for* angstrom unit.

a. *abbrev. for:* **1.** acre(s). **2.** Also: **A.** alto.

A. *abbrev. for:* **1.** acre(s). **2.** America(n). **3.** answer.

a-[1] *or before a vowel* **an-** *prefix.* not; without; opposite to: *atonal; asocial.* [from Gk *a-, an-* not, without]

a-[2] *prefix.* **1.** on; in; towards: *aground; aback.* **2.** in the state of: *afloat; asleep.*

A1, A-1, *or* **A-one** (ˈeɪˈwʌn) *adj.* **1.** physically fit. **2.** *Inf.* first class; excellent. **3.** (of a vessel) in first-class condition.

A4 *n.* a standard paper size, 297 × 210 mm.

AA *abbrev. for:* **1.** Alcoholics Anonymous. **2.** anti-aircraft. **3.** (in Britain) Automobile Association.

AAA *abbrev. for:* **1.** *Brit.* Amateur Athletic Association. **2.** *U.S.* Automobile Association of America.

Aachen (ˈɑːkən; *German* ˈaːxən) *n.* a city and spa in W Germany, in North Rhine-Westphalia: formerly in West Germany: the northern capital of Charlemagne's empire. Pop.: 239 200 (1987). French name: **Aix-la-Chapelle.**

Aalborg *or* **Ålborg** (*Danish* ˈɔlbɔr) *n.* a city and port in Denmark, in N Jutland. Pop.: 154 739 (1988).

Aalesund (*Norwegian* ˈoːləsun) *n.* a variant spelling of **Ålesund.**

Aalto (*Finnish* ˈɑːltɔ) *n.* **Alvar** (ˈalvar). 1898–1976, Finnish architect and furniture designer, noted particularly for his public and industrial buildings, in which wood is much used. He invented bent plywood furniture (1932).

A & R *abbrev. for* artists and repertoire.

AAP *abbrev. for* Australian Associated Press.

Aarau (*German* ˈaːrau) *n.* a town in N Switzerland, capital of Aargau canton: capital of the Helvetic Republic from 1798 to 1803. Pop.: 15 788 (1980).

aardvark (ˈɑːdˌvɑːk) *n.* a nocturnal burrowing African mammal that has long ears and snout and feeds on termites. Also called: **ant bear.** [C19: from obs. Afrik., from *aarde* earth + *varken* pig]

aardwolf (ˈɑːdˌwʊlf) *n., pl.* **-wolves.** a nocturnal mammal of the hyena family that inhabits the plains of southern Africa and feeds on termites and insect larvae. [C19: from Afrik., from *aarde* earth + *wolf* wolf]

Aargau (*German* ˈaːrgau) *n.* a canton in N Switzerland. Capital: Aarau. Pop.: 478 000 (1987 est.). Area: 1404 sq. km (542 sq. miles). French name: **Argovie.**

Aarhus *or* **Århus** (*Danish* ˈɔrhuːs) *n.* a city and port in Denmark, in E Jutland. Pop.: 259 155 (1989 est.).

Aaron (ˈɛərən) *n. Old Testament.* the first high priest of the Israelites, brother of Moses (Exodus 4:14).

Aaron's beard *n.* another name for **rose of Sharon.**

Aaron's rod *n.* a widespread Eurasian plant having tall

AB *abbrev. for:* **1.** Also: **a.b.** able-bodied seaman. **2.** Alberta. **3.** (in the U.S.) Bachelor of Arts. – **4.** *symbol for* a human blood type of the ABO group, containing both the A antigen and the B antigen.

ab-[1] *prefix.* away from; opposite to: *abnormal.* [from L *ab* away from]

ab-[2] *prefix.* a cgs unit of measurement in the electromagnetic system: *abampere, abwatt, abvolt.* [from ABSOLUTE]

aba (ˈæbə) *n.* **1.** a type of cloth from Syria, made of goat or camel hair. **2.** a sleeveless outer garment of such cloth. [from Ar.]

abaca (ˈæbəkə) *n.* **1.** a Philippine plant, the source of Manila hemp. **2.** another name for **Manila hemp.** [via Sp. from Tagalog *abaká*]

aback (əˈbæk) *adv.* **taken aback. a.** startled or disconcerted. **b.** *Naut.* (of a vessel or sail) having the wind against the forward side so as to prevent forward motion. [OE *on bæc* to the back]

abacus (ˈæbəkəs) *n., pl.* **-ci** (-ˌsaɪ) *or* **-cuses. 1.** a counting device that consists of a frame holding rods on which a number of beads are free to move. **2.** *Archit.* the flat upper part of the capital of a column. [C16: from L, from Gk *abax* board covered with sand, from Heb. *ābhāq* dust]

Abaddon (əˈbædˈn) *n.* **1.** the Devil (Revelation 9:11). **2.** (in rabbinical literature) a part of Gehenna; Hell. [Heb., lit.: destruction]

abaft (əˈbɑːft) *Naut.* –*adv., adj.* (*postpositive*) **1.** closer to the stern than to another place on a vessel. –*prep.* **2.** behind; aft of. [C13: *on baft; baft* from OE *beæftan,* from *be* by + *æftan* behind]

Abakan (*Russian* abaˈkan) *n.* a city in S central Russia, capital of the Khakass Autonomous Region, at the confluence of the Yenisei and Abakan Rivers. Pop.: 143 000 (1983 est.).

abalone (ˌæbəˈləʊnɪ) *n.* an edible marine mollusc having an ear-shaped shell perforated with a row of respiratory holes and lined with mother-of-pearl. Also called: **ear shell.** [C19: from American Sp. *abulón*]

abandon (əˈbændən) *vb.* (*tr.*) **1.** to forsake completely; desert; leave behind. **2.** to give up completely: *to abandon hope.* **3.** to give up (something begun) before completion: *the game was abandoned.* **4.** to surrender (oneself) to emotion without restraint. **5.** to give (insured property that has suffered partial loss or damage) to the insurers in order that a claim for a total loss may be made. –*n.* **6.** freedom from inhibitions, restraint, or worry: *she danced with abandon.* [C14: *abandounen* (vb.), from OF, from *a bandon* under one's control, from *a* at, to + *bandon* control] —**aˈbandonment** *n.*

abandoned (əˈbændənd) *adj.* **1.** deserted: *an abandoned hut.* **2.** forsaken: *an abandoned child.* **3.** uninhibited.

abase (əˈbeɪs) *vb.* **abases, abasing, abased.** (*tr.*) **1.** to humble or belittle (oneself, etc.). **2.** to lower or reduce, as in rank. [C15 *abessen,* from OF *abaissier* to make low. See BASE[2]] —**aˈbasement** *n.*

abash (əˈbæʃ) *vb.* (*tr.; usually passive*) to cause to feel ill at ease, embarrassed, or confused. [C14: from OF *esbair* to be astonished, from *es-* out + *bair* to gape] —**aˈbashed** *adj.*

abate (əˈbeɪt) *vb.* **abates, abating, abated. 1.** to make or become less in amount, intensity, degree, etc. **2.** (*tr.*) *Law.* **a.** to suppress or terminate (a nuisance). **b.** to suspend or extinguish (a claim or action). **c.** to annul (a writ). **3.** (*intr.*) *Law.* (of a writ, etc.) to become null and void. [C14: from OF *abatre* to beat down] —**aˈbatement** *n.*

abatis *or* **abattis** (ˈæbətɪs) *n.* **1.** a rampart of felled trees with their branches outwards. **2.** a barbed-wire entanglement before a position. [C18: from F, from *abattre* to fell]

abattoir (ˈæbəˌtwɑː) *n.* another name for **slaughterhouse.** [C19: F, from *abattre* to fell]

Abba (ˈæbə) *n.* **1.** *New Testament.* father (used of God). **2.** a title given to bishops and patriarchs in the Syrian, Coptic, and Ethiopian Churches. [from Aramaic]

abbacy

A PAGE

A PHOTOGRAPH OF A STICK

DANGER
PLEASE DO NOT LET
CHILDREN CLIMB ON
BARRIERS

A SIGN ON THE BARRIERS

ANIMALS

FURNITURE

A HOLE TO LOOK AT BIRDS THROUGH

TWO PEOPLE

A SHOP

A WALL

AT THE AIRPORT

A STONE WITH A SWORD STUCK IN IT

A PHOTOGRAPH OF A SHADOW ON A ROCK

A PHOTOGRAPH OF A BUCKET OF WATER

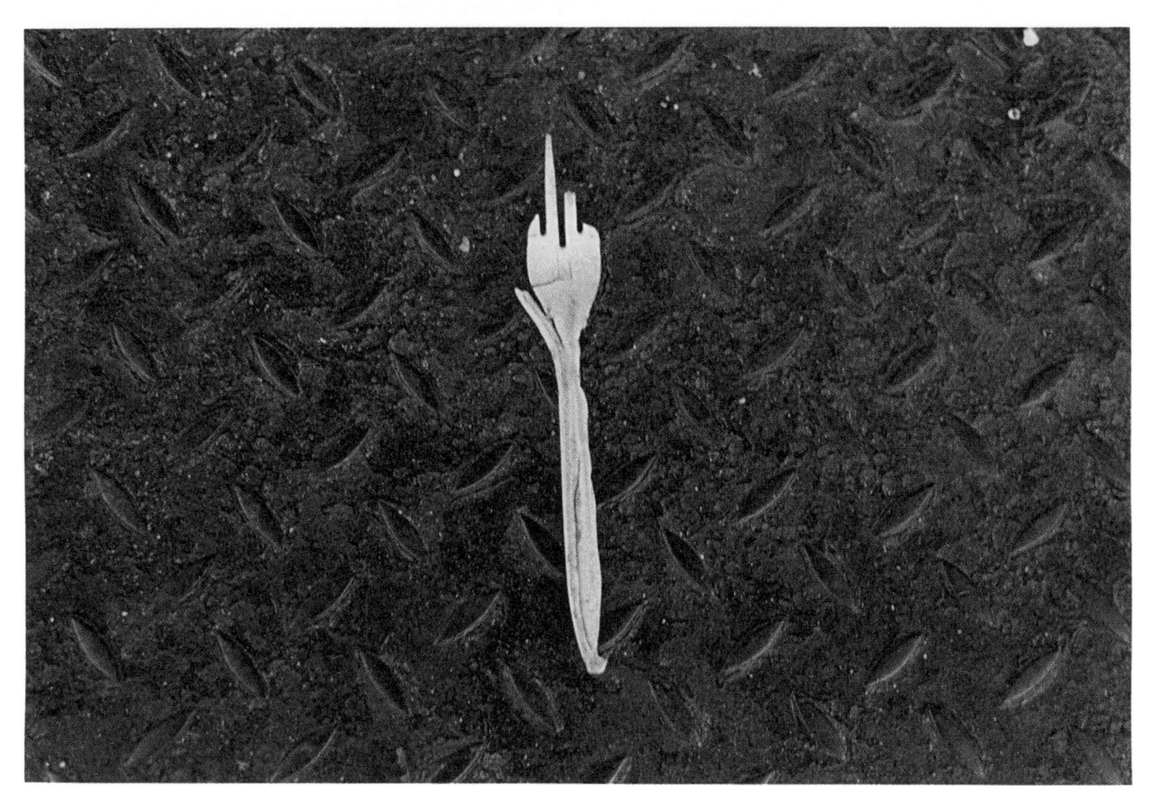

FORK

GHOSTS

A BLUR

AN ALLEY

A PHOTOGRAPH

A TREE

A PHOTOGRAPH OF BENT RAILINGS

A TREE WITH A HOUSE IN IT

A LITTLE MAN

A HUGE MAN

A MAN

A SWAN

NO EYE

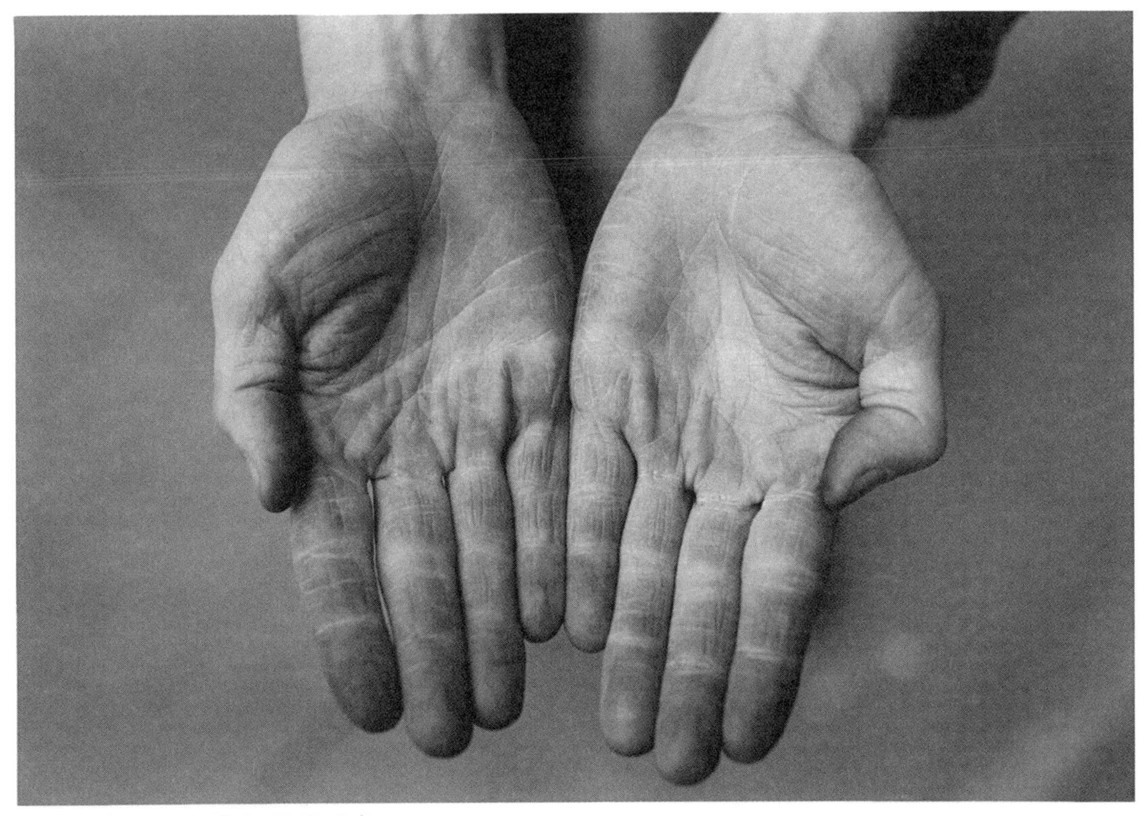

NOT CLEAN

AN AMBITIOUS PROJECT COLLAPSING

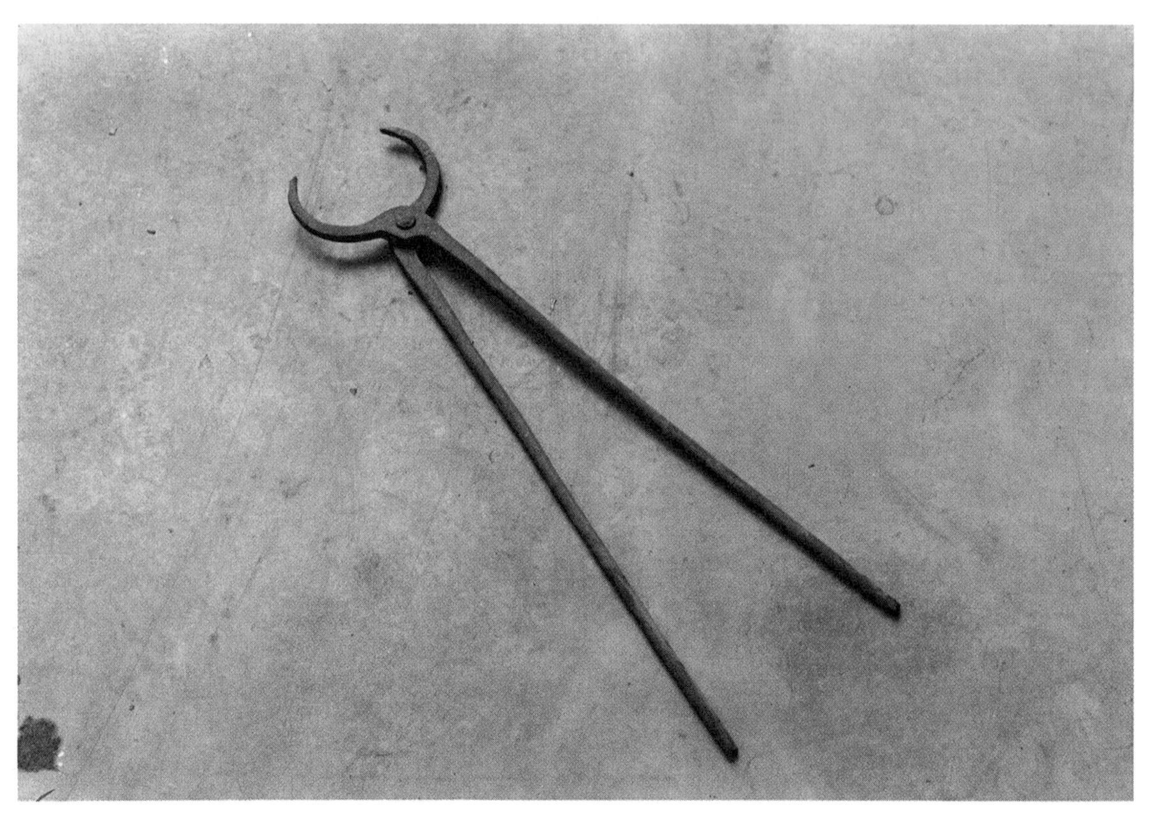

TO PICK UP HOT THINGS WITH

AN EMPTY ENCLOSURE

A PHOTO

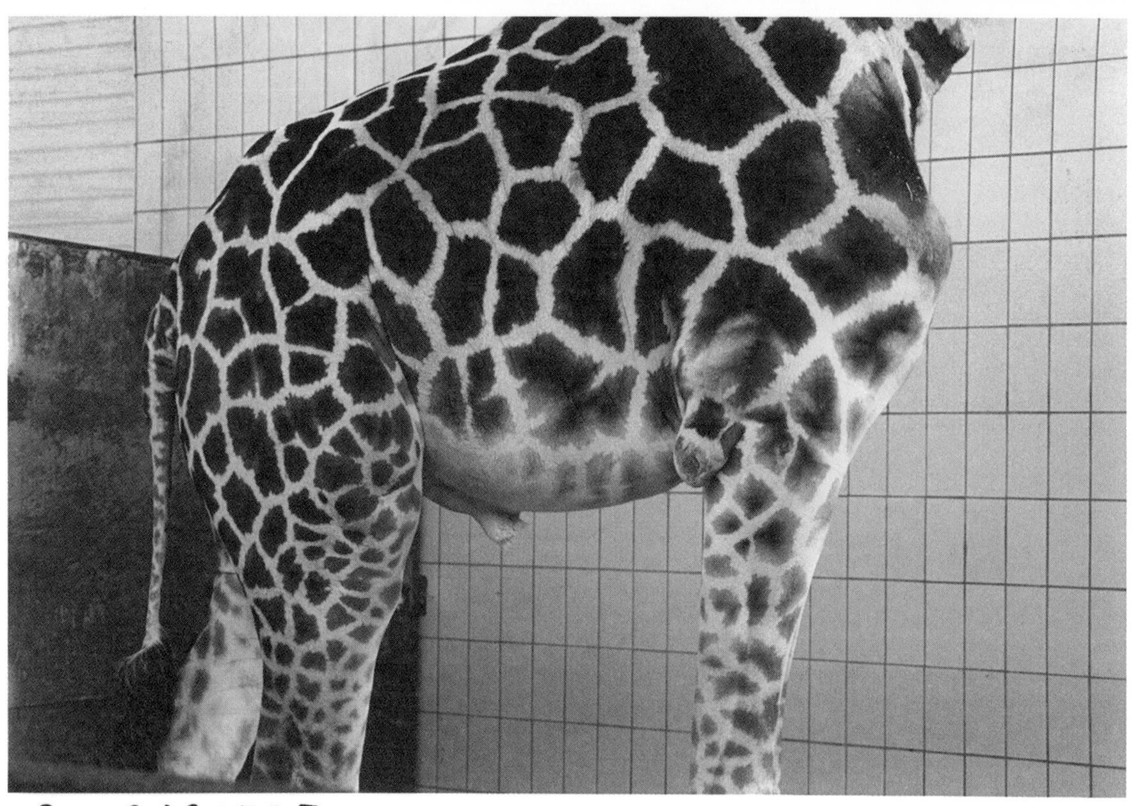

A GIRAFFE

A PHOTOGRAPH

THE ROUTE

THE SEEDS

NOT
RIPE

RIPE, DELICIOUS

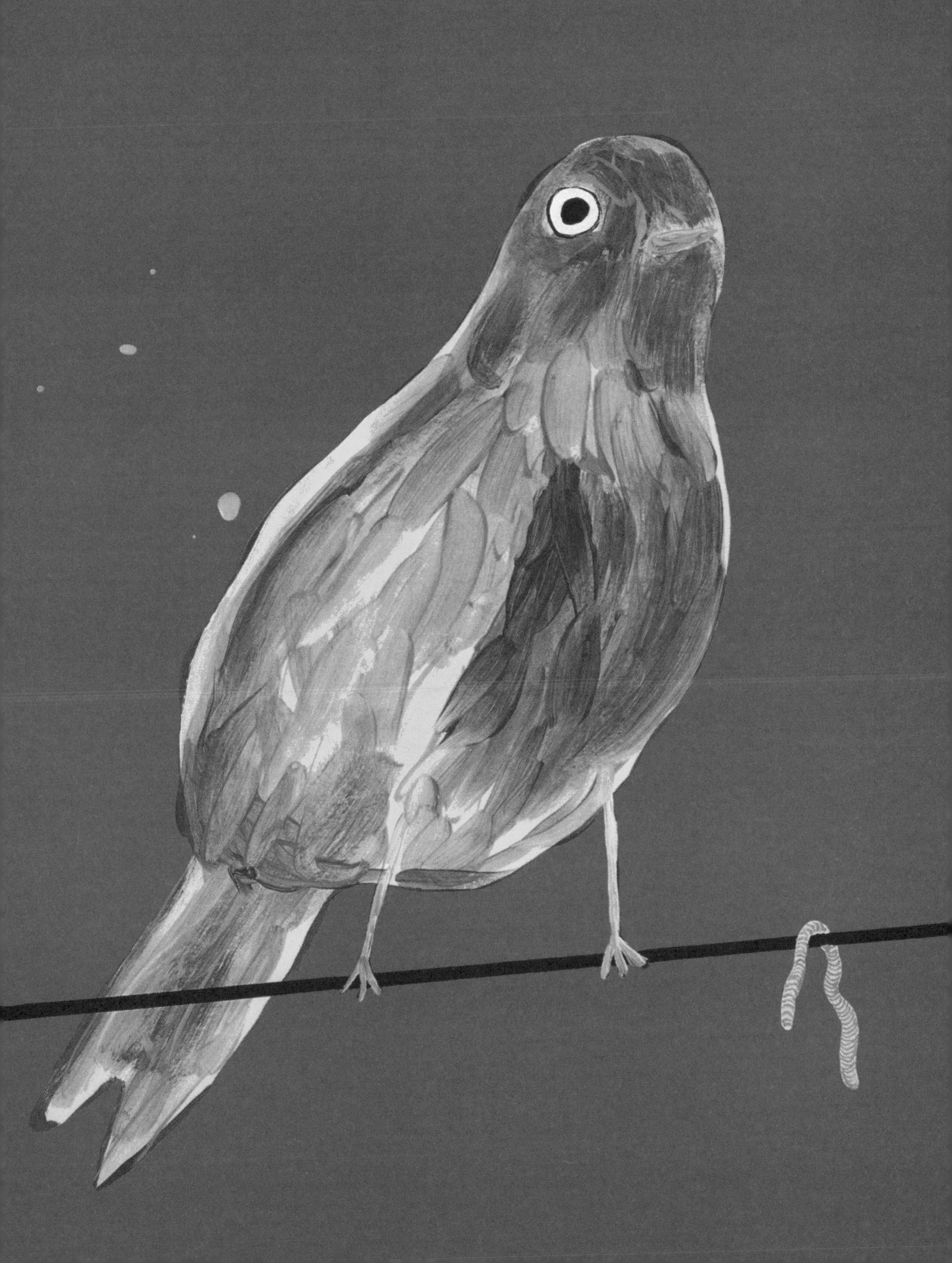

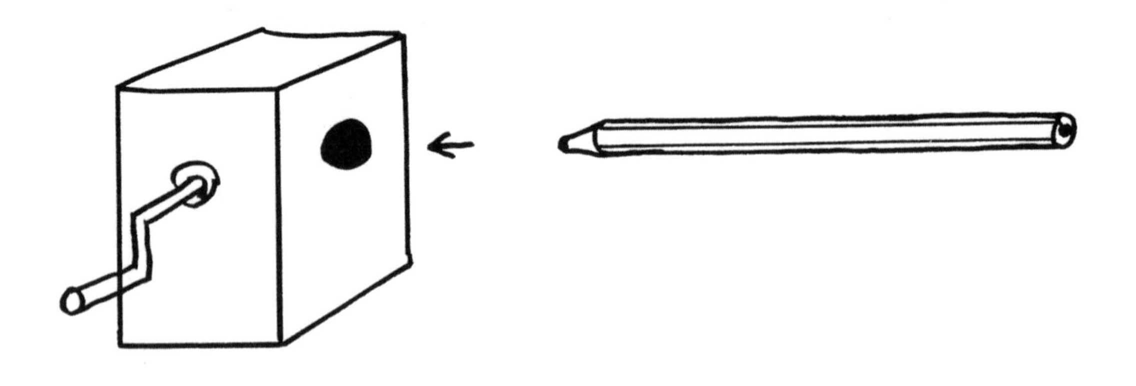

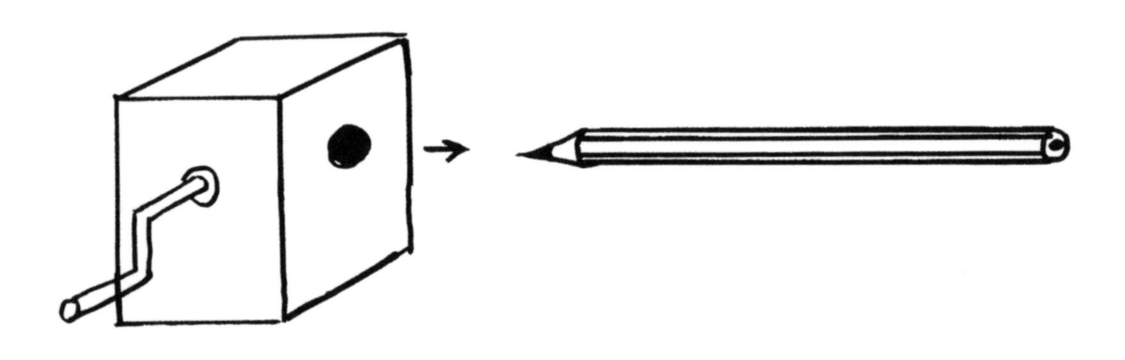

WHAT ARE
YOU GOING TO
DO ABOUT IT?

YOUR
BEST FRIEND

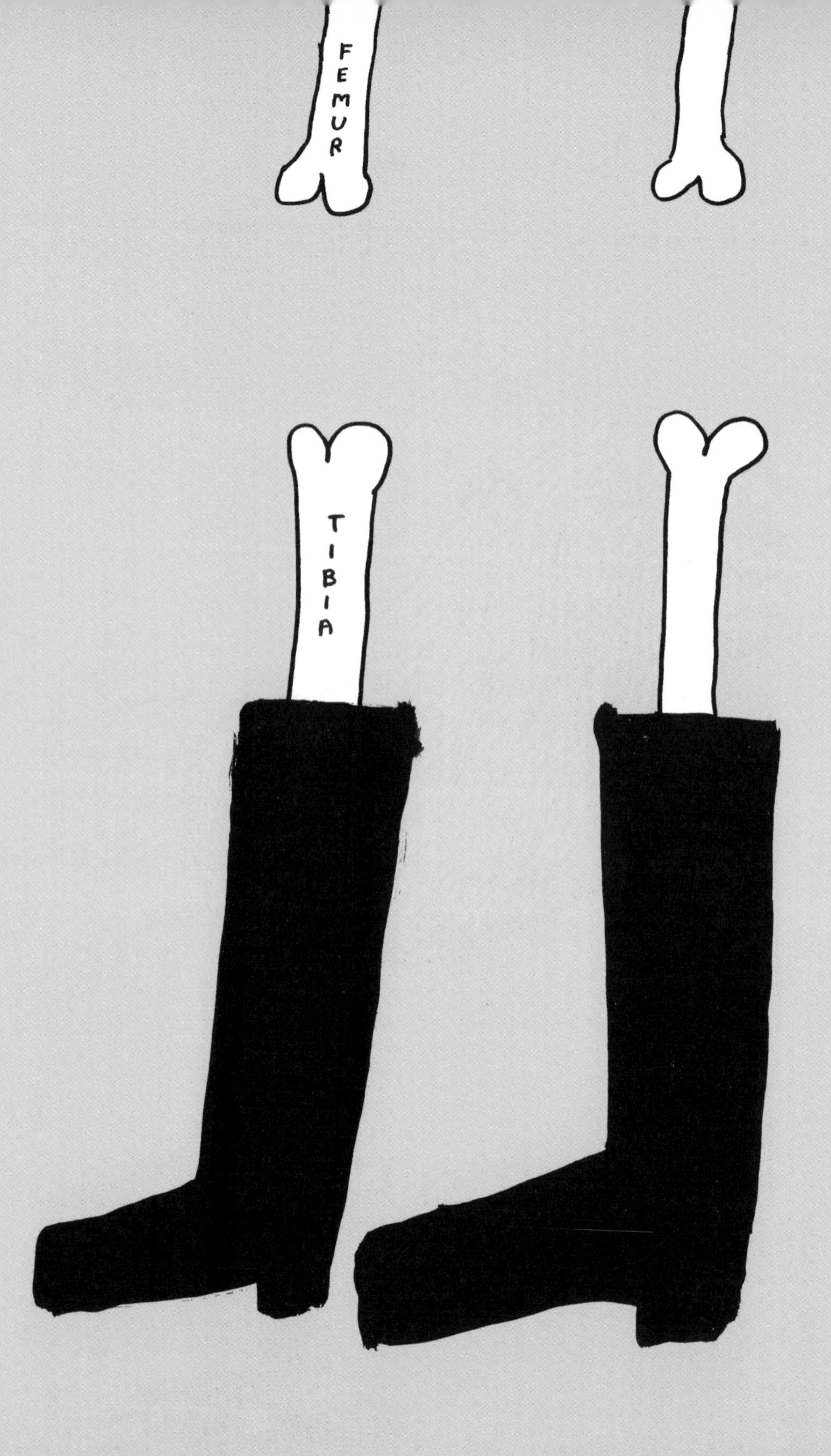
FEMUR
TIBIA

LEFT SIDE OF THE STREET

RIGHT SIDE OF THE STREET

EVERY-
THING
IS GOOD

LAUGHTER

RINGING OUT

ALL AROUND THE HOSPITAL

LIGHT IN THE GLOOM
SPOILING THE GLOOM

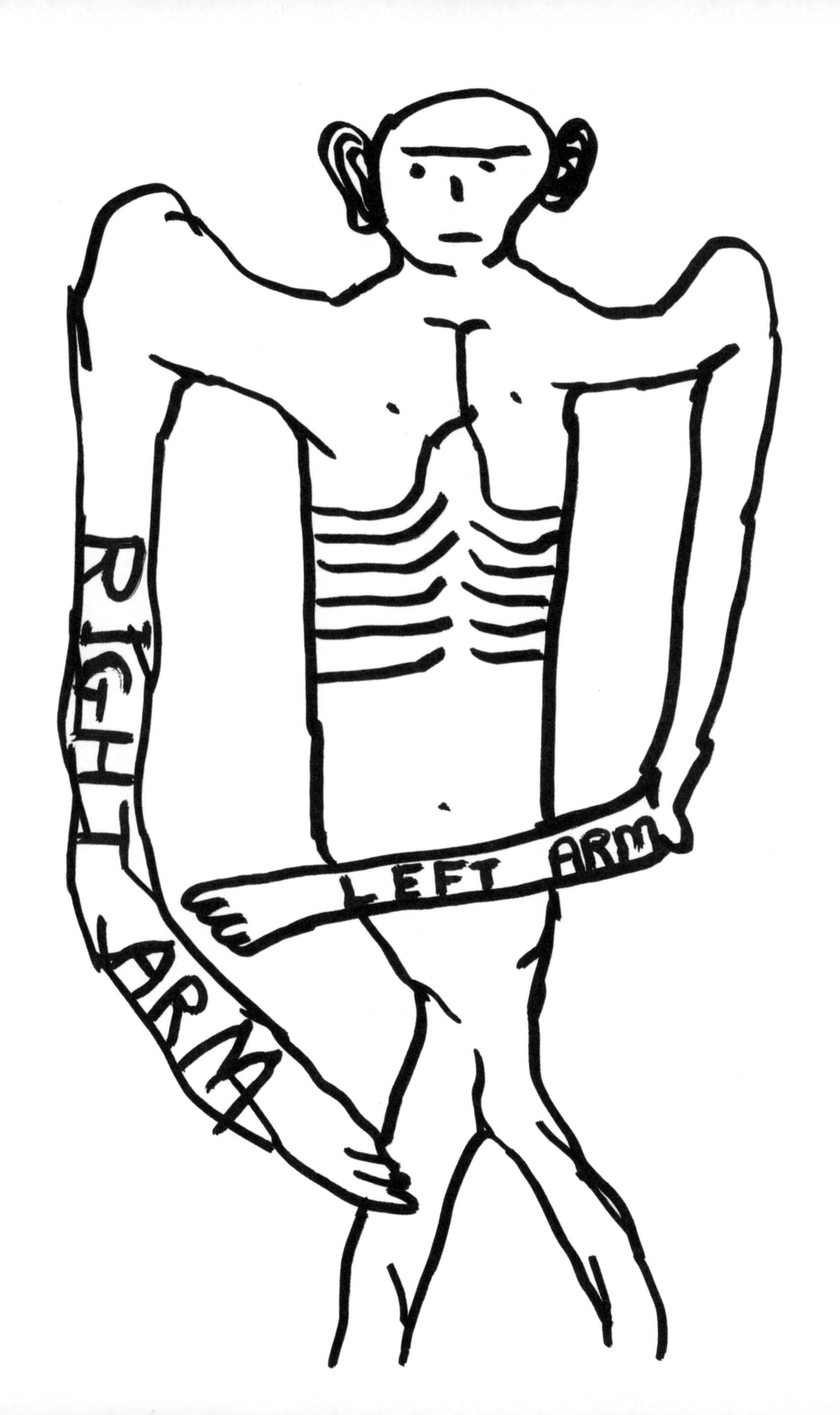
RIGHT ARM
LEFT ARM

HOW ARE YOU FEELING?

I'M FEELING VERY UNSTABLE AND INSECURE. I ALSO FEEL VERY WORRIED AND ANXIOUS ABOUT EVERYTHING

I ALSO FEEL TRAPPED AND I FEEL THAT I AM MUCH TOO FAT AND THAT PEOPLE ARE LAUGHING AT ME. I FEEL VERY FRUSTRATED AND DEPRESSED. I FEEL THAT I AM UNABLE TO MEET THE DEMANDS THAT HAVE BEEN MADE OF ME. I AM IN A BIT OF A RUT CREATIVELY AS WELL.

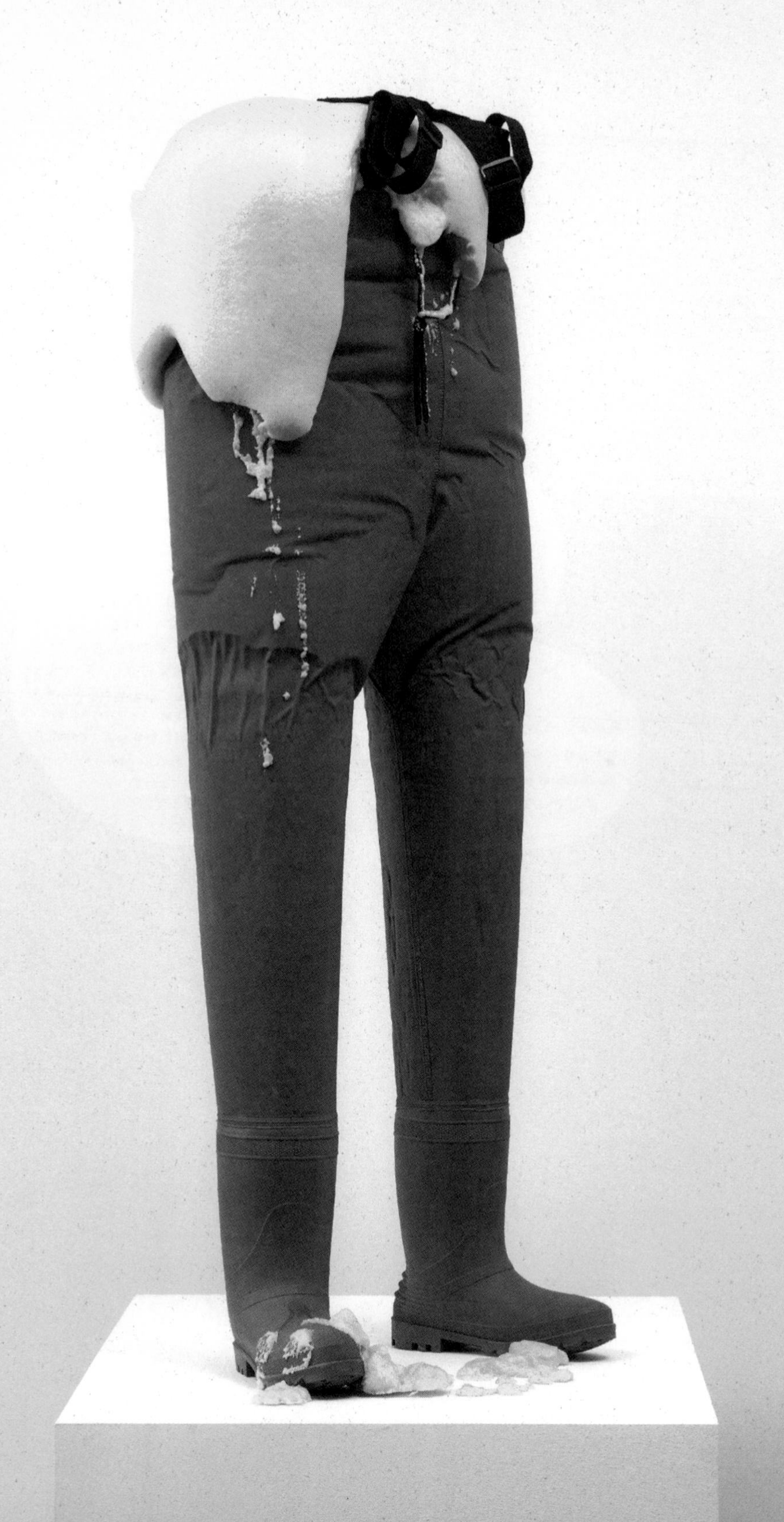

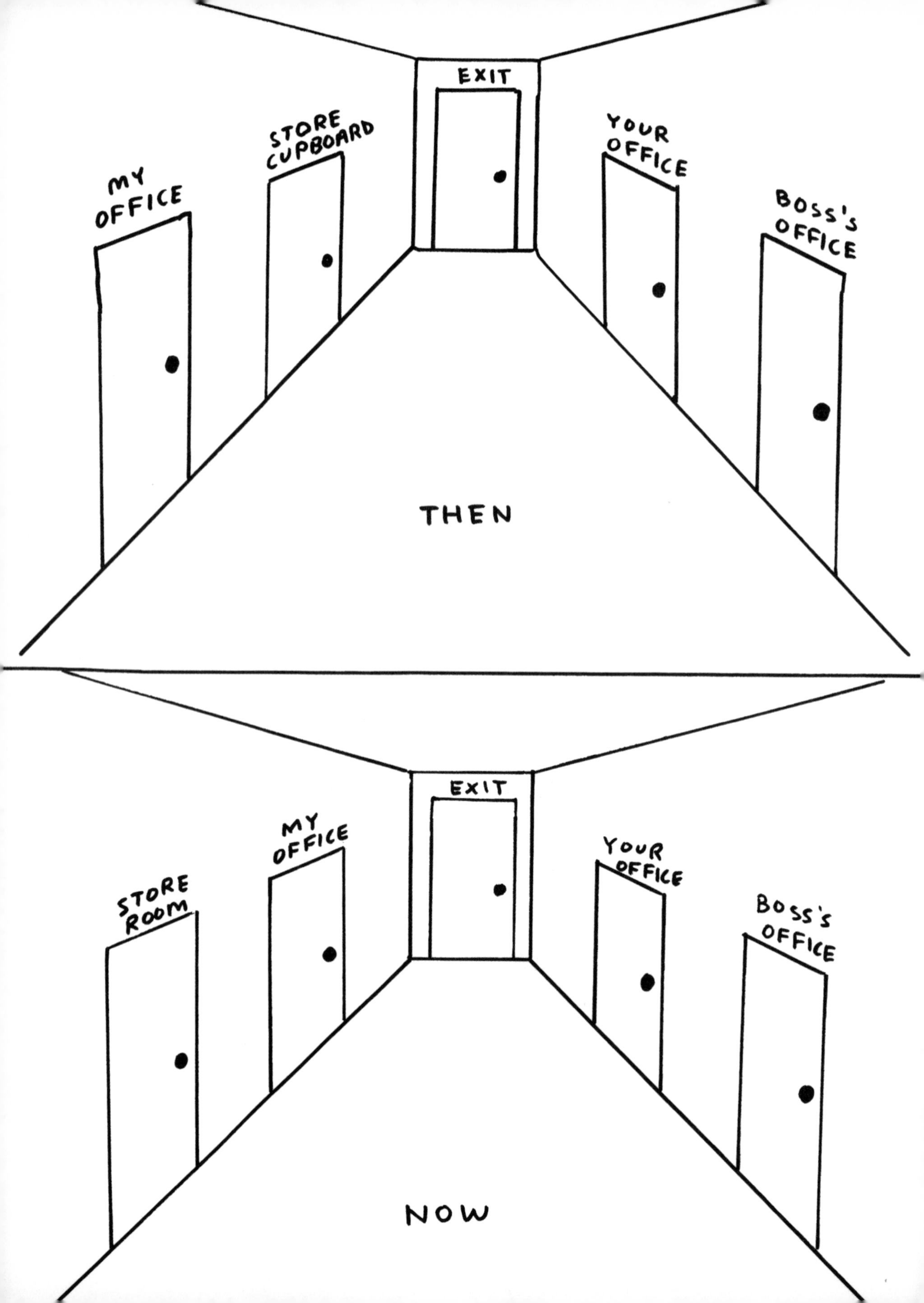
EXIT
STORE CUPBOARD
MY OFFICE
YOUR OFFICE
BOSS'S OFFICE
THEN
EXIT
MY OFFICE
STORE ROOM
YOUR OFFICE
BOSS'S OFFICE
NOW

TODAY IS MY

BIRTHDAY

PLEASE RELEASE
ME FROM JAIL

THE SURFACE OF THE EARTH

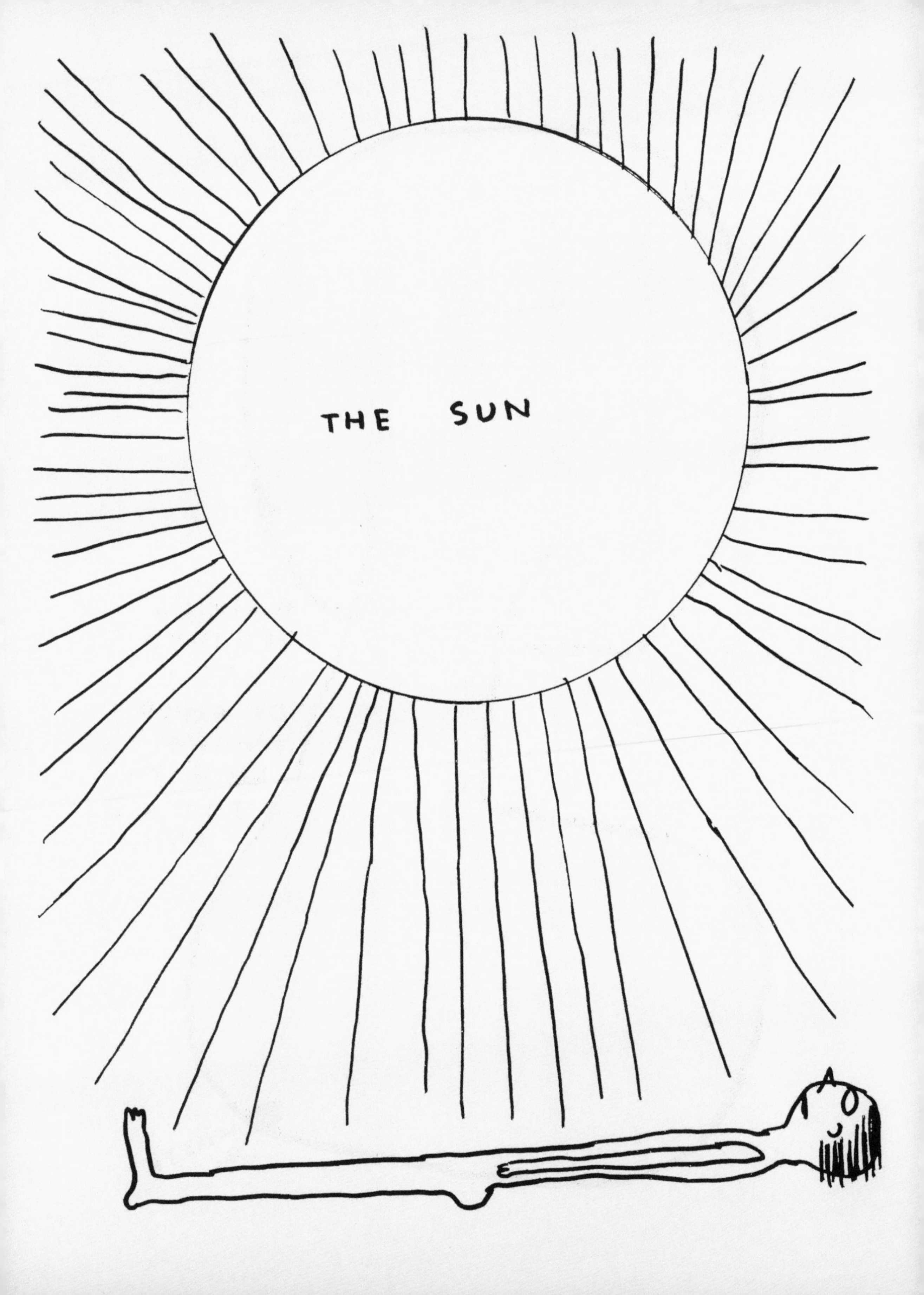
THE SUN

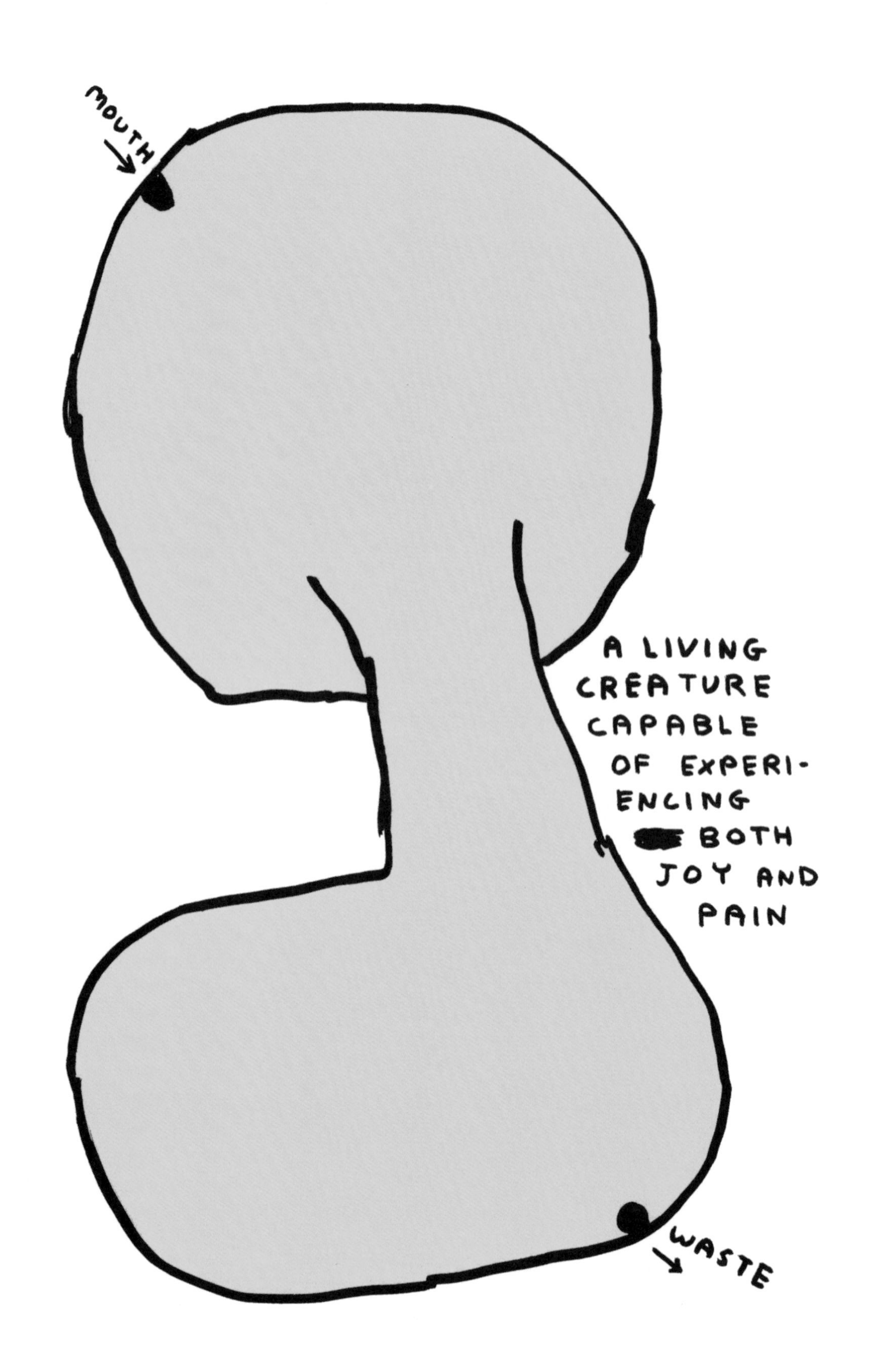
MOUTH
A LIVING CREATURE CAPABLE OF EXPERI-ENCING BOTH JOY AND PAIN
WASTE

IT DOESN'T MATTER WHICH ONE YOU DRINK

THEY ARE ALL POISON

I'M SO EXCITED
I'M GOING TO THE RIVER
TO DROWN MYSELF

SUN
BREAKS
THROUGH THE
CLOUDS

NOBODY,
KING OF NOWHERE,
GIVING A SPEECH

THE
CAT WILL
CATCH A
MOUSE
(YOU ARE THE MOUSE)

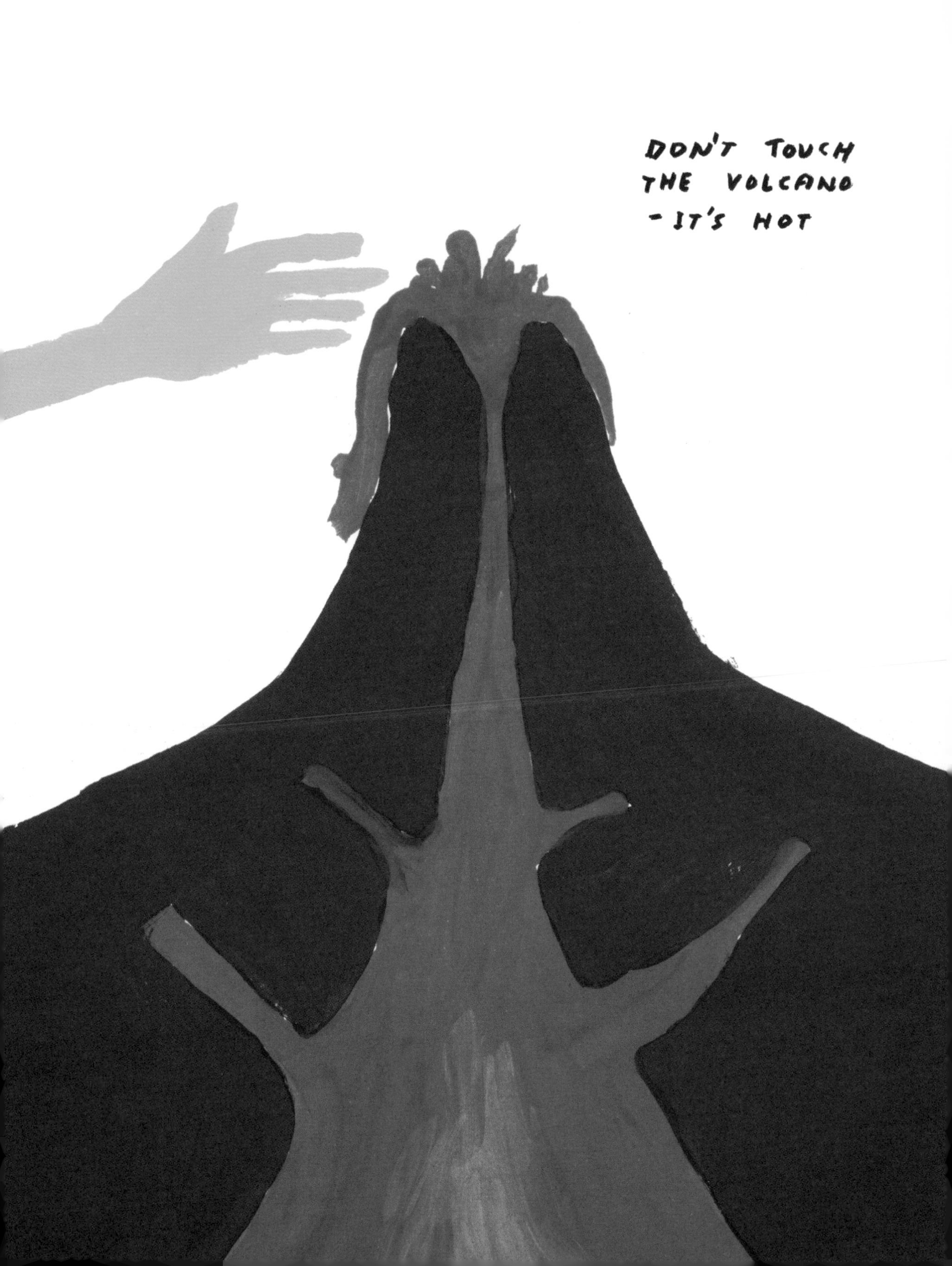
DON'T TOUCH
THE VOLCANO
- IT'S HOT

THING
OF
VALUE

TERRIBLE BURDENS PLACED BY WICKED MEN

GOD CHOSE
ME
TO MAKE
DECISIONS ON
HIS BEHALF

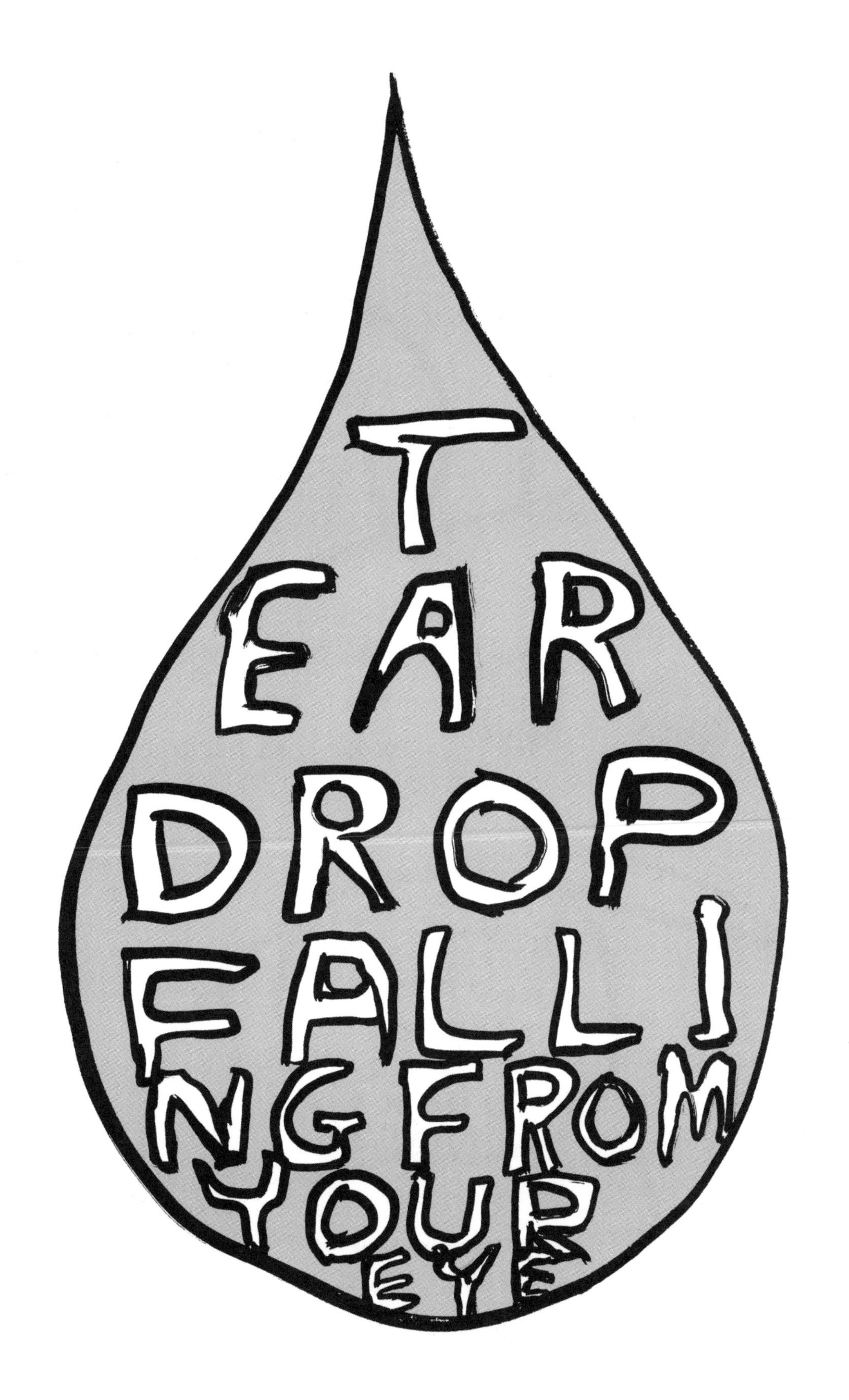
T
EAR
DROP
FALLI
NG FROM
YOUR
EYE

HE TOOK
OUT HIS
EYES

AND GAVE THEM
TO ME
TO HOLD

BUT I
DROPPED
THEM
AND
BROKE
THEM

I WAS SO
SORRY

IGNORE
THIS
BUILDING

SELF - CONFIDENT

RUG DOCTOR

RUG DOCTOR SAYS THERE IS NOTHING WRONG WITH YOUR RUG SO TAKE IT AWAY AND STOP WASTING HIS TIME.

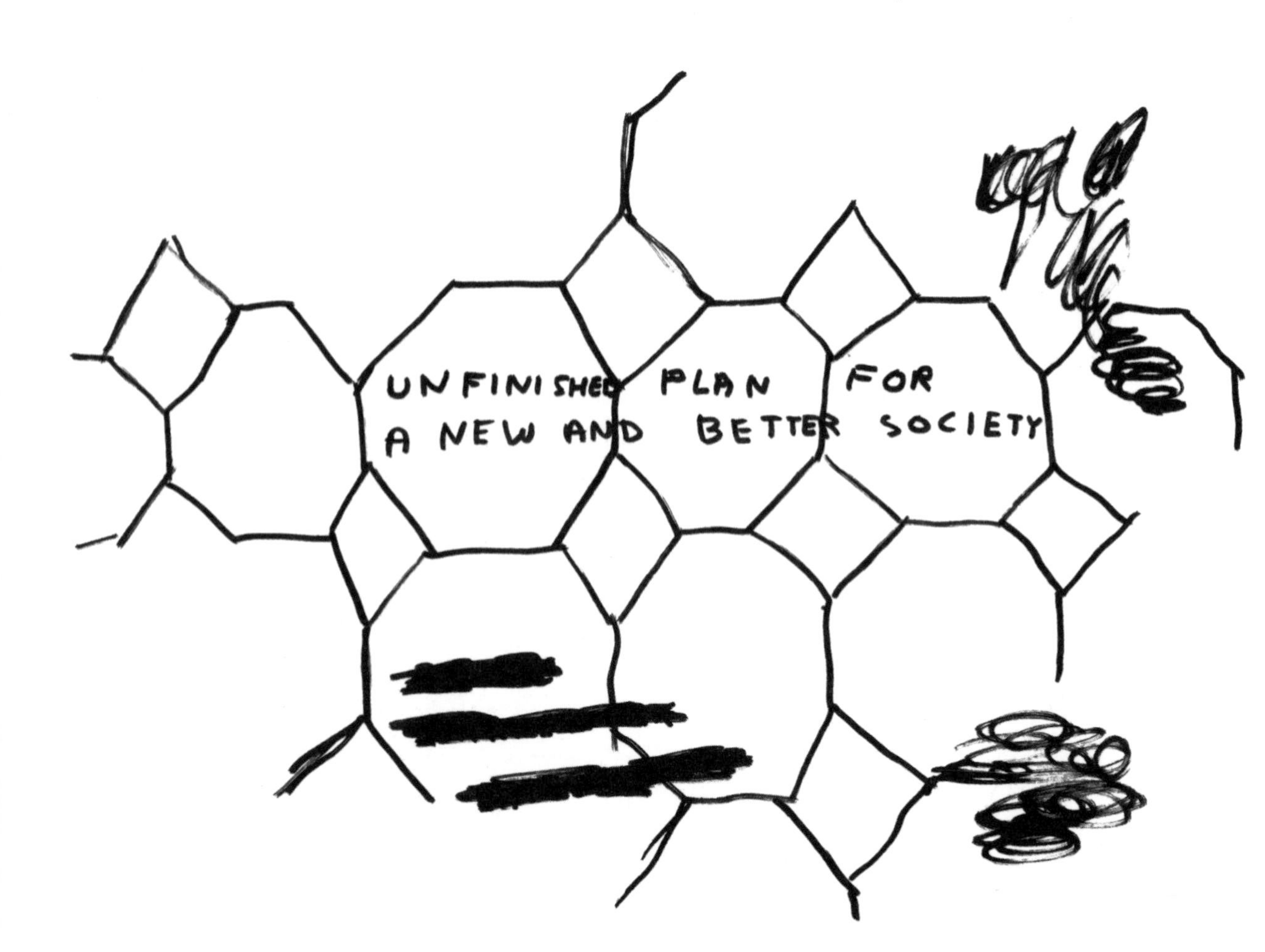
UNFINISHED PLAN FOR
A NEW AND BETTER SOCIETY

A LIGHT TOUCH FROM THE STUN BATON AND THERE WILL BE NO MORE DRUMMING

YOU ARE IN MY OINTMENT

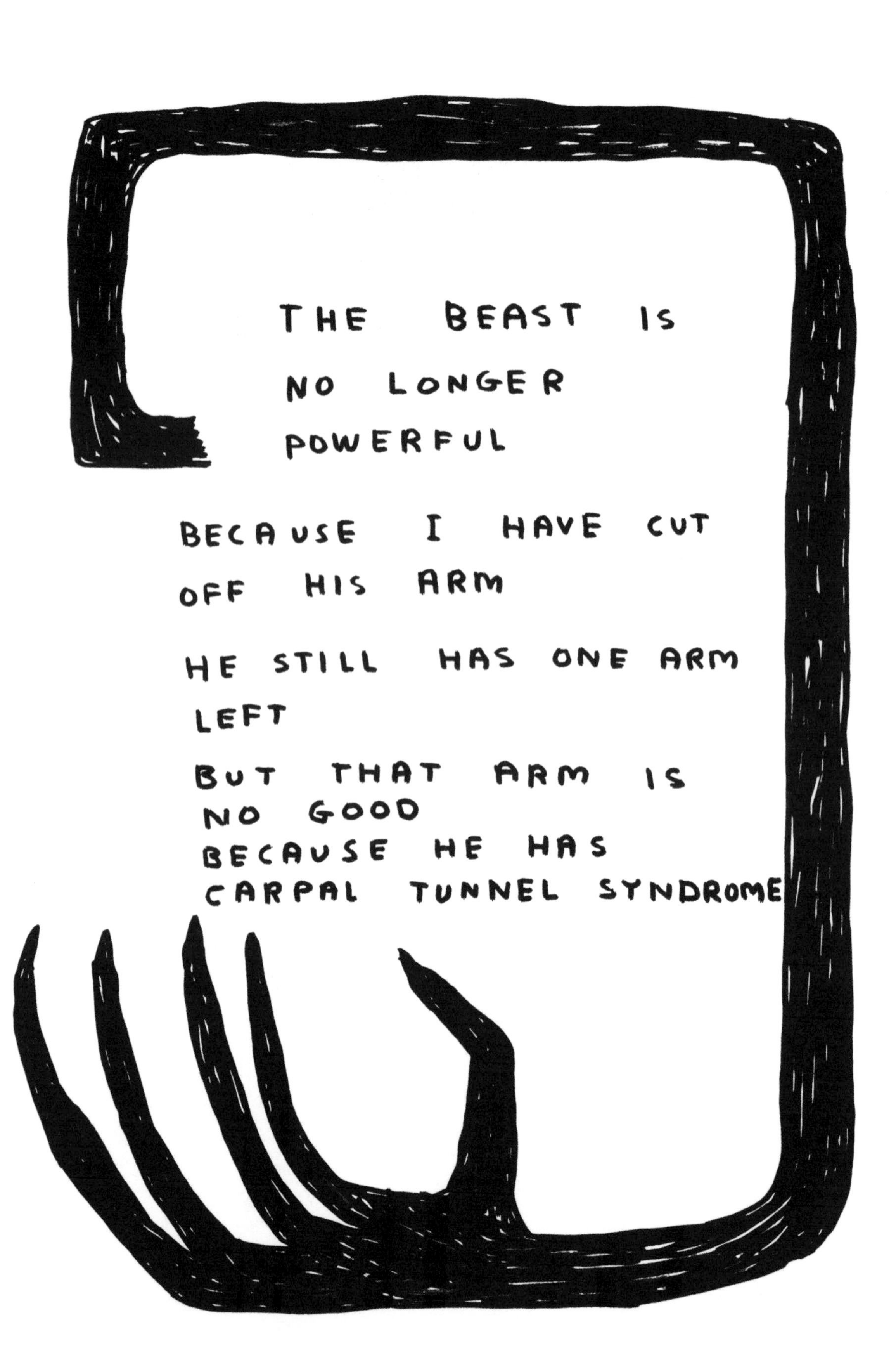
THE BEAST IS
NO LONGER
POWERFUL
BECAUSE I HAVE CUT
OFF HIS ARM
HE STILL HAS ONE ARM
LEFT
BUT THAT ARM IS
NO GOOD
BECAUSE HE HAS
CARPAL TUNNEL SYNDROME

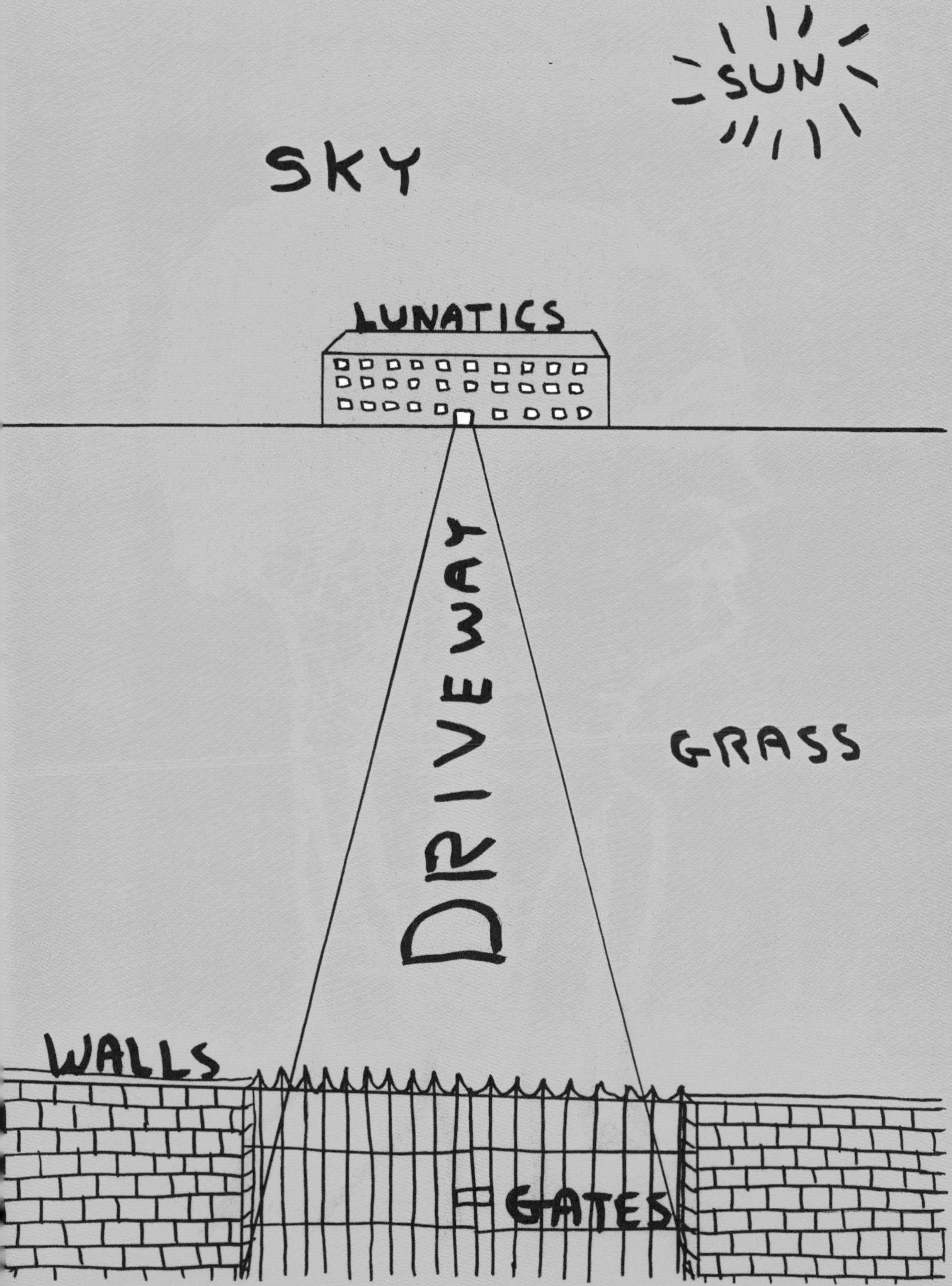

SUN

SKY

LUNATICS

DRIVEWAY

GRASS

WALLS

GATES

SPIDER WEB TATTOO

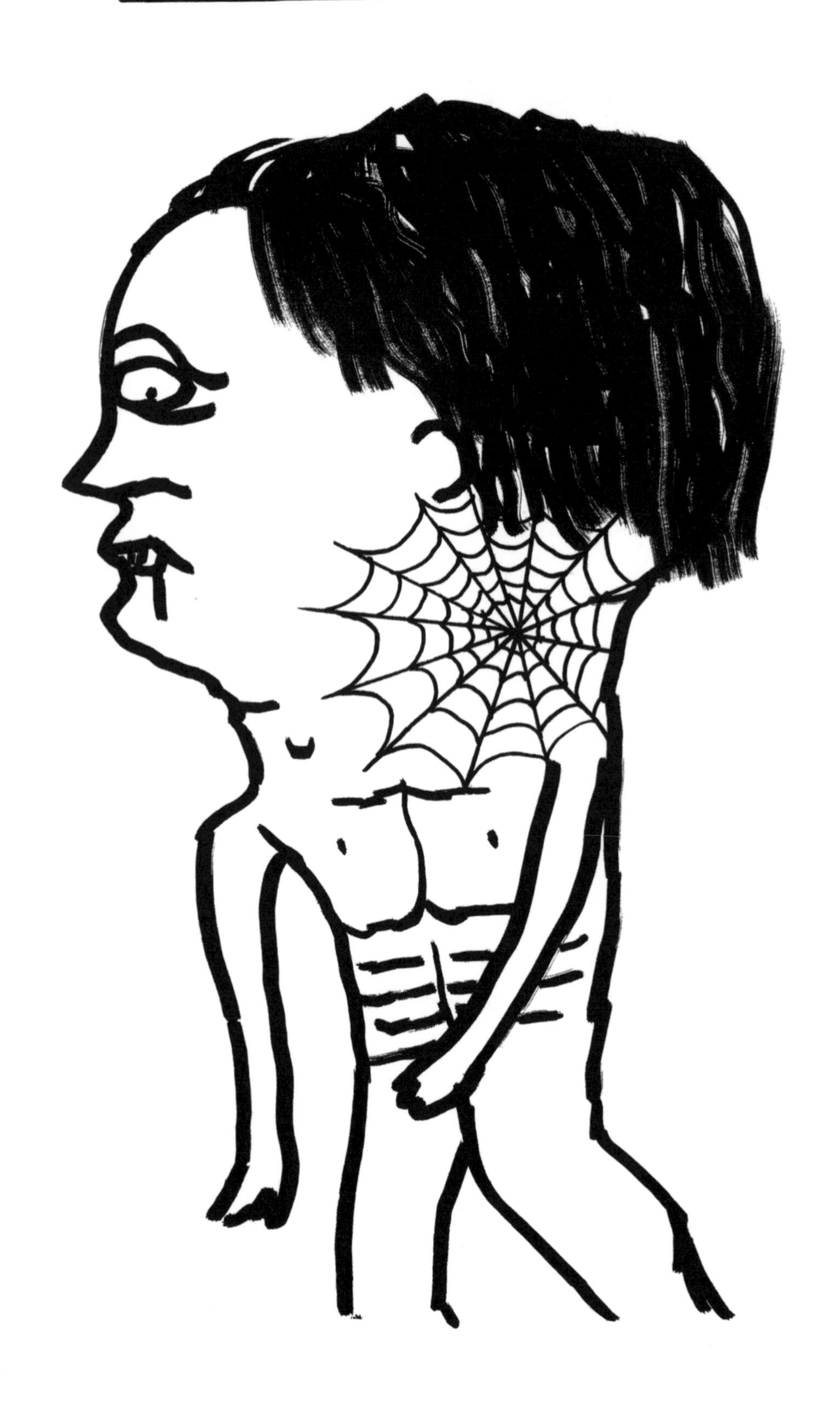

I REGRET
WHAT
I DID

UNOPENED HEADS

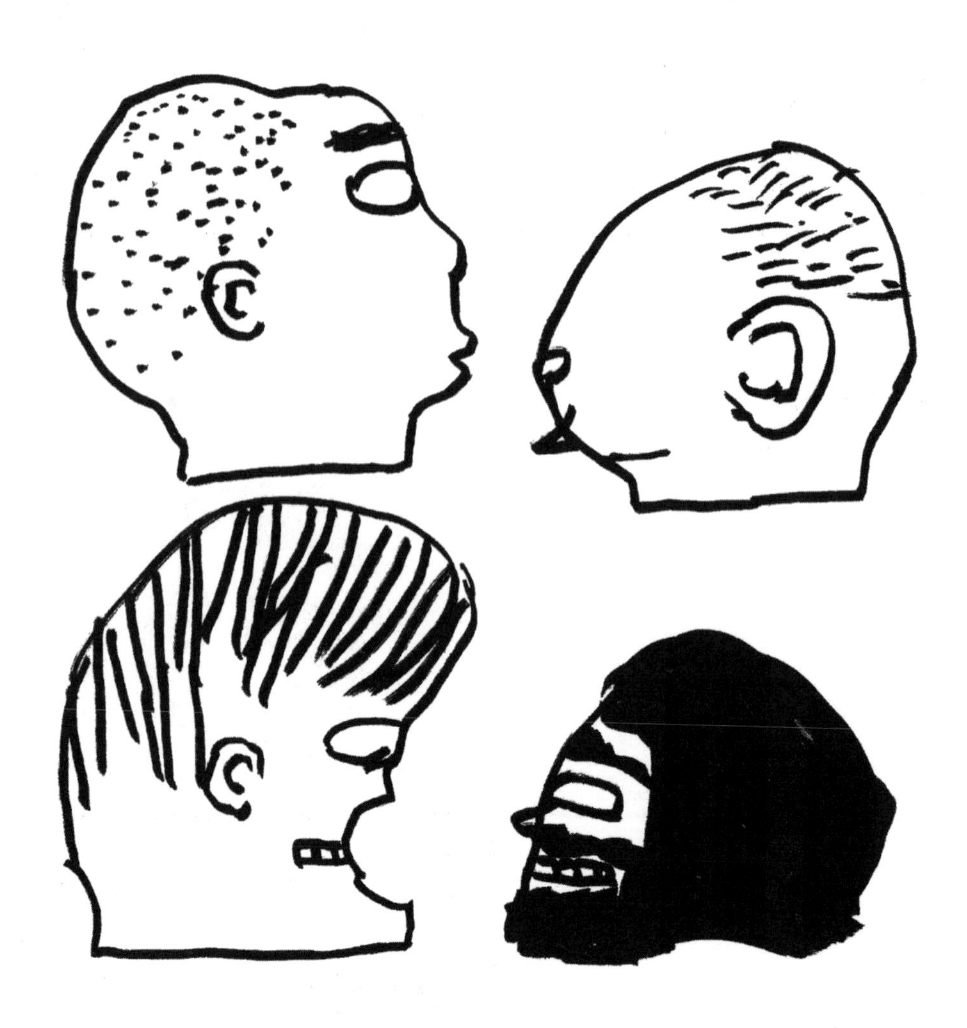

STAMP ON
THE EGGS
BEFORE THEY
HATCH

I'M FALLING
I'M FALLING
OH NO
I'M FALLING

I'M DROWNING
I'M DROWNING
OH NO
I'M DROWNING

YOU SHOW US NO RESPECT.
YOU ARE VAIN AND SELFISH. YOU EXPLOIT US. YOU ARE A TYRANT.
YOU CARE NOTHING FOR JUSTICE. YOU RULE THROUGH FORCE.
YOU ARE MOVED ONLY BY GREED AND THE LUST FOR POWER. YOU LEGITMATE YOUR ACTIONS THROUGH LIES.
YOU ELIMINATE DISSENTERS

PERVERSION

TEA OR COFFEE?

TEA AND COFFEE

A CUP OF TEA AND A CUP OF COFFEE?

NO, A CUP OF TEA AND COFFEE

I CAN'T DO THAT SIR.

WHY NOT?

BECAUSE IT'S OBSCENE

THAT'S TRUE BUT I AM BUSINESS CLASS

I'M SORRY I DIDN'T REALISE SIR. PLEASE GIVE ME YOUR CUP.

EAT IT QUICKLY BEFORE THEY TAKE IT AWAY FROM YOU

SHIT

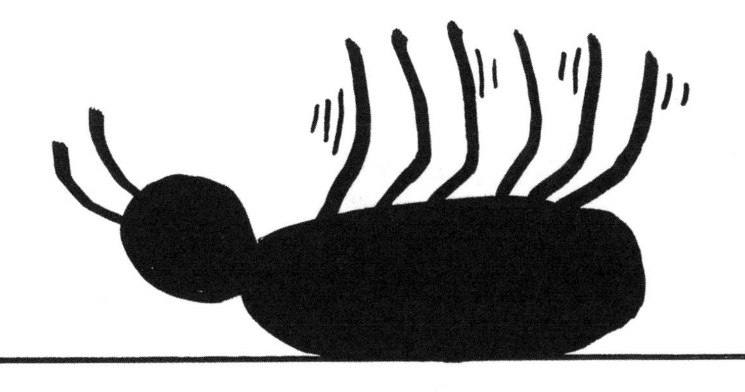
I WANT YOU TO
BE THERE
WHEN I DIE

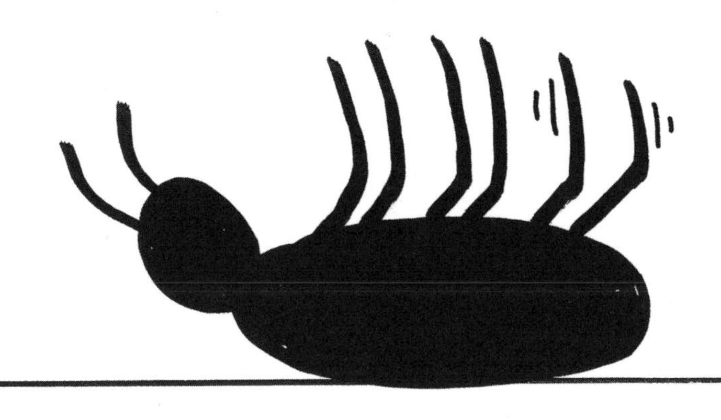
I DON'T WANT
TO DIE ALONE

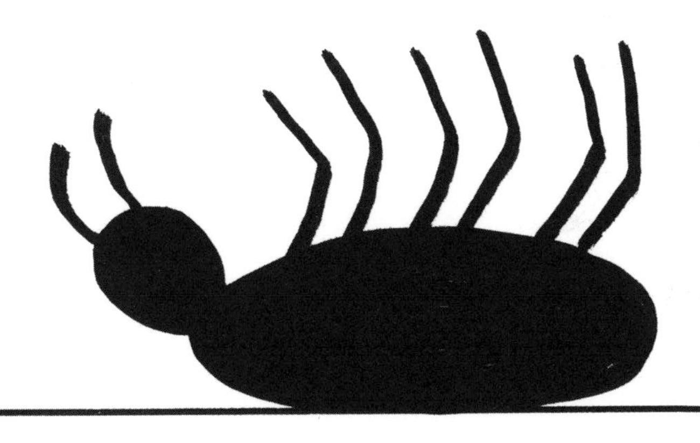
TO DIE ALONE
WOULD BE AWFUL

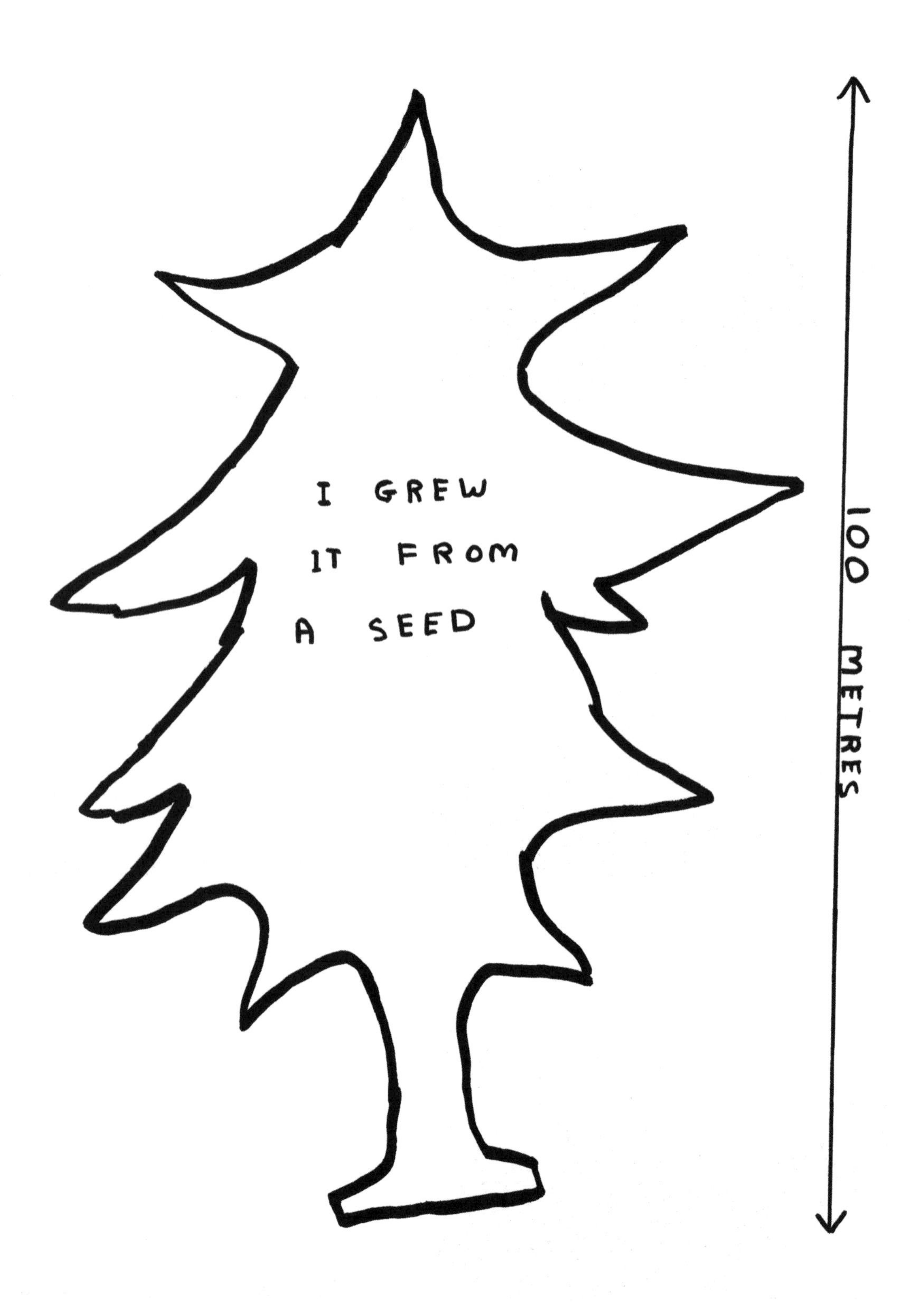

THEY MADE ME CUT IT DOWN

DOES THE OLD DOG DISPLEASE YOU ?
I CAN TAKE HIM OUTSIDE AND KILL HIM IF YOU WISH

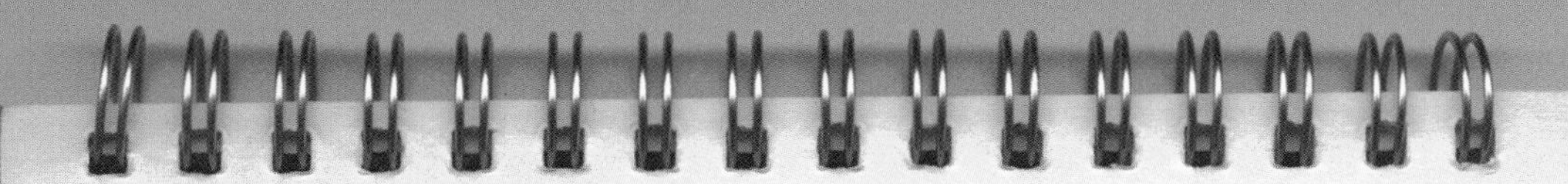

SPORT
MISERY

SOME WHISTLE SOME DON'T

CROCS WITH COCKS

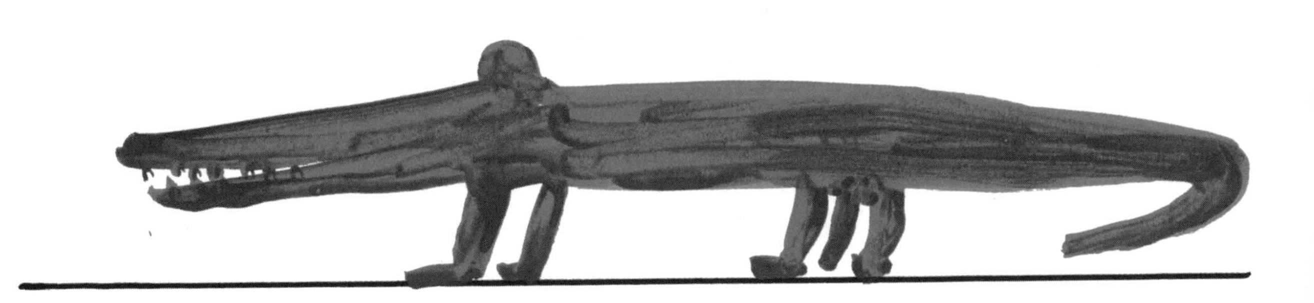

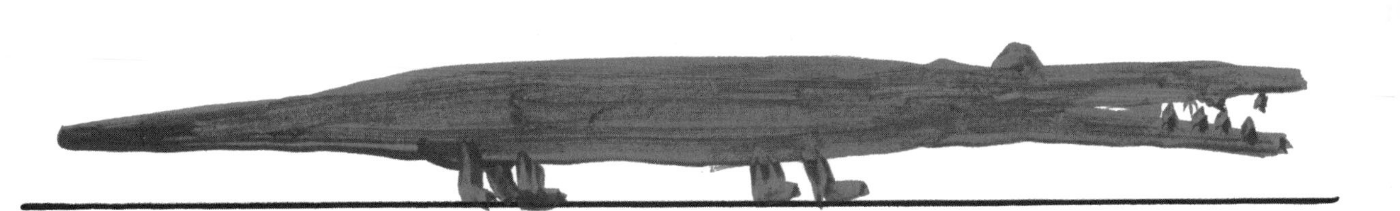

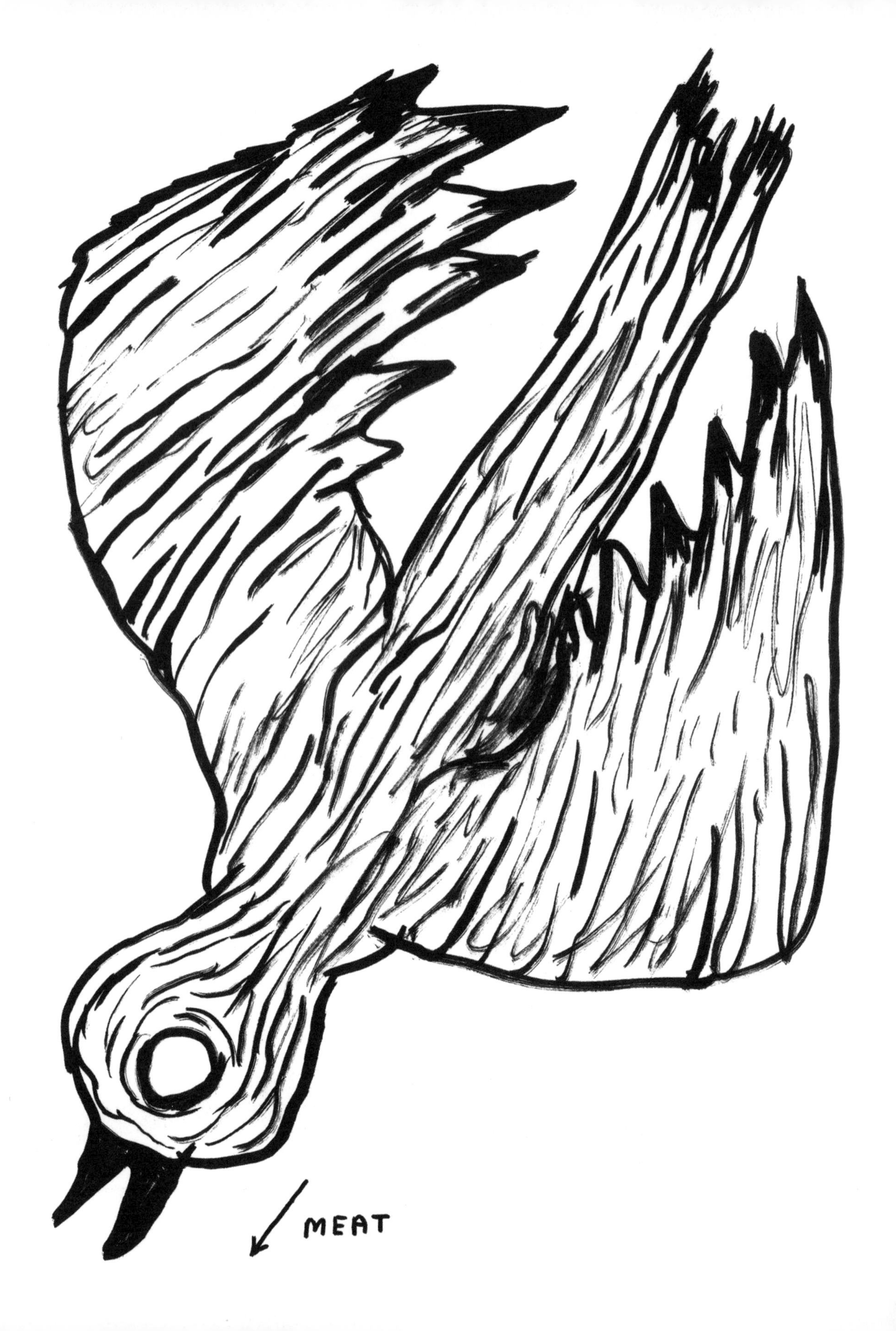
MEAT

WORLD'S LARGEST DIAMOND

OBSTRUCTING MY VIEW

TIME TO CHOOSE

I AM NOT GOD

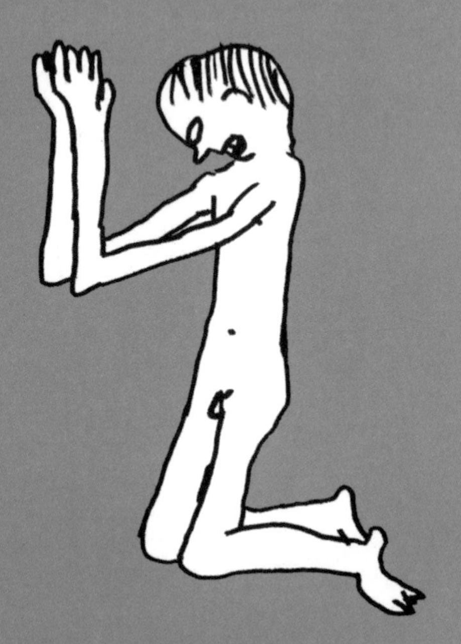
I'M NOT PRAYING I'M DOING YOGA

I'VE DONE NOTHING WRONG
SO WHY MUST I BE
KEPT INSIDE THE BOX ?

Q: DO YOU HAVE SIBLINGS ?
A: I HAVE A BROTHER
Q: AND WHERE DOES HE RESIDE ?
A: HE USED TO RESIDE ON THE HIGH STREET, THEN HE RESIDED IN THE SUBURBS, THEN IN A HOUSE NEAR TO THE RACE COURSE, THEN HE HAD A SPELL IN A SMALL VILLAGE MILES AWAY, THEN BACK TO THE HIGH STREET AND NOW HE RESIDES IN A HOUSE FOR THE CRIMINALLY INSANE.
Q: IS HE CRIMINALLY INSANE ?
A: NO, HE IS ONLY CRIMINAL BUT HE IS PRETENDING TO BE INSANE.
Q: HOW WAS HE CRIMINAL ?
A: HE FUCKED AND KILLED AND ATE SOME ANIMALS AT THE ZOO.
Q: WHAT ANIMALS ?
A: A LION, A ZEBRA, A GIRAFFE AND ANOTHER ANIMAL I CAN'T RECALL.
Q: A MONKEY PERHAPS ?
A: NO
Q: A TIGER ?
A: NO
Q: A SNAKE ?
A: NO
Q: A GORILLA ?
A: NO
Q: AN IGUANA ?
A: A WHAT ?
Q: AN IGUANA ?
A: NO
Q: A CHEETAH ?
A: NO
Q: AN ANTELOPE ?
A: I THINK THAT WAS IT

EVERGRADE
EVERGRADE
EVERGRADE
ANTI-
DEPRESSANTS

ALSO BY DAVID SHRIGLEY

SLUG TRAILS
MERRY ECZEMA
BLANKET OF FILTH
ENQUIRE WITHIN
LET NOT THESE SHADOWS FALL UPON THEE
DRAWINGS DONE WHILST ON PHONE TO IDIOT
BLANK PAGE AND OTHER PAGES
CENTRE PARTING
TO MAKE MERINGUE YOU MUST BEAT THE EGG WHITES UNTIL THEY LOOK LIKE THIS
WHY WE GOT THE SACK FROM THE MUSEUM
THE BEAST IS NEAR
HARD WORK
GRIP
DO NOT BEND
HUMAN ACHIEVEMENT
LEOTARD
WHO I AM AND WHAT I WANT
YELLOW BIRD WITH WORM
KILL YOUR PETS
LET'S WRESTLE
BLOCKED PATH
THE BOOK OF SHRIGLEY
PHOTOGRAPHS WITH TEXT
WORRIED NOODLES (THE EMPTY SLEEVE)
THIS IS A PAPER TRINKET FOR YOU TO WEAR
ANTS HAVE SEX IN YOUR BEER
HAND
MAN IN A ROOM
RED BOOK